THE LOVING TOUCH

THE LOVING TOUCH

CONSULTANT

DR ANDREW STANWAY MB MRCP

GUILD PUBLISHING
LONDON

Editor Nigel Cawthorne
House Editor Donna Wood
Art Editor Annie Tomlin

This edition published 1987 by
Book Club Associates
by arrangement with
Macdonald & Co (Publishers) Ltd
London & Sydney

A member of BPCC plc

Phototypeset by Input Typesetting Limited

Printed and bound in Spain

CONTENTS

INTRODUCTION 6

INTRODUCTION

It is often said that buying your first home is the most important act of your life. It is not. Nor is buying your first car, nor reaching the pinnacle of your career. More important than all of these is the ability to maintain a totally fulfilling sexual relationship with a cherished partner, and realizing the boundlessness of your own sensuality.

We have come a long way since sex was thought of as a bestial passion vented by an uncaring husband on his long-suffering wife. Thankfully, sex is no longer seen solely as a means of creating children which was otherwise best left alone. That society may have made women paragons of virtue in the drawing room, but it filled the streets with prostitution and disease.

These days, a good sex life is seen as a rightful part of an intimate relationship. In a partnership, a healthy sex life is the glue that holds you together.

Behind all this lies a completely new philosophy. Sex is no longer a regretable inconvenience, nor a shameful pastime indulged in only by the dissolute. Nor is it a hobby like stamp collecting or gardening. It is the very stuff of life itself.

But there is so much to learn and so little time. From puberty to the dying embers of old age you will make love thousands of times. Even if you stay faithful to one partner for all of that time, it is doubtful that you would ever get bored. There is always something new to be discovered in the act if you are doing it with someone you love. The problem is rather, with all the intimate sensations there are to feel, how do you fit it all in?

Remember, though that when you are making love, you are not only making love to someone else. You are doing it with yourself. It is only when you are as close to someone else as you are in lovemaking – which, after penetration, is as physically close as you will ever get to another human being – that you can endure the loneliness of looking deep into yourself. The French call the moment of orgasm *la petite morte* – the little death. Sex, perhaps, is the only practice we ever get for dying.

When you are young and taking your first hesitant steps into the world of sex, everything seems mysterious. And there is no one you can ask.

Parents are embarrassed. School teachers are often ill-informed. Priests, youth leaders, social workers all have their moral axe to grind. Older sisters and brothers snigger to hide their own ignorance. Friends are as ill-informed as you are. And no one else takes you seriously.

The Loving Touch aims to give you a deep understanding of lovemaking, its targets and techniques and the profound role it plays in all our lives. It helps you take the first steps to love by studying body language, flirting and kissing. It helps you assess possible partners and even examines the role of virginity in this and other societies.

It looks at your sexual awakening, examining

the complex sex signals that go on between us and the role of masturbation in learning about your body and your sexual response. It gives you a step-by-step guide to overcoming inhibitions and looks at the problems and pitfalls of first-time sex.

There is sound advice on contraception and a study of the strategies of seduction. And if a love potion is required, there's an ABC of aphrodisiacs.

The arts of intimacy must be understood if they are to be enjoyed. Why are some people promiscuous while others are faithful? What is an orgasm? What turns people on? These questions are answered. And there is a guide to sensual massage and intimate touching.

The speciality sex section looks at advanced foreplay, love games and quickie sex. And it examines some of the hardware that people employ as erotica and in fetishism.

To become an expert you will need to know about advanced lovemaking, the G spot and the possibilities of attaining simultaneous orgasm. And you will also learn how to prolong the pleasure by making love last longer, deep penetration and improving and multiplying your orgasms. Positions are important too. There is so much more to be enjoyed than unadventurous man-on-top sex.

Everybody has sexual problems at some time in their life. If you come too soon or cannot come at all, *The Loving Touch* helps you understand these conditions and gives sensible, straightforward advice on how to overcome them. It looks at sexually transmitted diseases, including down-to-earth examination of the killer disease AIDS, and tells you how to move towards lower-risk sexual behaviour.

But not everyone wants a regular relationship with someone of the opposite sex. Some choose to be homosexuals, lesbians, bisexuals or even to remain celibate. It is that choice that is the most important decision in your life.

Although most of the artworks in this book do not depict men wearing condoms, we do recommend the use of them, especially in a new relationship, or where you have not known your partner very long.

CHAPTER ONE

THE FIRST STEPS

BODY LANGUAGE

*Can you tell how someone feels just by
watching how they move? The answer is yes,
but like any other language you must know
how to interpret the finer points of body talk*

Our bodies talk. Every time we look at someone else, speak to a member of the opposite sex, have a drink, sit down or walk about – whenever we are in any type of social setting – we give out messages. These messages tell the receivers about ourselves, about our feelings towards other people, about our comfort and discomfort in the situation, and in many cases, about our willingness and availability for any sexual encounters.

It is important to know what actions and movements make the right and the wrong impressions, and which ones convey the 'right' and 'wrong' signals. If we are shy, then we tend to give off impressions that warn people away. If we are confi-dent, then we tend to give out body messages that make other people more interested – or at least we try to. If we like someone or hate someone, then it can show very clearly.

SOCIAL SKILLS

Psychologists have explored body language messages very carefully and have found that they are conveyed by a whole system of 'non-verbal cues' – behaviour that does not involve speech. These cues are carefully organized in most social settings and they form the basis of the social skills that lie beneath the actions that we take for granted in our everyday lives.

Direct eye contact, knees pointing towards the other person, are two major signs of interest

One arm stretched over the back of the sofa, one leg crossed over the other – a typical open posture

they have to lean to correct for turning a corner.

Similarly, in social behaviour, we all carry on quite happily without necessarily being able to say what the rules are, nor even knowing if we are giving off the right messages. Yet the more aware we become of the messages our bodies can convey, the more care we can take to ensure that we are giving off the right one – and not giving off the wrong one.

TALKING BODIES

Almost any part of our body that is visible to other people is capable of sending out messages. Our choice of clothing tells people something about us – so does the way that we sit or stand. Gestures and hand movements are informative. The way we look at other people can convey messages more power-

Direct and prolonged eye contact – a sure sign of deep mutual attraction

The man's arms folded tight across the chest and the woman's legs close together – the basic message here from both of them is 'keep your distance'

Like any skill, it is easily mastered by some people, but not by others. Like any other skill, however, people can improve by practice and training – or, in many instances, simply by thinking about it carefully.

It is rather like riding a bicycle. Almost everyone can balance on it and move it forward, but hardly anyone could tell you exactly how they are doing it, how they manage not to fall over, how much they have to turn the wheel to balance and how far over

fully than speech. The distance at which we stand from someone else in order to talk to them – that matters too.

Three types of messages are given out by body talk – how you feel about yourself (whether you are shy or confident, for example, or whether you are telling the truth or lying); how you feel about the other person (whether you like them or dislike them, trust them or disbelieve them); and how you feel about the relationship or the conversation or the setting for your encounter (whether you feel relaxed or tense, excited or bored, comfortable or uncomfortable).

Allowing someone to touch you by straightening a tie or brushing a shoulder shows acceptance

Once you realize that these messages are passed on by such simple things as posture (the way you stand), spacing (the closeness at which you stand to people) and eye movements (how much you look at people and when, relative to your speech), a whole new world of social encounters opens up before you.

LANGUAGE OF AVAILABILITY

When we are open to an approach by someone else, or willing to be, we stand in a way that indicates it.

We face people when we want to speak to them, for example, even though they could still hear us even if we faced another way. We look at them and catch their eye, even though we could still speak to them without doing so – bar staff and waiters do not usually serve customers who do not catch their eye first. And by refusing to let you catch their eye people can refuse to be drawn into conversation with you. It is as simple as that.

POSTURE SIGNALS

Availability can also be indicated by posture. Postures can be 'open' or 'closed'.

An open posture is one where the body is open to view and access by other people – as where someone sits with their arm over the back of the chair and the ankle of one leg resting on the knee of the other leg.

Someone adopting a closed posture might sit with their legs close together and their arms folded tight across their chest. In the first case the basic message is 'come on', and in the second it is 'keep your distance'.

The classic open posture that signals availability in men is when they stand with their feet apart, lean their backs on to a wall and put one hand on the belt of their trousers or in their pocket.

An open posture by women is one where the knees point towards the attractive person rather

than away from him. But women tend to use their eyes rather more than men to produce the same effect, and frequent glances towards a fancied male are a major sign of interest.

Once contact is established, there are other ways to sustain interest and maintain messages of availability. Glancing frequently at the partner's eyes, encouraging them to talk, smiling and agreeing with them are all ways of indicating that you are interested – and available as well.

These are known as 'reinforcers', and will encourage the person to relax, and to feel welcome and attractive.

THE LANGUAGE OF DESIRE

When availability turns to desire the same means are used to intensify the relationship, but now another area of non-verbal behaviour becomes important – that of touch.

While desire can be indicated initially by the eyes, by posture and by other non-verbal behaviour, the most agreeable indicator is closeness or proximity. Just as we can talk of a 'close relationship', so people really do sit closer to one another when they like their partner.

As a preliminary step, sometimes they will begin to check out the possibilities by touching one another fleetingly on the arm or shoulder before moving in closer, and then making contact in a more prolonged way.

The first indicator of desire is frequent looking, particularly in the area of the eyes. The length of gaze also increases, and the amount of direct eye-to-eye contact goes up dramatically, when two people fancy one another.

PHYSICAL CLOSENESS

Once it is established that the partners are interested in one another, then desire can be communicated by deliberately exploring the other person's face with the eyes when he or she is looking at you.

At the same time as this sort of exploration, the distance between the two people decreases, and they move closer together. These two 'cues' – increased eye-contact, plus physical closeness – are very powerful signs of desire.

This helps to explain why we find it so hard to look people in the face when we are cramped up against them – in a lift or on a crowded subway train, for example.

If we did, we would be signalling that we really did fancy them.

INCREASING INTIMACY

As the relationship becomes more intimate, so we are able to tolerate more intense combinations of eye contact, physical closeness and intimacy of conversation. In less intimate settings, we tend to compensate for one of these if it suddenly becomes more intense. If the conversation suddenly becomes

Constant glances indicate attraction by a female. Relaxed, leaning posture indicates male availability

more personal, for example, then the two partners in a formal encounter will look at one another less. They may also lean back from each other so as to increase the physical distance between them – keeping the overall intimacy level at about the same rate. This has been observed in interviews, where personal questions and answers are often given.

In intimate encounters, the more eye-contact, 'personalness' of conversation topic, and physical closeness, the better the partners will feel and the more strongly they will feel towards one another.

As the distance decreases, so the likelihood of touching goes up. Partners will brush up against one another, hold hands, put their arms around one another, or cuddle up to one another in order to increase touching.

Since there are well-understood rules about touching this signals attraction and desire very powerfully.

TIE SIGNS

Once a relationship is established – or sometimes even when it is forming – we use another set of signals called 'tie signs' to indicate ownership and possession. A good example of a tie sign is a wedding ring, but it can be as simple as the act of holding hands. Both things say, 'There is a relationship here. Do not interfere or try to get involved'.

READING THE SIGNS

Desire is one thing, but acceptance is quite another. The fact that someone accepts the advances of another person is also indicated by non-verbal cues. One interesting example of this is known as 'mirroring', and takes the form of copying the gestures and postures of a partner.

We sometimes do this unconsciously, finding that our partner has a hand up to the chin (and so do we), or the partner is leaning forward (and so are we), or we both lean back and cross our legs at more or less the same instant. We mirror powerful people and people that we like – and we definitely do not mirror people that we do not like. So, one sure sign of acceptance of another person's interest is when we find that they are mirroring what we do.

This is my territory – isolating a partner by leaning over her is the language of ownership

THE IMPORTANCE OF TOUCH

Another sign of acceptance is permission to touch. We do not let people touch us unless we like them, and not drawing away from a touch is a sign of liking and approval. For this reason, many available people place themselves in a position or a posture where the other person can touch them more easily. Or they may set out to touch the person in a less obvious way, such as straightening a tie or scarf, brushing something off their shoulder or pushing their hair out of their eyes.

Touching the person on the arm or hand is a signal too, and we all enjoy being touched even when we do not realize it has happened. Research in the United States has shown that librarians who touched people's fingers when they handed back a book were preferred to those who did not.

Just as gaze and proximity indicate liking and availability, so they also indicate acceptance. We look more often at people we want to encourage, and move closer to them as well.

This acceptance – and sometimes the whole process – can be subconscious. It is often considerably more obvious to an outsider than to the person involved that someone is strongly attracted to him or her. We seem to be more aware of the fact that two people are gazing into one another's eyes and sitting close together than we are when we are one of the two people.

When it happens to us we just enjoy it, but when we see it happening to other people we can actually interpret it and we realize what it means. They like and fancy one another.

Lovers stare at one another more often and for longer periods than platonic friends. They sit closer together, touch one another more and express agree-ment with one another more often. One important skill for relating to other people, then, is the ability to recognize the meaning of the non-verbal cues that other people give out towards us.

THE LANGUAGE OF REJECTION

Many advances – if not most – result in failure. The body language of rejection uses the same non-verbal cues, but works through the opposite of all the other signals.

To reject the advances of someone else we can adopt a closed posture to stop them approaching us in the first place. We can avoid eye-contact to discourage them from talking to us and increase our distance if they still do not get the message.

If all that fails, then we can place ourselves in a position that makes it difficult for the other person to touch us and can explicitly comment on any attempts to do so – which is both a little rude and very off-putting.

INTERPRETING SHYNESS

People who are shy and find it difficult to look others in the eye, or to give other messages of availability, are therefore giving out a message that says they are uninterested. Research has shown that when observers see videos of shy people talking to someone else, they assume that the shy person does not actually like the person they are talking to.

But when the shy person's friends see the tape they do not reach the same conclusion. Unfortunately, if a shy person does not know the person that he or she is talking to, then that person will assume that they are disliked, or that the shy person is not available for a relationship and is rejecting them.

ASSESSING YOUR PARTNER

How people look, dress, talk and move will all provide clues about their sexual performance. And even how they decorate their home will hint at life in the bedroom

It is said that the most crucial period in an encounter between two people is the first four or five minutes. The impressions formed in this time will tend to persist and even be reinforced by later behaviour.

In those first few minutes, we do more than simply decide whether or not we like someone, we make judgements about their character, personality, intellect, habits and talents.

The way we view people, and our own deep-set prejudices about their looks and clothes, will also cause us to prejudge their behaviour in bed.

In a survey carried out in the United States, and reported in the *Journal of Personality and Social Psychology* in 1984, Dr Karen Dion showed photographs of attractive and unattractive people to a large group of men and women, asking the group to rate them. The attractive people in the photos were seen as more sexually warm and responsive than the others.

Most of us see good-looking men and women as more desirable. And because they are more likely to elicit a sexual response from us, we assume they will be good in bed.

FIRST IMPRESSIONS

Our initial contact with other people is eye to body – we look first at their bodies before we establish eye contact, so what we choose to wear is important. Clothes reveal something about our income, status, occupation and personality. They also tell people how we see ourselves and how we wish to be viewed.

But men have more difficulty than women in estimating a potential partner's personality and possible behaviour in bed. This is not because men are less sensitive, but because of a woman's chameleon-like ability to change her style of clothes, and with them, seemingly, her personality. In ski pants, she can be boyish and companionable. In a slinky jersey, a sex kitten. In a smart suit, businesslike

With her steady gaze and open smile this girl is clearly at ease with her body. And her foot pointing forward is assertive without being threatening. Probably a playful, uninhibited lover

Unkempt hair and clothes show a man who cannot quite get things right, but it is not too serious. Sloppy dressers can make enthusiastic lovers when all the outside layers are removed

and perhaps unapproachable.

Clothes can be the gauge of someone's mood, but they provide only a broad guide to how a person will perform in bed. In a recent study of obsession, it was found that obsessively neat dressers, for example, do not necessarily perform badly in bed. As long as they can set the time – and preferably the place, too – they can enjoy sex as much as the next person.

But they do take a long time to arouse. They tend to have a take-it-or-leave-it attitude to sex, enjoying it when it is going on, not missing it when it is not. They are also less likely to indulge in the hugging and kissing that makes for an all-round successful sex life.

At the other extreme, the sloppy dressers who look as if they are colour-blind – the girl who has always got a ladder in her tights, the man who has never got matching socks – usually make up in enthusiasm for what they lack in finesse in bed. But

they are quick learners.

When a man and woman prepare for a sexual encounter, even though they may not have said a word about their intentions to each other, their bodies are already making preparations.

Their muscles become slightly tensed. Body sagging disappears and they stand up straighter. There is less jowling in their faces and bagging round the eyes. They pull in their stomachs and tighten their leg muscles.

Even their eyes seem brighter, while their skins may blush or go pale. There could even be changes in their body odours, harking back to a more primitive time when smell was a tremendously important sense in human sexual encounters.

GESTURES

As these changes take place, they may begin to use certain preening gestures – he may adjust his tie, she may stroke her hair. They then position themselves in such a way as to cut off any intrusion from a third person, by facing each other and probably leaning towards each other.

So we can tell from the way two people move their bodies, from their unconscious gestures, that they are keen to get to know each other more intimately. But can we go even further and estimate whether they will enjoy sex with each other?

It is well known that most of us choose our partners from within a small, tight circle. They usually live within 16 km of us, come from the same background, are educated to the same level and either work with us or enjoy the same hobby.

We know from assessing these details about such a person, however unconsciously, that we will probably be compatible. But what about in the bedroom?

SIGHT, SOUND AND FEELINGS

Everyone perceives his or her world with three basic 'senses' – sight, sound and feelings. But for every man and woman, one of those senses is dominant to some degree. Discovering which sense is the most important to a potential partner can tell you a lot about how they are likely to behave in bed.

To discover which of the three senses is dominant, ask a simple question, such as 'What's your flat like?' If he or she replies along the lines 'It's blue with pale cream carpets,' the chances are they are visually dominant. If they say, 'It's about two miles from town on a quiet road,' they are more likely to be auditory (highly sensitive to sound). Those who reply, 'It's in a house with lots of other single people and I love living there,' are feelings of people whose emotions dominate.

VISUAL PEOPLE

Visualizers, as the name implies, react very strongly to visual imagery. They like to kiss with their eyes open (men are more likely to be visualizers than women – 70 per cent of men kiss with their eyes open compared with only 3 per cent of women) and make love with the lights on.

Visualizers find it hard to express their feelings, so you will usually have to be the one leading the way in lovemaking. But they are really turned on by visual gimmicks such as wearing suspenders and black stockings. A visualizing man will enjoy seeing the silhouette of his erect figure as a shadow on the wall.

You can tell visualizers by their bedrooms – lots of magazines strewn around, pictures on the wall, perhaps even a television. At first, you may think they are slow on the uptake. But what is actually holding them up is that they are pausing to look you over first before they get aroused.

AUDITORY PEOPLE

You can distinguish auditory people by their sideways eye movements as they conduct long private

By donning a suit – the traditional uniform of the business world – a woman takes herself outside of a sexual sphere. She is professional, serious – to be treated as a person, not a sex object

Here the signals are confusing. The boyish look can still be a turn-on, particularly tight-fitting ski-pants, but the crossed arms and taut features are defensive, warning someone to keep his distance

The casual dress shows an easy-going nature, self-confident but not arrogant. And the way the man holds himself implies an ease about his own body which may well translate itself into the bedroom

conversations in their head. When seated, they often hold their hand to the side of their head as if they are talking on the telephone, for the same type of reason.

Sensible rather than fancy dressers, their bedrooms will probably be untidy, but with a superb stereo standing in the corner.

They are great talkers in bed, asking you how you like it, and letting you know very clearly how they are enjoying it. Their orgasms tend to be very noisy affairs.

FEELINGS PEOPLE

Feelings people wear their hearts on their sleeves and are always kissing and hugging their partners. They may have silk or satiny sheets on the bed and produce oil from the bedside table for you to massage them.

Turned-on by touch, they prefer making love

with the lights off and are into protracted foreplay. Because they are so sensitive, they can suffer from impotency quite easily. They usually take a long time to come. Feelings people are usually quite athletic, and dress comfortably rather than fashionably.

These are just basic outlines of types of people. Within these three general types, there are lots of other signs to watch out for which will help you to assess someone's future performance in bed.

HERE'S LOOKING AT YOU

Eyes can be a real give-away. When we are interested in someone, our pupils dilate. Research shows we like people with dilated pupils better than those with contracted pupils. What this implies is that someone showing interest in and perhaps desire for you is likely to arouse your interest in them.

Psychologists researching into mental illness

discovered some very interesting facts about what eyes reveal about your personality.

After the initial eye contact, you usually break gaze to the left or the right, that is to say you look to something or someone to the left or right of the person you are interested in.

Evidence suggests that left-breakers tend to be imaginative and creative, enjoying the sensual pleasures of life, both in bed and out. Long, unflickering looks are used by those who seek to dominate, who always like to be on top in bed, take the initiative and hate being told what their partner likes. Rapid scanning movements mean they are excited and eager lovers, with more enthusiasm than style.

Students of body language also found that where people are active, with many non-verbal movements – gesticulating with their hands, moving from one foot to another – they are considered warm, affectionate, good lovers, considerate in bed, unselfish and energetic. When they are mainly still, they are thought to be cold, selfish, concerned only with their own pleasure.

People who are very expressionless and immobile in their body language are afraid of what they may reveal. They are more likely to cut off the visual aspect of lovemaking completely, by only making love in the dark and refusing to undress until the lights are off. So look out for fidgets – they are more likely to give you an exciting time in bed.

VOICES

No matter what our words are, the emotion behind them carries a message. Our breathing affects the pattern of our voice, its speed and its punctuation.

Long pauses between our words tell the listener we are slow to arouse but unstoppable once we get going. Too short a pause, however, sends a message of coldness and indifference. A fast talker could be trying to hide his or her embarrassment, and may need a lot of coaxing in bed. A slow talker signals a mature and sensitive lover, while too slow a talker indicates complete lack of interest – someone who would get more of a thrill from speeding down the motorway than from sex.

The type of pauses that in a public speaker signals uncertainty and confusion can, in an intimate relationship, indicate vulnerability, which for some is a turn on.

So do not write off hesitant speakers – out of the public eye, they can be kind and sensitive lovers.

Rhythm is also very telling. On first meeting, we usually ask 'How are you?', stressing the 'are'. If, however, we stressed the 'you', the simple greeting becomes more intimate and the person greeted becomes more interested. If the rhythm pleases us, we are likely to find the speaker more appealing.

Certain types of 'give-away' behaviour will be more relevant for one sex than the other. So analysis of men and women will be different.

MEN

■ Some people, particularly men, make love according to stereotypes. If, for example, you have been put on a pedestal by your partner who treats you like precious china, you can assume that, once in bed, he will expect you to behave like his definition of a lady – no taking the initiative, not too much overt enjoyment and probably no oral sex.

■ A man who bites his nails and knuckles is looking for security, in a symbolic return to the comfort of his mother's breast. He is likely to go for big-breasted women and may derive the most enjoyment from lovemaking while he is sucking and playing with his partner's breasts.

■ If a man's head is thrust forward, it shows he is an aggressive lover, enjoying rough-and-tumble foreplay and lots of biting and scratching.

■ A man with a straight back is not very flexible and will probably be unimaginative in bed.

■ Retracted shoulders reveal suppressed anger, which could possibly explode during sex.

■ Square shoulders indicate maturity, the hallmark of a caring lover.

■ Bowed shoulders signify selfish lovers whose only concern is their own orgasm.

WOMEN

■ Women tend to be far more physically private than men, so it is wrong to assume that because a girl fobs you off when you start kissing her passionately on the street that she does not want or like sex. Women tend to regard early passionate behaviour in public as teasing rather than genuine, because it cannot go anywhere – at least not yet.

■ When a woman crosses her legs and adjusts her skirt, she is cutting off the possibility of an approach. Women who spread their hands across their chest in a defensive manner may be afraid of sex.

■ Women who sit with their knees and feet together or parallel and slightly crossed at the ankles have a desire for neatness and orderliness in their lives and are unlikely to be spontaneous in bed.

OTHER INDICATORS

■ At the disco, take a good look at the way your partner dances. The way they keep time to the music and the way they move signals their feelings about their own body. If they are in tune with their own bodies, they are more likely to tune into yours.

■ People who stand with their arms held loosely down the sides of their body are usually openminded about sex, taking it naturally in their stride. Those who lean backwards when seated, or stand with their arms folded across their chest, are more likely to have problems in the bedroom. Folded arms usually indicate a 'hands off' attitude.

■ If, when you are talking with someone, they smile and lean forward, they are likely to be open and receptive in bed.

FLIRTING

The silver screen elevated the act of flirtation to an art form. More passion could be implied in the lighting of a cigarette than in the most explicit sex scene, and often was

To flirt is to show an interest – usually sexual – in another person, and to do it playfully. The object is to make it clear, but not too clear, that it is not really serious although, depending on how things go, it might be.

TESTING THE GROUND

Flirting forms a very important element of the whole social game, because it is sexual but indirect. It allows us to 'say' sexual things or to send sexual

messages without committing ourselves to them. It saves us from being embarrassed or humiliated if the other person does not think of us in the same way.

It is unacceptable in our society to go up to a person and make immediate sexual suggestions, except in very unusual circumstances, such as when a prostitute approaches a client. We cannot approach a stranger and say 'I fancy you, let's go to bed', because the person is most likely to reject the advance, slap our face or call the police.

Instead we can test out the atmosphere and establish his or her likely response to a sexual overture by flirting first. A wink, a smile, a suggestive comment are all possible openers. In this way, we can show our interest in the other person playfully, without charging straight into a sexual proposition. In addition, we can try to entice the other person to think that sex might be a nice idea, particularly if they choose us as their partner.

Flirting, at its most successful, can achieve a good deal. It helps us to arouse the other person's interest, it hints at sexual availability, it suggests that we are nice to know and it may even indicate that we are quite proficient lovers too. Given all these possible effects, it is clear why flirting is so popular.

HOW WE FLIRT

Skilled flirters have an assortment of techniques at their disposal. They can engage in eye games (winking or gazing) or games involving body language.

Eye gaze has been found in many experiments to be the most powerful signal of intimacy and sexual interest, and it is known to play a major role in flirting too.

Looking fixedly into someone's eyes implies that you really like them. If they return your gaze, the chances are that things will turn out well for you.

Most of us have experienced the quickening of the pulse which happens when someone attractive

(including the eyes) and spoken language. In experiments social psychologists have found that the use of the eyes and the other nonverbal elements of behaviour have roughly four times as much effect as the verbal elements, particularly in a sexual context.

BECKONING WITH OUR BODY
Other flirtatious behaviour generally involves us moving in a suggestive way or displaying our body in sexually stimulating ways, or emphasizing our sexual outlines, by means of behaviour rather than dress.

One way of drawing attention to ourselves in a sexual sense is to run our hands across sexually associated parts of the body such as our hair, or to play our tongue around our lips or to stroke and caress parts of our body, for example by running a hand slowly up and down our thigh.

SEXUAL BANTER
Flirtation is not entirely a matter of body language and almost always has a verbal element to it as well. The spoken side can take on a number of forms, from innuendo to sexual jokes, to outrageously bold advances.

It can involve remarking on the sexual content of someone else's speech or taking their comments as if they were making sexual overtures, by adding a phrase such as '. . . as the actress said to the bishop'.

By indicating that your mind is tuned into sexual themes and inferring that the other person's is as well, you are demonstrating the sexual possibility in the encounter and inviting the other person to think about it also.

Sequences for doing this are quite well known and can even become fairly standardized. For example, studies of homosexual encounters have revealed that, in the 1950s when homosexual behaviour was illegal, the sequence for a homosexual pick-up was quite predictable, and was arranged so that the sexual theme was introduced cautiously.

A male homosexual would approach another male by asking for a light for his cigarette and giving a smile. He would make a remark about marriage or the in-laws and ask why the pick-up was out so late. He would then suggest a drink, but when they arrived at the nearest pub, would say that the atmosphere was unfriendly and suggest going to another nearby pub that had a good atmosphere. This one would be a known 'gay bar' and if the pick-up made no objection, the subject of sex would be mentioned explicitly.

Heterosexual encounters do not run to such a clear-cut formula because sex is not necessarily the ultimate goal, and, even when it is, the preamble tends to be much longer and more convoluted.

Generally, the main feature of heterosexual flirtation is that it gently and indirectly reminds people

Part of Marilyn Monroe's fascination lay in her ability to appear both little-girl vulnerable and sex-idol vamp. Here the baggy jumper contradicts her sexuality, but the look is flirtatious and the black tights lead the eye tantalizingly upwards

makes eyes at us at a party, but there are other body signals that hint at sexual interest as well. The most common ones are to do with the bodily postures or stances that we assume, and the gestures that we make with our hands.

So we can flirt with our bodies as well as our eyes. Leaning towards the other person (particularly with our lower body), touching them (even the slightest touch will have an effect) and emphasizing our own sexuality by the way that we stand or the way that we move can be effective. Additionally, we can draw attention to ourselves by the parts of our own body or clothing that we touch, stroke, or even caress.

Flirting divides itself into body language

of sexuality and leads on to, and then emphasizes, the sexual side of an encounter.

WHY WE FLIRT

We flirt in different ways according to the purpose that we have at the time. For example, we may occasionally flirt just for the fun of it and because it makes us feel good to see that someone else can be aroused by our behaviour and might actually desire us, even if both of us know that the arousal will go nowhere.

Research studies at Lancaster University, England have shown that most of us rarely believe that other people find us attractive or that they might desire us sexually. For that very human reason, the discovery that they respond well to playful sexual overtures takes us by surprise and boosts our egos.

IN THE OFFICE

Flirting can also be used as a way of handling conflict or difficulties at work. If a colleague or superior of the opposite sex challenges something that we have done and we know that we are in the wrong, then a flirtatious response can help to take the steam out of the situation and to give us back some of our self-esteem.

Flirting shows that we can have some influence on the feelings and behaviour of the other person. We can make them respond as sexual beings, where all persons are more or less equal and no one has any natural superiority over another. In a sexual sense, the concept of bosses and office juniors becomes meaningless.

ON A DATE

Flirting can also serve as a means of breaking the ice. Experiments by social psychologists have found that approximately 50 per cent of all human beings experience some degree of anxiety about dating members of the opposite sex and more than 60 per cent of all shy people actually panic about it.

One of the big issues in establishing a relationship involves presenting an attractive and desirable front to the other person. For this reason we unconsciously straighten up and smooth our hair down and make other gestures when we see someone who appeals to us.

Another way to make ourselves seem attractive and desirable is to flirt outrageously. This serves two functions. It emphasizes the sexual nature of the encounter and simultaneously adds a certain degree of flippancy that helps us to laugh and feel more relaxed.

WHAT MEN AND WOMEN WANT

Do men and women flirt in the same ways? Current research suggests that they do it slightly differently.

A study by Ron Riggio and Stanley Woll conducted in 1984 showed that women were more attracted to very expressive males who used lots of body language and showed their intentions very clearly. Men, however, were attracted to less expressive women who were more subtle in their body language.

It appears that women prefer to know that the man feels sexually confident and they gauge this by his body language, while men prefer a somewhat 'submissive' woman who allows them to play a major role in the encounter. Men evidently like to hog the floor when it comes to expressiveness in sexual contexts and women comply as part of their techniques for getting their man.

PLAYING HARD-TO-GET

One of the most commonly accepted ways of exciting interest from a sexual partner is teasing and playing hard-to-get. This method was even practised in Ancient Greece so it has a long if not venerable tradition.

But does it work? It is a high-risk strategy, since we might keep our partner hanging around too long and he or she might lose interest. Does uncertainty about our commitment make us seem more attractive or does it prompt the other person to go after someone more obviously available?

Several research studies in the United States have established that those people who play hard-to-get are probably not using the most effective technique available, unless they also give a very strong hint that they are not so hard-to-get for the right person.

KNOWING WHEN TO STOP

The trick is to appear selective, but not too selective. Studies by American psychologist Elaine Hatfield indicated that those who played hard-to-get for everyone risked ending up alone.

Those who played hard-to-get for almost everyone, yet were available to one particular person, were regarded as highly attractive. So flirting like this works only if you can couple the 'hard-to-get' act with a 'but I might be available to you if you keep trying' act.

A study conducted in 1984 by Rex Wright of Maryland University established a further advantage to this sort of behaviour. Not only is it a good sexual ploy, but we assume that moderately selective people are nicer, more attractive and better people than those who are either always available or never available. It is as though they have to be selective in order to keep their dating behaviour under control.

If they were not selective they would be overwhelmed with offers because they are such attractive people. But they are not so unavailable or difficult that we would have no chance with them.

Those people who are too selective are thought to be conceited and probably not worth the effort of chasing. Unselective people are thought to be

Dress, posture, eyes and lips are all involved in this flirtation. By cupping Albert Finney's chin in her hand, Diane Cilento allows her fingertips to suggest a kiss

desperate and so are regarded as unattractive just because of that.

There has to be some point to the chase. The trick is to make it clear that we are worth wooing and that, with a bit of extra effort, we can be won.

FLIRTING AND SEXUAL MOVES

One problem with flirtation is that because it is indirect it is open to misunderstanding. Unfortunately, some men are rather inept as distinguishing the playful flirt from the big sexual come-on.

Men tend to assume that their level of arousal is reciprocated by the woman and their judgement in this may be further confused if they have been drinking alcohol. So, if they feel particularly aroused themselves, they will assume that the woman they are flirting with does too.

The less experienced or the more socially anxious

the man is, the more these errors can occur.

The chance of misunderstood signals are aggravated if the men have been drinking, since this simultaneously increases their arousal, decreases their inhibitions and diminishes their ability to discriminate between the flirtatious joke and the serious sexual invitation.

Research has shown that men who have been drinking are more likely to read sexual content into particular stories than are men who are sober. Similarly, they tend to interpret women's behaviour as sexy and inviting.

But despite the occasional misunderstanding, flirtation is almost always enjoyable. People feel good when a flirtatious approach is reciprocated and are spared bruised egos when an advance is rejected. They find out where they stand and can decide where to go from there.

The resting of hand on thigh draws attention to Hedy Lamarr's sexuality, but Victor Mature's loving gaze makes it clear that subtle body signals and gentle flirtation are not necessary

KISSING

Kissing marks the beginning and often the end of a sexual relationship. It can be the first confession of desire, and when that stops the relationship is probably over

Scientists have discovered that kissing really is a matter of personal chemistry. At puberty, groups of sebaceous glands develop inside the mouth and at the edges of the lips which produce substance called semiochemicals.

These semiochemicals are biological signals which rest on the skin and are transmitted by touch, as in during kissing, when they are passed from one person to the other and cause heightened sexual desire.

BIOLOGY TAKES OVER

If you have ever felt that kissing is contagious – that having kissed someone you could carry on for ever – there is a biological reason for that, too. As passion rises, each partner releases even more semiochemicals, thus increasing their kissability.

During sexual arousal, mouths become swollen and red. This is more noticeable among women, whose mouths are usually slightly larger than men's and who sometimes exaggerate this natural tendency by wearing lipstick.

WHY MEN PEEK

But lip size is not the only difference between men and women when they kiss. Canadian anthropologist Pierre Maranda found in one experiment that 97 per cent of women kept their eyes closed when kissing, compared with only 30 per cent of men.

This does not mean that women are more likely than men to find their partner's looks unappealing – but that closed eyes allow them to fantasize while still enjoying the experience of the moment.

Men, however, who are more visually stimulated, find that keeping their eyes open heightens their own desire.

WHEN THE KISSING BEGINS TO STOP

The way you kiss not only reveals a lot about the way you love. Like a thermometer, it can measure the warmth and degree of intensity of your relationship.

The Marriage Guidance Council has found that kissing is one of the first activities to go when a relationship is breaking up. Surprisingly, couples find it easier to continue making love than they do to kiss each other.

It is because of the extremely intimate nature of the sexual kiss, for example, that prostitutes usually refrain from kissing their clients.

LOVE GOES

Couples who give each other perfunctory kisses on

Not a clutcher afraid of losing his lady but a more practised seducer, this Romeo raises his Juliet's face to meet his and then plants a tender kiss on her lips

22

the cheek may well be showing the signs of growing apart and not want to be close to each other any more.

Kisses plonked on the forehead may show that your relationship is retarded and that your partner still regards you as an immature child, not a passionate adult. Sex between partners who rarely kiss each other tends to be rushed, with very little body touching. It is easy to fall into a situation where kissing becomes just another social function rather than a symbol of your feelings for each other.

THE CARING KISS
Taking time to kiss each other deeply will help to ensure the relationship remains strong and caring. If your partner is still giving you full-blooded kisses on the mouth, the chances are your sex life is satisfying and also fulfilling.

And then, as passion heightens, the lips will naturally search out new territories to explore and conquer – the erogenous zones of the ear lobes, nipples, clitoris or penis. Together with the tongue and the lips themselves, these are the most sensitive areas of the body. And kisses on the ear lobes or even the tips of the fingers show that you are prepared to spend time pleasing each other.

HARMFUL EFFECTS
Kissing may be good for the soul but it is not always good for the body. Doctors have discovered that kissing has the same effect as stress – thyroid activity shoots up, glucose production rises and the body's production of insulin stops.

Kissing can also spread disease – transferring up to 250 different bacteria and viruses. And every time you kiss your heart beats much faster. According to research carried out in the United States, this can cause your life span to be reduced by three minutes.

The good news is that each kiss uses up three calories. But the bad news is that you will need 1,000 kisses to lose just 0.5 kilos in weight – and those kisses may take 50 hours off your life span!

AS GOOD AS TOOTHPASTE
Dentists are pleased to report that kissing is good for the teeth. It encourages saliva, which washes off food particles and also lowers the level of acid in the mouth. This can help prevent the build-up of plaque and may lessen tooth decay.

FROM KISSING TO HANDSHAKE
Historically, kissing has always been an integral part of social intercourse in England. In medieval times, knights on the jousting field would kiss each other before taking part in a tournament. And in the 16th century, hosts would signal their welcome to guests by inviting them to kiss each member of their family – on the lips.

Although not returning his kisses the lady is clearly willing. Her part seems to be to provide the appetizer to the main course, and to that end she proffers first her cheek, then the nape of her neck

TIPS AND TECHNIQUES

TRY THESE
Ticklish tongue tracing *Run the tip of your tongue round your lover's lips, inside and out, and then over and around his or her tongue.*

Nibble, nibble *Gently kiss the corners of your lover's lips. Keep going from one side of the mouth to the other until your partner demands you go further.*

Lots and little *Plant a hundred little kisses on your partner's parted lips, working up to a crescendo.*

The searching kiss *Push your tongue hard into all the recesses of your lover's mouth.*

The rhythmic kiss *With your mouth held over your partner's, thrust in and out with a strong, stabbing movement. Many couples find that this can bring almost unbearable excitement when accompanying intercourse.*

It was only when the Industrial Revolution forced small, closed communities to break up and to go to the cities in search of work that lip kissing evolved via hand kissing into the handshake greeting we are familiar with today.

KISSES THAT GIVE YOU AWAY

Just as you can tell a lot about a person by their style of dress, their type of home and how they speak, so you can also learn a good deal about them by the way that they kiss:

■ Closed-eyed kissers can be true romantics at heart, falling in love as often as other couples quarrel, despite knowing that the ending may be unhappy.

■ Open-eyed kissers can be realists, but they are also fairly safe to fall in love with. Once they meet the partner of their dreams, they are often eternally faithful.

■ Kissers who begin with a short peck followed by another slightly longer one, before joining lips, hide a passionate and sensual nature behind that slow build-up. They are not the sort of people who commit themselves quickly, but once a decision is made, they stick to it.

■ Cuddlers have been around long enough – or are intuitive enough – to appreciate the pleasures of anticipation. Usually soft-spoken, they seem to have endless poise and confidence and reveal this side of their nature in bed with lengthy and exquisite foreplay.

■ At the opposite extreme is the public kisser, the type who grabs every opportunity to grab you. Acting like red-hot lovers on the street, in the pub, at a party, they only get a kick out of kissing when there is an audience. For them, the sexual thrill comes mainly from other people's belief in their sexual prowess.

■ Clutchers initially appear confident and strong, giving the impression they are running the relationship and can get out any time it suits them. But deep down, lovers who always hold on tightly to one part of your body while kissing may be terrified in case you discover their basic weakness and then leave them first.

■ All-over kissers tend to live their whole lives to the full. Whether eating, drinking or making love, they concentrate totally on the task in hand.

The practice of hand kissing stems from chivalric times when the gesture indicated respect and obedience. It is occasionally still used this way, although more often than not it is just a beginning....

Usually optimistic people, they view each encounter as a new and exciting experience.

■ Lovers who kiss with their mouths closed may have closed minds as well. Closed lips signal a taker, not a giver.

■ Puckered-lips kissers are very similar to closed-lips kissers. While the act of puckering seems to say 'come on', the reality of kissing puckered lips reveals a definite rejection. These kissers want everything their own way in kissing or in life.

■ The vacuum kiss occurs when two people open their mouths and, instead of caressing and exploring, suck inwards as though trying to draw air. Soon, the mouths adhere so tightly together that there is pain instead of pleasure. Vacuum kissers are often quite violent personalities who like to rush their partner into lovemaking rather than let them decide for themselves. They may also have a jealous disposition.

■ French kissers are gentle versions of vacuum kissers, letting their tongues explore at leisure, and enjoy. They can make wonderful friends, as well as lovers, just as their deep kisses ensure that they can taste all their lover's feelings, so they share all their friends' sufferings – and also joys – too.

They crave intimacy with another person to the extent that they sometimes leave themselves open to disappointment. They have no inhibitions about letting other people know what they want and to this end can be surprisingly outspoken.

DO'S AND DONT'S

■ *Do not give wet, messy kisses. You normally swallow before kissing, but make sure that you do.*

■ *Do not go on and on with the same kiss for too long. One of you might get bored. Ring the changes by trying different sorts of kisses.*

■ *Do not give loose-lipped sloppy kisses. It always feels better to have a firm mouth against yours.*

■ *Do keep your mouth in tip top condition. Poorly kept teeth and smelly breath are a real turn off, and an insult to your lover. You would not dream of intimately caressing your partner with oily, muddy hands, yet a lot of people attempt long, deep kisses without a thought for the condition of their mouths.*

■ *Do visit a dentist regularly, clean your teeth thoroughly and frequently and use an antiseptic mouthwash to keep your breath fresh.*

■ *Do make sure that you and your lover eat the same strongly flavoured foods at the same time.*

■ Hand kissers are usually so charming that although you know their sincerity is only skin-deep, you fall for them anyway.

■ Ear nibblers show something other than a knowledge of the body's erogenous zones. Ear nibbling can be a way for shy people to avoid direct confrontation.

This self-consciousness shows itself in everyday situations by an unwillingness to put themselves forward until confident they have something worthwhile to contribute.

It is important to differentiate between nibblers and biters, especially since a nibble can easily turn into a bite.

■ Persistent love-bite kissers are human grafitti artists, leaving their mark wherever they go and on whoever they go with. A love-bite may be an owner's brand as much as a sign of passion.

But whether kisses are violent, loving, passionate or gentle – between partners or among family and friends – one thing is as true today as it has ever been: kisses always tell the truth about how much you love or are loved.

LIP PLAY

Kissing is a sensual art vital to lovemaking but many of us are unaware of the exciting variety of pleasures it can give. By learning the erotic techniques of kissing, a couple can do much to change their sex life.

Throughout the time leading up to lovemaking you will have been showing your affection for your partner in occasional kisses, hugs and light touches.

Now you will want to take that contact a stage further. Kisses which have consisted of pressing the lips on the cheek, the neck, a hand or an arm will now move to the lips and become more directly erotic.

THE KEY TO SENSUAL FOREPLAY

The mouth is highly responsive. Second only to the genitals on the sensitivity scale, and with greater mobility than either the penis or the vagina, it offers a great variety of sensual pleasures. The mouth also gives us the ability to taste, which means that with the nose so near, we can experience touch, taste and smell at the same time. With all the potential enjoyment and excitement to be derived from oral contact, kissing techniques are clearly of great importance in lovemaking.

THE IMPORTANCE OF TECHNIQUE

Kissing should not be restricted to mouth-to-mouth contact. The mouth is perfectly equipped to feel and taste every crease and crevice of the body.

Kissing your lover's erogenous zones is the most intimate and stimulating act of foreplay. Start loveplay with the feet by kissing them both all over. Give sexy, soft kisses to the sensitive arch of the instep and plant tiny, pursed-lipped kisses on the toes. Stretch the palms of your lover's hands taut, and lick and kiss them all over.

Attack the responsive area behind the knees with firm, forceful kisses with just a hint of teeth behind the lips. Continue up the legs to the inside of the thighs. Reckless, rapid kisses all over the inner thigh will excite both the giver and the receiver.

Put your face right against your lover's thigh as you press your lips down. Sink your mouth into the buttocks with sharp, strong kisses. Trace the spine with your tongue and sprinkle light kisses either side. Pamper the shoulders with kisses and drive your lover wild with desire by alternating soft with firm kisses on the back of the neck, and by nuzzling the ear lobes.

KISSES SWEETER THAN WINE

In Ancient Rome, kissing apparently had a function. Anxious husbands concerned at the amount of wine that their wives were drinking during the day, would return home and taste their partner's lips to discover whether they had been drinking that day. The Romans were so keen on kissing that they had three words for it.
Osculum – the kiss to the cheek between friends
Basium – the kiss on the lips
Suavum – the lover's kiss.
But the emperor Tiberius banned the practice when lip sores became endemic throughout the population.

THE GREAT PRETENDERS

These are some people who kiss anyone and everyone – lovers, ex-lovers, teachers, colleagues, even traffic wardens. They give the impression of having lots of love to give, of warmth and affection, but underneath they are terrified of physical contact. While they keep up the facade, their partner is often bewildered by their lack of passion.

A woman's breasts respond far more to oral caresses than to any other. A man should try sucking the tip of his lover's nipples sensually and then pushing as much of her breast into his mouth as possible, taking the nipple gently between his teeth and flicking his tongue back and forth across its hardened tip.

Kissing plays a vital part both in foreplay and after lovemaking is over. It makes your lover feel wanted and cherished

VIRGINITY

In Christian cultures, the traditional white wedding symbolizes the virtuous virginity of the bride, but in some societies, virgins are feared, not revered

Whether or not virginity is regarded as a desirable state in itself, cultures sometimes have beliefs that virgins have extraordinary powers.

In medieval Europe, for example, people believed that only a virgin could capture a unicorn. Eastern European peasants for example, (Rumanian and Bulgarian) apparently believed that male virgin soldiers were impervious to bullets.

One of the most unfortunate myths is that if a man has syphilis or some other venereal disease, he can be cured by having intercourse with a virgin. Rural Serbians and natives of the island of Jamaica believed this, and undoubtedly other myths have existed and probably continue to exist.

RITUAL DEFLOWERING

Virgins have been, and still are, considered to be especially dangerous for one reason or another. The Gond of India are said not to admire virgins, because they somehow store up too much psychic power. And in several societies men do not want virgin brides and a man might complain bitterly if he should discover that he has just married one.

In these societies, the bride has to be deflowered by some man other than her husband. This man may often have special status as a *shaaman* or medicine man – someone who has great psychic power of his own – as with the Kagaba of South America. Among some Eskimos only the daughter of a chief has to be deflowered by a shaaman.

The Kamchadal of Eastern Siberia require a stranger to be the first to have intercourse with a virgin – or with a widow who wants to re-marry.

The Russian writer and traveller Krasheninnikov, writing in 1764, reported that for a while the Kamchadal were in despair because no strangers were showing up. But then the Russian Cossacks appeared on the scene and saved the day.

A custom known variously as *jus primae noctis* 'law of the first night' or *droit du seigneur* 'right of the (feudal) lord' has been reported from various societies, including medieval European societies. A chief, feudal lord or some other high dignitary has the right, or possibly the obligation, to deflower all of the women who are under his jurisdiction.

This custom or one very like it has been described for the Marshallese and Tongans of the Pacific, the Seri of Central America, the Zande of Central Africa and the Dard of Central Asia. The justification, or even motivation, for this custom is probably the same as, or similar to, that for ritual deflowering. It is not necessarily insatiable lust on the part of a chief, but a belief that virginity is too powerful and dangerous for the average man to cope with.

In theory, a virgin is either a woman who has never had a penis inside her vagina – or a man who has never inserted his penis into a vagina.

This means that many people with extensive sexual experience would still count as being virgin. For example, a woman who has enjoyed oral or anal sex can still be a virgin.

So can a woman who has used a penis substitute – a dildo or a finger – as long as she has not been penetrated by a real human penis.

Men and women with exclusive homosexual experience could also be defined as being virgins. The Marquis de Sade wrote about 'taking the virginity of someone's mouth or anus' as well as vagina, but this way of speaking is not usual.

SCOTTISH DEFLORATION

The question of whether there really was such a custom anywhere in Europe has not been settled. Some conservative historians say that it occurred only in a few parts of Scotland at some early point in the Middle Ages – if it occurred at all. Other reconstructions are more expansive and suggest that not only European feudal lords but even some monks were involved in the ritual.

Possibly the earliest record of ritualistic deflowering comes from the writings of Herodotus, the Greek historian of the 5th century BC. He writes that in Babylon every woman had to have sexual intercourse with a stranger in a temple dedicated to the goddess Mylitta (a deity Herodotus equates with Aphrodite, goddess of love). Every woman had to do this once in her life.

Herodotus does not say so explicitly, but it is likely that the act took place before the woman married. And, if this is the case, it suggests that a fear of virgins is a very ancient belief.

VIRGIN BRIDES

Fear of virginity can be contrasted dramatically with the enthusiasm some societies have shown for female pre-marital virginity, and the horror expressed if a bride is not a virgin.

One consequence of this other extreme was the development of a defloration mania. Brothels in 19th-century Europe – and later – were hard pressed to provide virgin prostitutes and had to resort to 'cosmetic virginity'. Vaginal canals were treated with alum to make them tighter, and vaginal openings stitched together in imitation unbroken hymens.

In societies where virginity in brides is important, marriage is usually looked on as a contract between two families. Part of the contract is the guarantee by the bride's family that she is 'intact' and will produce children only by her husband.

Since this was the general western view of things until fairly recently, it may come as a surprise that several societies consider it more important for an unmarried women to prove that she can produce children at all, rather than dwelling on questions of future paternity.

In such societies, marriage occurs when the woman becomes pregnant or has a child but not before.

A variant of this was the custom of 'handfasting' formerly practised in Scotland, in which intercourse was tacitly permitted before the marriage itself.

ENSURING VIRGINITY

In pro-virginity societies, parents have used various means to ensure that their daughters would remain intact. Chaperoning and seclusion are common techniques. But in many societies in Africa and the Middle East (seldom elsewhere) more drastic measures are taken.

Operations are performed on the sex-organs of little girls either to cut down on their sexual feelings

In some cultures, adult virginity is simply unimaginable. The anthropologists Smith and Dale report the following conversation with an Ila man from south-eastern Africa. They were trying to discover the Ila word for 'virgin'.

Anthropologist: 'What would you call a woman who has grown up without ever knowing man?'

Ila man: 'Well, I should call her a fool.'

It turned out that there is no special word for 'virgin' in Ila, as is also the case for several other languages including Abipon and Tukano of South America and Pukapukan and Trukses of the Pacific.

or to make it physically impossible for a girl to receive a penis into her vagina.

To reduce interest in sex, the clitoris is cut off in an operation which is known as clitoridectomy – or female circumcision.

This practice is almost only performed in societies that circumcise boys, but male circumcision is a considerably more common custom.

To make intercourse virtually impossible, the opening to the vagina is sewn shut in a procedure known as an infibulation or pharaonic circumcision. Despite its name, it seems that the Ancient Egyptians did not practise it.

It occurs at present almost exclusively in Muslim societies found in Ethiopia, Somalia, the Sudan and Southern Egypt. On the day of the wedding, a midwife comes to the cut the vagina open.

Both clitoridectomy and infibulation have come under severe attack by international feminist

In some cultures, the marriage contract stipulates that the bride be a virgin. Here, 18th-century wedding guests are checking that the bride is – or was – 'intact'

groups. But although these practices have been made illegal in at least one country, Egypt, they continue in others.

CHASTITY BELTS

Historically, it was probably infibulation that triggered the invention of chastity belts, which were created in Europe in the Middle Ages.

Crusaders undoubtedly came into contact with infibulated women and brought back home with them from the Middle East the notion that women could be 'closed off' or 'locked up' in some way.

The belief that the Crusaders fastened chastity belts made of metal on to their wives before they had been in the Holy Land seems to be pure myth.

THE BROKEN HYMEN

Attitudes about the unbroken hymen have ranged from indifference to intense concern. Some groups – the Gond of India and the Kaska of Canada – apparently have no idea of the existence of a hymen at all. At the other extreme, most traditional societies of the Middle East, Africa and Europe have made an unbroken hymen almost a fetish.

The theory that an intact hymen is proof of virginity does not necesssarily hold up. Cases have been reported of women who have had sexual intercourse many times, but whose hymens were so elastic that they have not broken. Among such women are a few prostitutes, and even some women who have given birth.

Whether unmarried girls were fitted with chastity belts is still unclear.

Chastity belts are still available and are manufactured commercially by at least one firm. In Britain in 1971, a decision that chastity belts were an item of apparel, and therefore subject to an 11 per cent sales tax was challenged by a 70-year-old widower and Labour Member of Parliament. The grounds were that there should be no tax on protecting a lady's virtue.

In the Caucasus, unmarried girls wore chastity corsets that were fastened with numerous knots. On the wedding night, the groom was supposed to undo all the knots one by one.

PROVING VIRGINITY

Many societies require that brides undergo virginity tests of one sort or another. Usually this means that a girl would have to stain a bed sheet or some clothing with the blood from the hymen, ruptured in first intercourse.

Sometimes such a sheet or other piece of evidence is displayed publicly to wedding guests or other members of the community. Similar customs have been observed in many European societies, for example among peasants in Greece, Russia, Italy, Africa, the Far East and the Pacific.

The rules about female virginity are essentially concerned with ensuring that a woman will bear only her husband's children. Today, this can be accomplished with efficient contraception, which has brought about the most serious challenge to the idea of virginity as a virtue in the entire history of the Judaeo – Christian culture.

CHAPTER TWO

SEXUAL AWAKENING

SEX SIGNALS

Why are some people sexy and others not?
What attracts us to someone we have not
even met? Do our clothes, gestures and
actions say more than we think they do?

Even before two people have exchanged a single word, they may well have had a lengthy conversation – in terms of body language. The human body is constantly sending out conscious and unconscious signals to social companions, particularly people we feel sexually attracted to. And this leads to the question – what makes an individual attractive?

Some years ago a national newspaper printed photographs of 12 women, and invited their readers to place them in order of sexual attractiveness. The results were contrary to the idea that 'beauty is in the eye of the beholder' and that everyone has their own unique ideas of what makes others attractive.

People agreed with each other most of the time about who was most attractive, least attractive, second most attractive, and so on. The survey also contradicted another frequently made claim – that men's ideas and women's ideas of what makes a woman attractive are quite different. They were not – men and women found the same faces attractive. Nor did age make much difference to the way the photos were judged.

WHAT'S IN A FACE?

Exactly what makes a particular face attractive to people is difficult to pinpoint, but in the past a great deal has been written about the importance of facial proportions. Other attempts to analyze the sexual attractiveness of faces have concentrated on the size and shape of individual features. This approach tends to end up with an 'attractiveness' score which largely depends on points given to various features of the face.

Another possibility which may help to explain

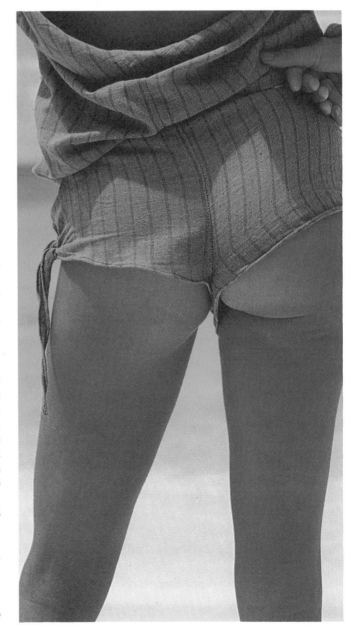

A scantily clad figure is often more of a sexual turn-on than a naked body. These barely covered buttocks, held at a slight angle, throw out strong and confident sexual signals, which could be interpreted by some men as an invitation to intimacy

sexual attraction of certain faces is that they remind us of babies and very young children, and that when we feel drawn to these forms we are answering an innate call to love and protect and care for the young of our species.

If this is true we would expect that the more a head resembled the domed head of a baby the more attractive it would be. Also we might expect women to be more prone to this effect than men, and indeed they are.

When 330 men, women and children of various ages were shown profile drawings of faces, they liked those with domed foreheads best, and they were especially attracted to foreheads which were much more domed relative to the rest of the face. The effect seemed to depend on the onset of adolescence. Girls began to show preference for domed foreheads

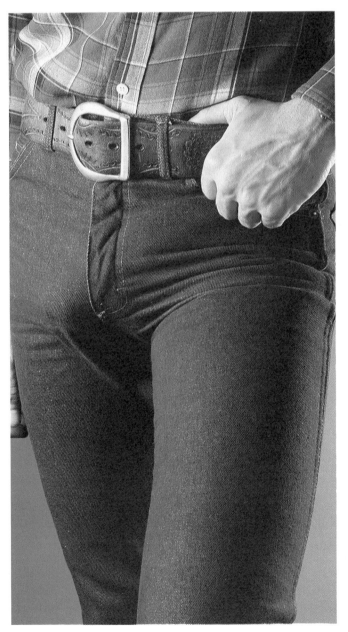

when they were around the age of 12, but in men the preference emerges much more slowly, and never becomes as strong as in a woman.

Ideas of facial beauty are not, however, standard worldwide. Looking at the whole range of human societies, there seem to be no general standards for what makes a face sexually attractive, with one possible, if unsurprising, exception. No one, it seems, finds a poor complexion attractive, perhaps because a clear complexion is seen as a sign of good health – an obviously desirable characteristic.

FACIAL FEATURES
The face is the part of the body first noticed in an encounter, and there are three features which have special significance in women – the eyes, lips and cheeks.

The eyes are the most striking feature of the face, the one that is always looked at first. Women often use make-up to make their eyes look large.

The eyes also send out sexual signals, in two ways. The pupil of the eye becomes larger when the person likes what he or she is looking at. This is especially so if they are looking at another person. Also, people observe very closely a set of unwritten rules, one of which says you do not look at people for any length of time unless you are prepared to consider some relationship with them.

If you do not want a relationship, you collect such information about them as you feel you need when they are not looking back, or in glances so fleeting the other has no time to realize you have made them.

The sexual significance of the lips is obvious – kissing – but it is sometimes claimed that for women they have a less obvious significance, because they 'echo' the powerful, but forbidden, sexual signal of the lips of the vagina.

The lips, too, are made up by many women, who often change their shape to an ideal width and give them a richer colour making them resemble the lips of the vagina even more strongly.

The similarities between the two are obvious, as are the differences. The argument that the human lips have evolved their prominence as a genital echo would seem to be strengthened by this desire to accentuate the similarity between the two – a desire which may have arisen partly because humans started wearing clothes and covering their genitals.

The argument faces problems, however, for men also have lips so the 'echo' cannot have any relevance to their anatomy.

The cheeks are significant because they are the main area to blush. Blushing results from blood

Clothes not only cover the human body – they can also accentuate certain areas. Encased in a pair of tight jeans, a man's penis presents a clearly visible bulge to the interested eye. A hand strategically placed in a belt can act as an effective 'arrow'

circulating in the surface blood vessels, and is part of a general pattern of physical response, which may or may not be sexual. It can just as well be embarrassment, or indignation.

Women tend to blush more readily than men and, rightly or wrongly, it is often interpreted as a sexual invitation. Make-up often includes reddening the cheeks, which is perhaps an attempt to capture a permanent blush. In the past, when illness abounded, it may have been an attempt to make the wearer look healthier than she really was.

BREASTS AND BUTTOCKS

Two parts of the body everyone immediately associates with sexual attraction, besides the face, are the female breasts, and the buttocks. It is often said that men can be divided into three categories, coarsely referred to as 'breast men', 'buttock men' and 'leg men'. Indeed, research has shown this to be true, but there seem to be two types of 'leg men' – those who like large thighs and calves, and those who prefer slim legs.

The characteristics of these different 'types' of men, in terms of personality, habits, interests and outlook, were found to be very different. It appears that extrovert men prefer women with large breasts and buttocks, while introvert men feel overwhelmed by well developed women and are more at ease with thinner women.

The reason for this may well lie in the sexual significance of the female breasts and buttocks.

The adult female human is the only primate to possess a pair of swollen mammary glands when she is not producing milk. This shows they are more than simply a feeding device. One school of thought is that they mimic a primary sexual zone – the buttocks – and this gives the female a powerful sexual signal, particularly when she is dressed in such a way as to emphasize her breasts.

The buttocks are more pronounced in the female than the male and this is an uniquely human feature. If a human female were to bend down and present her buttocks to a male in the same way that the female ape adopts her invitation-to-copulation posture, the genitals could be seen, framed by the two smooth hemispheres of flesh. This association makes them an important sexual signal, and if a woman slightly emphasizes the movement of her buttocks as she walks, it acts as a powerful and obvious erotic signal to a male.

HAIRY CHESTS AND BROAD SHOULDERS

Surveys of what physique women prefer in men found that they prefer men of average build, but if the man's physique is to deviate it should be bigger above the waist, rather than below it, or around it. Women, in fact, have a very reliable preference for Vs rather than pears.

The studies also found differences between women who preferred different physiques. Women

---

IN SEARCH OF THE PERFECT HUMAN FACE

There are no universally accepted standards of facial beauty and attempts to quantify it through such methods as male and female beauty contests are notoriously unreliable. Psychologists working in the United States have attempted to discover which facial features are regarded as most attractive in both men and women. The survey worked by people attributing points to certain features, and suggests that the most popular 'perfect face' for both men and women would be oval-shaped.

■ *The mouth to chin distance should be less than the height of the forehead*
■ *The width of each cheek ought not to be greater than the width of the mouth*
■ *Hair straight*
■ *Eyes large and preferably blue*
■ *Eyelashes long*
■ *Nose straight in profile and 'diamond-shaped' from the front*
■ *Mouth neither too wide nor too narrow.*

The most attractive nose shape was found to be straight – followed by upturned – for both men and women. But in men a "Roman nose' was thought to look better than a 'droopy nose', while for women, it was the other way round.

The resulting composite face should in theory be perceived as beautiful. However, in reality even the most beautiful face is not symmetrical. The left and right hand sides may have the same proportions, but they are not mirror images.

When photographs of a face are cut in half, and the two right hand sides (centre) and the two left hand sides (bottom) are stuck together, the resulting two faces look completely different.

---

who liked well-built men tended either to be interested in competitive sports, or raised in a fatherless home. Perhaps they chose an idealized male figure, to compensate for the father they never had. The woman's own physique also played a part, but in an unexpected direction – smaller women preferred larger men.

Other surveys of this type have found strong evidence that men and women systematically misjudge what turns on the other sex. Men think women like a man who has a muscular hairy chest, broad shoulders, and a large penis, but the women in the same survey said they actually liked small buttocks and a tall slim physique.

Looking further afield to non-western societies, the reports of anthropologists make it very clear

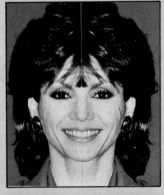

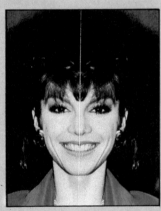

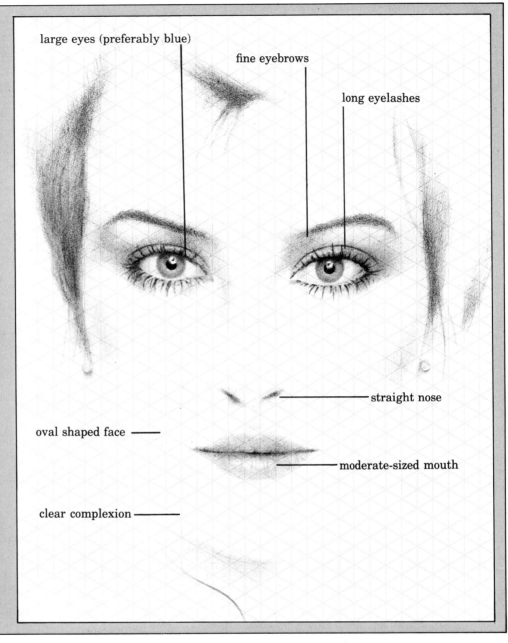

large eyes (preferably blue)

fine eyebrows

long eyelashes

straight nose

oval shaped face

moderate-sized mouth

clear complexion

that there are few universal standards for the body beautiful. There are societies where tall and power-fully built women are preferred, others where thin women are in demand. Many societies like women to have a broad pelvis, and wide hips, but at least one society specifically dislikes these features.

Most other human societies are not as 'breast conscious' as our own, but those that are again have widely different ideas about the right size and shape for the breast, some preferring long pendulous breasts, others upright, well-rounded ones, others simply going for sheer size.

Some cultures set great store by parts of the body we in the West pay little attention to, such as the lower leg, and value especially small shapely ankles, or fleshy calves.

THE BODY AND CLOTHES

Humans wear clothes, not just for warmth, but to cover the genitals, and in most societies the female breasts.

Clothes can of course do more than simply cover bits of the body we are not allowed to show off. They can also be used to mould the shape of the body – the bra being the obvious example.

Clothes may also be used to get around the taboo on displaying the genitals. Women today often wear shorts or jeans which are tight enough to display the outline of the vagina, even at the expense of some comfort. Similarly some men wear jeans so tight that they create a suggestive bulge in the region of the groin, reflecting the long-forgotten 'codpiece' of the 15th and 16th centuries.

MASTURBATION

Masturbation is an important part of lovemaking. Most people think of it as a solitary activity, but as a shared experience it can be one of the most exciting ways a couple can learn about each other's needs

Masturbation is a source of interest to almost everyone, if only because most of us do it.

Yet there are probably more myths and old wives' tales concerning masturbation than about any other area of sexual activity. There are stories of it leading to blindness, blood loss, impotence – the list goes on for ever.

All these claims are false, but over the years they have served to give masturbation an extremely poor press. And although nearly everyone masturbates, a large number of people are still extremely secretive about it.

DOES EVERYONE MASTURBATE?
Almost all men and women masturbate from time to time. It has been said that 90 per cent of men admit to masturbation and the other 10 per cent are liars.

Some people – including about a third of all women – say that they cannot remember a time in their lives when they have not masturbated. Others date its beginnings from puberty, while yet others seem to start when in a permanent relationship.

But it will almost certainly have started earlier. Almost all babies play with their genitals. And most parents are aware that their toddlers sometimes masturbate, although whether this kind of genital stimulation ends up with what adults would call an orgasm, is difficult to tell.

MORE WAYS FOR A WOMAN
Masturbation is almost certainly less common among females than among males. But this is partly because it is more difficult to define – and hence quantify – with women.

With men, masturbation involves direct stimulation of the penis, and generally ends in ejaculation. But for women almost any part of the body can be a source of arousal and orgasm, and stimulation can give an infinitely more variable sensation.

There may be social as well as physical reasons for the fact that some women do not practise 'overt' masturbation, but stimulate themselves in less obvious, indefinable ways. Parental influence is probably an important factor.

Parents of both sexes generally tend to be more tolerant when their boys handle their genitals than when their girls do.

By stimulating themselves without directly handling their genitals girls can pretend they are not doing it.

Some girls masturbate by sitting on their heels, others while riding their bicycle. Masturbation may become attached to activities which involve 'legitimate' gential contact, such as washing the vulva or even urination – the permutations are endless.

In 20 years' clinical experience, one expert in this area has collected more than a hundred non-genital ways that women masturbate.

REASONS FOR DENIAL

Most definitions of masturbation imply that it ends in orgasm. So if it does not, a woman may think of herself as not masturbating.

This kind of self-delusion is not confined to women. Some men are brought up to feel guilty or sinful about sex.

In later life, they may masturbate the way other men do, but block off the consciousness of an orgasm. Some may rub their erect penis with no intention of ejaculating, and so think that they are not masturbating.

People who feel guilty may confine their masturbation to between waking and sleeping, and so feel able to deny masturbating because they are not fully conscious.

These systems of denial indicate how guilty many people feel about arousing themselves sexually. Yet masturbation is a valuable experience, not simply a pleasurable one.

It is the way most of us first learn about how our bodies respond to sexual stimulation. Just as we learn to talk before we hold a conversation, most of us masturbate before we learn to make love.

HOW MEN MASTURBATE

The most usual method of male masturbation, at least from adolescence onwards, is to stimulate the rim on the head of the penis by encircling it with the fingers and then moving the hand up and down in a pumping action.

The main stimulation of the rim is done by the thumb and index finger, but the remaining fingers encircle the shaft of the penis with varying degrees of grip in different men. Some men use their other hand to stimulate their scrotum, anus or other parts of their body.

Most men stop at some stage as if to prolong the pleasure – others 'tease' themselves by coming to

the edge of orgasm and then stopping and repeating this a few times.

Some men even stop altogether at this stage and get up and do something else, only to continue later.

How much pressure is used is a matter of personal choice – some men use more than others. The guideline is not to use too much – too much pressure can be painful.

Variations consist of lying face down and using the flat of the hand to press the penis on to the mattress or floor while making copulatory movements.

HOW WOMEN MASTURBATE

Women masturbate in a variety of ways, but the most usual method is to lie on their back and stimulate the vulva with one hand. A few women stimulate only the vagina when masturbating, but the majority usually stimulate the clitoris either directly or indirectly.

The variations on this theme are vast. The whole vulva may be stroked or massaged, or one specific area – particularly the clitoris – stimulated.

The edges of the inner lips might be rubbed or

trapped between the fingers using either a vertical or circular motion.

Some women stimulate themselves so lightly it is like a butterfly, some use an intermediate touch and others use heavy pressure.

On reaching the plateau stage of arousal, women usually change the type of stimulation and, as orgasm approaches, the clitoris may be ignored entirely in favour of another body area. Most women stop and then start in a teasing way, although some women race to orgasm as quickly as possible.

They may insert one or two fingers into the vagina and rotate them or move them in and out. This can sometimes be related to a fantasy that they are being penetrated, and can serve to slow things down for a while, and so prolong the pleasure.

A few women put an object of some kind into their vagina. Everything from vibrators and dildos to candles and cucumbers are, and have been, used. There are obvious dangers to using such objects – they could get stuck.

It is during masturbation rather than intercourse that women demonstrate their greater sexual capacities compared with men. Where a man will usually stop masturbating after ejaculation, many women experience multiple orgasms during masturbation – up to 50 at one session.

LEARNING THROUGH SHARING

The aim of these sessions is for the couple to become totally at ease with their partner watching as they masturbate, so that both can learn to masturbate the other as well – or even better – than he or she does.

First set the scene – ensure that the room you choose is private, warm and relaxing. If you find it relaxes you, perhaps have a little drink – not too much – beforehand. Use music too, if this helps get the mood right. Have a bath or shower together, if this turns you on, and then perhaps massage one another lovingly as you become aroused. Then take it in turns to teach your lover what you like best.

WATCHING THE WOMAN
This can be more tricky for many couples, because some women may feel shy, and find it difficult to relax sufficiently to have an orgasm, even if they usually have them without any trouble.

The secret here is to start off by cuddling and setting the scene as before, then ask the woman to masturbate with the lights down low or even off

while you hold her or caress her.

Slowly, over another session or two, increase the light level as she becomes excited and oblivious to her surroundings, and then note:
■ her body and leg position
■ what she does with both her hands
■ where she puts her fingers to stimulate her vulva or clitoris
■ the type, size and pressure of movement at each stage of arousal
■ whether or not she puts fingers into her vagina
■ if she stops stimulating herself, and then restarts
■ facial, breast, vulval, clitoral and skin changes
■ if she makes noises or cries out at orgasm
■ what she does at the moment of sexual climax
■ what changes occur as she calms down.

Now cuddle up and talk about the effect the experience had on you both. Most men find watching their woman masturbating intensely arousing, possibly because it declares her to be a full-blooded, sexy woman.

WATCHING THE MAN
Cuddle him if he likes and observe:
■ the exact position of his hand
■ the location of his fingers on his penis
■ how much pressure he uses
■ the rate, extent and type of movement
■ the changes that occur in the penis, scrotum and testes
■ other bodily changes, including his breathing rate, facial expression, muscle contractions
■ any other areas of the body he stimulates, for example his anus, the 'root' of his penis or testes
■ the amount of pre-ejaculatory secretion
■ the size and force of the initial spurt and the speed and force of further spurts
■ the stage at which he stops
■ the changes that occur as he calms down.

When he has relaxed, cuddle up and perhaps talk about the experience.

MUTUAL MASTURBATION
Once you are at ease with watching each other masturbate and have learned all you can, you can make the most of mutual masturbation.

But once you know how best to excite your partner and produce the best quality of orgasm for him or her, it is best to stick to whatever produces this on most occasions you masturbate.

(**Left**) His enjoyment
leads to a moment that
many partners like to
share visually – the
point of ejaculation. The
hand pressure, position
and speed of stimulation
is highly individual from
man to man. Watching
his climax develop is a
shared erotic event

(**Above**) Her enjoyment
of reaching a climax
through masturbation is
a powerful turn-on for
him and a rewarding
guide to the timing and
techniques that he can
bring into play when he
next comes to stimulate
her. Masturbation is far
from a selfish experience

OVERCOMING INHIBITIONS

Any sexual inhibition – even something as simple as a fear of making love with the lights on – can be overcome using a simple training programme. But why do we suffer from such fears and what can we do to rid ourselves of them?

DISSATISFACTION

The trouble with shyness and inhibitions is that they prevent people from getting the best out of sexual pleasure. Even many so-called liberated women who can ask for, or even demand, exactly what they want sexually, can be dissatisfied in bed and find little joy in sex. It is as though the conscious mind is saying 'go on do it – you'll love it' but their much more powerful unconscious mind puts the brakes on and prevents them from enjoying it.

At the other end of the spectrum are those who never initiate any form of sexual activity. They believe, usually quite unconsciously, that they have no sexual needs because they are really 'sexless'. They are prepared to go along with their partner and 'do their duty' but to do anything more makes them feel so anxious that they cannot enjoy it. This picture can be seen in both sexes but tends to be more common in women. Sex is only at all pleasurable for such a woman if she can 'blame' her partner for making her do it. This absolves her from the guilt feelings because the matter is out of her control.

An inhibited man married to such a woman may well be unable to initiate sex for similar reasons and, as a result, they have a very quiet sex life. This can work out well until one or the other realizes

that other members of the opposite sex are not the same and then trouble can start.

SIMILAR LEVELS

Everyone is inhibited to some extent about something or other when it comes to sex. The best marriages are probably between individuals whose levels of inhibition are about the same. Problems arise when two people who have very similar levels of inhibition pair up and subsequently become unbalanced as one loses his or her inhibitions faster than the other. The less inhibited one then wants to do and enjoy all kinds of sexual pursuits that the other cannot cope with.

This is where trouble can start. The less inhibited partner may look outside the relationship to find satisfaction, as may the more inhibited one – but for different reasons.

HOW INHIBITIONS SHOW UP

There are many ways that sexual shyness, reluctance and inhibitions show up. At the most obvious end of the scale, the inhibited person is so wary of sex in its many forms that he or she simply avoids situations in which anything is likely to occur. This can easily be seen in the late-night movie-watching man who rarely goes to bed at the same time as his wife. He cannot cope with the sexual demands he knows will come and so avoids the situation.

The next most common group of inhibitions show up as anxiety, fear and guilt. Anyone suffering from these feelings derives little or no pleasure from sex when he does do it, for the same reason.

Occasionally, such people, and there are many of them, go ahead and actually enjoy a sexual encounter only to be overcome with guilt and anxiety afterwards. Whatever the scenario, they all result in the avoidance of certain situations, poor performance, little pleasure, or all three.

But inhibitions are not quite this simple because many people are inhibited in one situation and not in another. Perhaps the best example of this is the man who is inhibited within his marriage, and may even be impotent, but in extra-marital sex, say with a prostitute, he functions perfectly well. Unconsciously, such a man sees his wife as pure and 'nice' and cannot bring himself to ask for what he really wants. As a result, he rarely becomes really turned on and so performs badly, or not at all. When with a 'dirty' or 'forbidden' woman outside his marriage, he can become uninhibited and really enjoy himself without any fear of being rejected for having such 'filthy' needs.

CHANGING FASHIONS

The trouble with inhibitions is that they are so personal and at the same time so governed by fashion. Fifty years ago, oral sex was considered a perversion and to be inhibited about it was not only acceptable but normal. Today, with the fashion for oral sex and the notion that 'semen is good for you', many women are branded as inhibited simply because they have not yet taken this new message on board.

Given that all inhibitions are learned, they can be unlearned if the individual is willing. Perhaps surprisingly, the best starting point is to discuss with your partner what you each mean by love. During such a session, both partners usually reveal that they have their own unique ideas about the subject and their own stereotypes which they expect their partner to fulfil. So it is that a woman who does not like to be on top during lovemaking might believe that the very nature of intercourse is that the man should be on top providing all the action while the woman's role is to lie there and receive it. Any other behaviour is seen by her as 'unloving' and, therefore, quite unreasonable.

INHIBITIONS AND LOVE

Just because a woman cannot go along with something sexual does not necessarily mean that she does not love her man, yet many men put such conditions on their lovebond. 'Any woman who really loved me would do . . .' is a common cry. But this can be a very false definition of love. That particular woman may indeed love him, but might be totally unable to show it in ways that the man thinks she should.

For the woman who wants to shed her inhibitions and make love with the lights on, the first step involves lying naked under the bedclothes in the dark. With the lights now on, the man should kiss and cuddle her. They couple can peel away the bedclothes and cuddle, first with the light off, and then with it on

On the other side of the coin are those women who, liberated by society's current awareness of female sexuality, realize only too well what their needs are, yet say nothing for fear of appearing tarty in their partner's eyes. It is a sad fact that, in millions of homes, one partner may be fantasizing about something they would like to do, and which their partner might very well be prepared to do, yet the subject is never discussed. They may even look elsewhere for satisfaction – often with disastrous results. During such discussions, the most amazing revelations come about as each individual begins to reveal his or her real self.

PLAY A GAME

Make a list of sexual subjects which cause problems to you in your relationship and put each on a small slip of paper. Suitable subjects might include penis size, oral sex, breast size, occasional impotence, PMT, semen, talking during intercourse, love, who initiates sex and so on. When you are both relaxed, perhaps after a small drink, take it in turns to pull one out of the pile unseen and share your thoughts about it. Say what you think about it and honestly try to be understanding about your partner's point of view. Some couples find that going to a pub, or for a country walk, provides the right kind of atmosphere. Be positive and reassuring and take your partner's point of view seriously.

As a follow-up to this kind of discussion, some people find that talking to their parents can be very helpful. In this way, they can come to a better understanding of the way things were during their childhood. Things you could never understand or forgive may now fall into place – so emphasizing the background to inhibitions in adulthood. Understanding your parents' inhibitions can be a great help in sorting out your own.

TAKE TIME

Invest more time and care in your lovelife generally. If you want your partner to be less inhibited in a particular way, a good start is to ensure that he or she is being made love to in a way that really pleases them. An individual who feels taken for granted, is bored, or frankly turned off much of the time is very unlikely to want to behave in an uninhibited way.

Do not forget, too, that sex reflects the rest of your relationship out of bed. No one will feel free to behave in an uninhibited way if they feel generally unloved, are bored, tired, or ill, for example.

START TO ENJOY SEX

Make a positive effort to act more sexually in general. To at least some extent, we can 'act' in a more uninhibited way and achieve what we want. For example, some women who have trouble enjoying orgasms during intercourse are greatly

The woman should now be ready to take a more active role. With the lights on, she may now feel ready to take off her clothes in front of her partner. From there, it is a small step for the woman to relax in front of him as he removes her clothes

helped if they act (like an actress) in a frankly sexy way.

At first this seems a little false but, as many such women have found in practice, it gets them over the first hurdle and before they know it they really are enjoying their orgasms.

Come to terms with the fact that a certain amount of prohibition makes sex more exciting – Freud said that if sex were not so 'naughty' it would not be nearly so much fun. In western cultures, the very fact that something is prohibited, or even makes us somewhat inhibited, can add to our delight. Looked at this way not all inhibitions are bad.

USE YOUR FANTASIES

Start to change your fantasies while you masturbate or make love. If you have a rather poor-quality sexual fantasy, consciously extend it a little when you are very aroused until what you were too 'inhibited' even to fantasize about becomes acceptable and enjoyable to you. Many inhibited people are always spectators in their sexual fantasies and others never end up having intercourse although they may well do everything else. Slow, stepwise improvement in the quality and excitability of the fantasy helps the individual so that he or she is more likely to be able to behave in a less inhibited way in real life.

As time passes, reveal more and more of yourself (and not just your sexual self) to your partner and you will be amazed at the way in which it loosens your inhibitions.

We all want to be fully understood by somebody, preferably by our partner, but this cannot happen in a vacuum. Both partners need to make an effort to share more of themselves. By opening up generally, most people automatically find themselves becoming more uninhibited, even without much effort.

A couple who grow in this way slowly shed their inhibitions over the years and by their forties are often totally in tune with one another.

LEARN WHERE TO DRAW THE LINE

Accept that everyone has a 'final position' on certain things – a line which they will not venture beyond. Although these lines can be bent a little, this is often the most that can be expected. What every loving couple should aim for is to be sufficiently mature to be able to come to terms with their respective 'final positions' and not to make an issue out of them. If the line is drawn at an unacceptable distance from where you want to be, and you have not been able to sort things out, it may make sense to seek professional advice.

THOUGHT STOPPING

Thought stopping is a simple do-it-yourself psychological technique that uncouples negative thoughts such as guilt and anxiety from your thinking and substitutes positive, helpful thoughts. It works because the brain can only cope with one emotion at once and because one emotion can flood out another.

The moment a negative thought comes into your head that makes you feel anxious, fearful, or guilty and which inhibits you from doing something you or your partner want to do, shout 'STOP' loudly and crash your hand down on something. Quickly replace the thought with another, positive one that pleases or excites you. To do this you will need to get a bank of exciting and pleasant thoughts ready. After a very few shouts you may find that you can just say 'stop' to yourself and you can dispense with crashing your hand on anything. Some people find it useful to keep an elastic band around their wrist which they snap against the skin when negative thoughts start to enter their heads at this stage of training.

The positive thoughts you substitute for your negative ones need not be anything to do with sex at all. They can be as different as having your first novel published, winning at Wimbledon, growing a prize-winning rose, or whatever would be most blissful for you.

Practise thought stopping eight or ten times a day, or whenever a negative thought enters your head. Over a few weeks, the number of negative thoughts you have should reduce.

FIRST TIME SEX

More often than not, making love to someone for the first time is a disaster. Why do so many opening nights turn into experiences that couples would rather forget?

In every relationship there comes the time that you first make love. It could be within the first few weeks, or after months or years of knowing each other. But whenever it happens, few people find it is something they enter into blithely without a care in the world. Most people, however experienced, are somewhat nervous, a little embarrassed, concerned that everything should go well – and unsure of what they should expect from each other.

THE VERY FIRST TIME

The very first time you make love in your life has a particular impact. This unique experience tells you a little about sex – but by no means all.

Certainly, after thinking and wondering about

it for so long, you at least find out how it works – often difficult to imagine, no matter how much 'theory' you know.

It is rarely absolutely wonderful. Girls particularly, for whom orgasm is by no means automatic, may worry that sex has been over-rated, and they never will enjoy it the way others seem to and the way they have read about in books and magazines.

Some girls are deeply ignorant. Donna was very hazy about the mechanics of sex, and based most of her knowledge on a steamy, romantic book that stopped short of describing the act itself. 'I was just 15 when I made love for the first time, and I can hardly credit my stupidity. I didn't think I'd actually done it, because I was under the impression that you saw stars and heard music – and nothing of the sort happened to me!'

Robert knew exactly what was supposed to happen, but thought it sounded very complicated and would involve strange gymnastic manoeuvres.

'I couldn't believe it when during some heavy petting and grappling on the sofa it just happened. I thought "Now this is easy!" – I remember the occasion for the glow of pride I felt, nothing romantic. It was a sexual burst – not even very sensual.'

Some people are quite well organized about planning their first sexual experience. Perhaps it is with someone they have been going out with for a while, and they have considered contraception, and provided themselves with protection.

Others get 'carried away' – and just hope and pray there is no resultant pregnancy or sexually transmitted disease.

The question of first time sex is more important today than it used to be. Now that so few people marry their 'first love' and stay married forever, most people have a series of first times – the sexual beginning to each new relationship that they have.

FIRST TIMES

Some 'first times' turn out to be one-night stands – but the main difference is that one or both partners

I couldn't believe it when it just happened. I thought 'Now this is easy!' I remember the occasion for the glow of pride I felt, certainly nothing romantic

go into it believing that it is the first time of many.

Whereas a one-night stand might seem a waste of effort unless it results in personal sexual gratification, the feelings accompanying a 'first time' are more complex.

It is seen to be the beginning of what could turn out to be an important relationship. That means that although your own sexual concerns are important, they are not more so than your lover's.

What is just as important is finding out how you 'fit together'. While making love, you are picking up clues to a different side of the other's personality, while also showing something of your own.

So what happens after sex has finished is equally important – whether there is tenderness, humour or a feeling of togetherness.

As Chris said, 'There are things that you can only tell about someone else when you go to bed with them. People are more themselves when they are literally stripped naked. I remember a girl who came across as so sexy – the way she danced was an open invitation – but in fact she had no sensuality, she was probably the least sexual girl I've been to bed with. Her dancing was copied from people she'd seen, it was not an outward expression of inner sexiness.'

WHEN SEX IS RIGHT

Before going to bed with someone new the decision has to be made – whether it is a lightning impulse, or the result of long deliberation. You have to decide when the moment is right – should it be within weeks, or should you get to know each other well first?

There is no hard-and-fast rule. Sometimes the impact of meeting is so great, every instinct tells you it is right, that you go to bed together as soon as you can.

Impulsive sex is no longer considered healthy. It can be a mistake if one person coerces the other into it, either by getting them drunk, or by some kind of emotional blackmail – a man might say, 'Are you frigid or something?'; a woman's come-on might be, 'Prefer men, do you?'

More often people wait to make love. You do not usually feel relaxed or secure enough with the other person to want to make love immediately – you prefer to get to know them better first, discuss it together, weigh up the risks involved and choose your moment and place carefully.

ACTING ON IMPULSE

Spontaneous sex, with its suggestion of uncontrol-

When the big moment comes I think 'Oh no! The cellulite on my thighs! My breasts are too small! After that wonderful meal my stomach must be absolutely enormous!'

lable passion is a very attractive idea – but it is not without its practical problems.

Protection from disease and contraception must be considered, and cannot be left to chance. The onus is no longer on the woman – if there is a pregnancy she will be the person most intimately concerned but both partners will wish to diminish the risk of catching AIDS by using the sheath. If she is not protected in any way, she should say so.

Sam is not unique when he says, 'These days I never ask a woman if she's on the Pill or something. Now that I'm involved with women in their twenties I just assume it's OK. When I was at school and university I was paranoid about an unplanned pregnancy and always checked up – but more experienced women have had to work out a solution before they've met me.' Since the AIDS epidemic men like Sam have had to change their attitudes.

A man should be aware that many women will abandon contraception when 'between' relationships. If he does not know she is protected he should use the sheath – or delay sex until they have discussed protection.

Paula always brings the subject up herself. 'I say, "You don't have to worry about contraception." That's partly because I use the cap and am slightly embarrassed about talking about it to someone I hardly know – some men aren't too keen on the idea. I hope that my remark will forestall the question "are you on the Pill?" to which I would have to say "no". I was once incredibly attracted to a man – and didn't have my cap with me. Regretfully I had to postpone going to bed with him – luckily it made it all the more exciting for both of us in the end.'

SEXUALLY TRANSMITTED DISEASE

The other major problem with someone you hardly know is bringing up the subject of AIDS or VD. If you do not know someone you can have no idea of the number of sexual partners they have had, or the possibility that they might be the carrier of a sexually transmitted disease.

It is not enough just to trust to luck and instinct. Different people have different ways of coping with this very difficult and personal question.

Vickie asks straight out. 'The idea of contracting something – particularly now that AIDS has spread to heterosexuals – fills me with horror. My usual ploy is to pretend that I had a bad experience once before – that I caught gonorrhoea from a lover, and consequently am particularly worried about it. That at least gives them the get out of saying that they suspect their ex-girlfriend might have been unfaithful, etc, etc.'

Ray tries to make a joke out of it, 'I usually say, "I'm perfectly clean, you know." That breaks the ice, brings the subject up – then we can have a little chat about it, and if there is something to be said it gets said. One girl admitted to herpes. She explained to me that it is not catching unless she is having an attack – so that was OK. It meant that later on, when she did have an attack she was able to tell me.'

OTHER PROBLEMS

There are other practical problems which arise from spontaneous sex, not very important in themselves, but that can cause embarrassment when you are with someone you hardly know.

If you have spent the night together there can

be the problem of not having a change of clothes for the morning. Some women feel insecure being seen without make-up, and men can have the problem of having to shave in the morning.

For these reasons it is worthwhile considering whether you should spend the night together, or leave before morning.

Micky is in no doubt. 'I always go home before morning – sometimes only just – at 4 a.m., say. I think it is important not only for the niggling practical problems, but also for the development of the relationship. Mornings after with someone you hardly know are more tense and difficult than anything that might have gone before. You might be ready for passion, but you are not ready for the kind of friendly cohabitation waking up together means. I like to know someone really well before I kiss her with unbrushed teeth, talk monosyllables over the newspaper – or can use the loo without embarrassment with her around. That's why I always manœuvre it so that the first few times happen round at her place, which leaves me free to go when I'm ready.'

THE DELAYED FIRST TIME

Generally, more people go to bed with each other for the first time after they have known each other for a while, and the attraction has grown.

This means that you can carefully choose the right time and place so that making love together has the chance of being really successful.

You can also talk over problems well in advance – such as contraception and VD – which is easier to do when you are not otherwise involved in tearing off each other's clothes. Most people find that in ostensibly 'general discussions' about life and love, it is possible to bring up these related matters, so that when the time comes for sex there are actually few practical things to worry about.

THE AWKWARDNESS

But whether the sex is unpremeditated or planned, it is a rare person who does not feel at least a little awkward engaged in sex with someone for the first time. For some people the embarrassment is so acute that the sex itself passes almost unnoticed.

It was not quite as bad as that for Alison, but she says she has never actively enjoyed first time sex with a new partner.

'I can't see how it could ever be really good. Quite apart from the awkwardness, there is just the inescapable fact that you don't know your way round each other's bodies. It's all a question of hit and miss and guesswork, going on past experience. As far as I am concerned it is just a promise for the future, a start. If it's even halfway good, then you can be quite sure it's going to get a whole lot better.'

Women, particularly, are often worried about whether their bodies are 'good enough'. And an anxious man might be impotent when it comes to

I can't say it completely screwed up my sex life, imagining my penis to be far too small, but it definitely didn't help. Certainly first times are still a bit nerve-wracking. I usually try to engineer it so that she doesn't see – or touch – my penis initially, or at least until I've made love to her once. Then if that seems to have gone OK I stop worrying and start to feel better about things

it. This is difficult to handle in any circumstances, but particularly when you do not know each other very well. But once you have taken the first step together – you can now take the next. It could be the start of something big.

CHAPTER THREE

LEARNING ABOUT LOVE

CONTRACEPTION

*Despite the availability of family planning
and an increasing range of contraceptives,
millions of women throughout the world still
risk unplanned pregnancy*

Every year two million American women have abortions, and the number of unintended pregnancies remains stubbornly high.

One reason is that information about contraception is often not reaching the people that most need it. As a result, couples and individuals often make the wrong decisions about the methods they choose, use them badly, or abandon them altogether. Others are not using contracption at all and simply taking a chance that they do not get pregnant.

It is not really surprising that this happens, since information about contraceptive methods is changing all the time. As methods are tested and researched, more risks and side-effects come to light and the more confusing it all becomes – for doctors as well as the consumers.

Choice becomes even more complicated as scientific research points to limiting medical methods of contraception to particular ages and groups of women.

At the same time women have learned to understand and appreciate their bodies far more and are less inclined simply to accept what they are prescribed. Increasingly, they are attracted by methods which they see as more natural, in keeping with the general trend towards a more natural lifestyle.

SHARING THE CHOICE

With the arrival of the Pill and IUD (Intra-Uterine Device) in the 1960s, women took responsibility for contraception and were relieved to have the means of preventing pregnancy under their own control. But many women now feel resentful that they shoulder all the risks and problems, while more men feel unhappy that they have no role to play.

Time and time again, studies show that men's intentions in terms of sharing responsibility for contraception are often very positive. Unfortunately, these same studies show that for most men there is a wide gap between intention and practice.

There is no ideal contraceptive, nor is there likely to be for decades. But good methods do exist. They all have advantages and disadvantages, and

Information from leaflets and Fact Sheets published by the Family Planning Information Service, October 1984 (revised 1985).		*When occasional usage is included.
METHOD	**EFFECTIVENESS**	**USERS**
PILL	Almost 100%	2,850,000
MINI-PILL	98%	228,000
DEPO-PROVERA	Almost 100%	Not known
IUD	96–98%	912,000
DIAPHRAGM, CAPS	85–97%	Up to 250,000*
SPONGE	75–91%	No available figures
SHEATH	93–99%	2 to 3 million*
'COMBINED' SAFE PERIOD	85–93%	570,000
FEMALE STERILIZATION	Occasional failures	1,140,000
VASECTOMY	Occasional failures	1,368,000
POST-COITAL (PILL)	97–98%	Not known
POST-COITAL (IUD)	Almost 100%	Not known
Effectiveness rates for reversible methods refer to the number of women out of 100 using the method for a year who do not get pregnant.		Post-coital effectiveness rates refer to the number of women out of 100 who do not become pregnant after using post-coital methods.

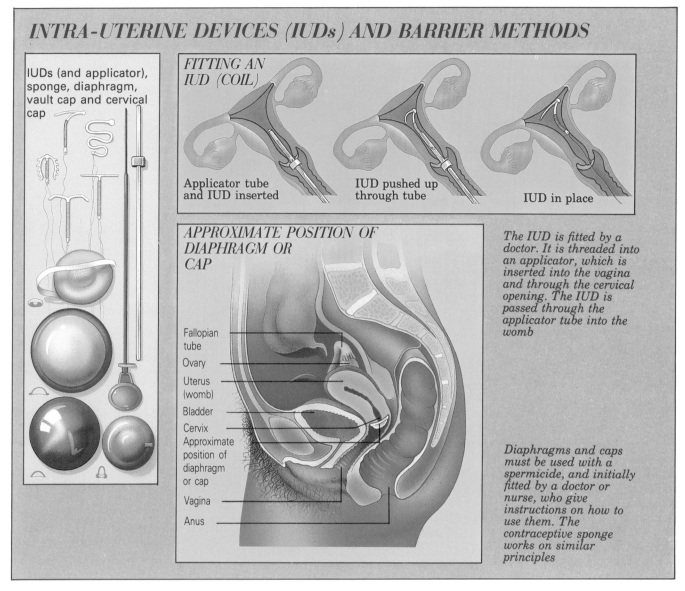

INTRA-UTERINE DEVICES (IUDs) AND BARRIER METHODS

IUDs (and applicator), sponge, diaphragm, vault cap and cervical cap

FITTING AN IUD (COIL)

Applicator tube and IUD inserted

IUD pushed up through tube

IUD in place

APPROXIMATE POSITION OF DIAPHRAGM OR CAP

Fallopian tube
Ovary
Uterus (womb)
Bladder
Cervix
Approximate position of diaphragm or cap
Vagina
Anus

The IUD is fitted by a doctor. It is threaded into an applicator, which is inserted into the vagina and through the cervical opening. The IUD is passed through the applicator tube into the womb

Diaphragms and caps must be used with a spermicide, and initially fitted by a doctor or nurse, who give instructions on how to use them. The contraceptive sponge works on similar principles

the way individuals or couples assess these very much depends on their lifestyle and attitudes to sex.

For many people there will be a different 'best method' at different times of their life. For couples the solution to sharing the responsibility may be to alternate between male and female methods.

Doctors and nurses can help you make a choice, and counselling services are gradually becoming more accessible to men as well as women, but in the end the decision has to be yours. A good choice of contraceptive can help you enjoy a relaxed sex life as well as protecting against unintended pregnancy.

THE PILL
When most people refer to the Pill, they mean the oral contraceptive which contains two hormones, oestrogen and progestogen, that stop women ovulating.

The Pill became available in the early 1960s and it gained popularity, with a few hiccups, to become the most used method of birth control and almost synonymous with contraception. But in the last 20 or so years a great deal of information has been collected on the effects of the Pill on women's health.

Some of this information is inconclusive and confusing, but it has resulted in more thought being given to minimizing side-effects and the production of a second generation of contraceptive pills which contain much lower doses of hormones.

THE PILL AND THE RISKS
To some extent it has also become possible to identify those women who might run risks from taking the Pill, such as smokers, those who are overweight or those with high blood pressure.

Since the publication of reports in October 1983, suggesting possible, but unconfirmed links between taking the Pill and breast and cervical cancer, women are increasingly questioning that crucial balance between reliability and safety.

THE 'SAFE PERIOD' METHODS

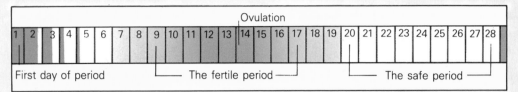

Ovulation

| 1 | 2 | 3 | 4 | 5 | 6 | 7 | 8 | 9 | 10 | 11 | 12 | 13 | 14 | 15 | 16 | 17 | 18 | 19 | 20 | 21 | 22 | 23 | 24 | 25 | 26 | 27 | 28 |

First day of period ———— The fertile period ———— The safe period ————

The principle of safe period methods of contraception is to learn to predict and recognize the time of the month when you are most fertile, and avoid intercourse at that time. Sex is restricted to 'safe' days, when you are less likely to conceive.

A woman is most likely to get pregnant at and around the time of ovulation – when the egg is released from the ovary into the Fallopian tube. This usually occurs about two weeks before the start of the next period, but there are various ways that a woman can pin-point the moment more accurately.

Since sperm can live for up to five days inside a woman, and an egg can live for about two days, a woman must not have sex for at least five days before ovulation and for several days after.

Calculating the time of ovulation (when sex should be avoided) can be done in several ways:
- *The temperature method*
- *The Billings (mucus) method*
- *The calendar method*
- *Combinations of these methods.*

The temperature method *The woman takes her temperature every morning on waking up, and keeps a special chart. Immediately before ovulation, body temperature drops slightly – after the egg is released, it rises to a higher level than in the previous week.*

The Billings (mucus) method *This method works on the principle that ovulation can be detected by changes in cervical mucus. The woman is taught to examine her mucus and to recognize changes – such as increased amount and 'wetness'*

The calendar method *The woman is shown how to calculate when she is most likely to ovulate by keeping a long-term record of her menstrual cycle. On its own this is very unreliable and not recommended.*

Combined methods *Combining methods and learning to recognize other 'symptoms' of ovulation increases reliability. With all these methods, skilled guidance is essential. See your doctor or family planning clinic for advice.*

These techniques are most successful for women who have regular periods.

The great attraction of the Pill has always been its reliability together with its convenience. For many couples the Pill is the only method which allows them to be completely spontaneous in their lovemaking without fear of pregnancy.

Many women are trying to weigh up the pluses and the minuses of taking the Pill. The most serious condition linked with the Pill is thrombosis, although the risk is very small unless you smoke or are overweight. Other side-effects include depression, weight gain, loss of sex drive and head-aches, although these can often be stopped by changing to a different Pill. It is worth remembering, however, that the Pill may protect against some diseases such as cancer of the ovaries and the lining of the womb, and rheumatoid arthritis. And it is certainly the most convenient form of contraception at present.

THE MINI-PILL

For some women looking to minimize the health risks of Pill-taking, a move to the mini-Pill will provide a good solution. Mini-Pills contain only one hormone, progestogen, and the dose is lower than the progestogen dose in the combined Pill. They do not stop ovulation but prevent pregnancy in other ways, such as thickening the mucus at the entrance to the cervix to make it difficult for the sperm to penetrate.

As it does not contain oestrogen the mini-Pill is not thought to contribute to the risks of thrombosis, nor have mini-Pills been implicated in cancer scares. On the other hand, they are less effective, and if a pregnancy does happen there is some risk of it being outside the womb – most probably in the Fallopian tubes. Women taking the mini-Pill also tend to suffer from irregular, or break through, bleeding.

Mini-Pills must be taken every day at exactly the same time each day to be effective. They are usually considered most suitable for older women and breastfeeding mothers.

LONGER-ACTING METHODS

Depo-provero is a synthetic progestogen which is given by injection. It is absorbed over a period of three months and stops ovulation. Its use has always been controversial.

IUD, OR COIL

An Intra-Uterine Device (IUD) is a small 2.5 cm-long flexible plastic device, now usually wound with copper, which is inserted into the womb by a doctor.

Coils come in a variety of different shapes and are normally replaced every two to five years, depending on the type. Although no-one knows exactly how an IUD works, it prevents an egg from implanting in the womb lining.

Like the Pill, the coil was introduced in the 1960s, but has never achieved the same popularity. One reason for this was that early coils were not usually a first choice for women who had not had a child, for they were rather large in relation to the size of the womb.

More recently, copper-wound coils are smaller, but now there are different reasons why these are not recommended to women who have not had children. The problem is that the presence of a coil makes a woman more susceptible to pelvic infection which can be difficult to deal with and which could affect her ability to conceive later on.

The failure rate of the coil is about the same as the mini-Pill and, like the mini-Pill, pregnancies that do occur happen outside the womb.

One of the main disadvantages of the coil is that it often causes heavier periods. There may also be bleeding between periods. One of the main advantages is that, once fitted, there is no further involvement by the woman, except to check now and then that it is in the correct place by feeling the threads. An internal check-up by your doctor every year or so is essential.

BARRIER METHODS

Men and women started using barriers of various kinds to prevent pregnancy thousands of years ago. The forms they now take are not much different in principle from the early versions.

Currently available are the diaphragm, cervical cap, vault cap and vimule cap. They are all made of soft rubber and fit over the neck of the womb.

They are used with spermicide cream or jelly, and inserted before sex to form a barrier to sperm.

The newest barrier, the contraceptive sponge, is already popular in the United States and is now available elsewhere.

It is less reliable than the diaphragm, and therefore only suitable for women for whom pregnancy would not be disastrous.

The male sheath is making a comeback – attractively packaged and styled. This is a reliable barrier method which rarely has any side effects.

'MORNING-AFTER' METHODS

Most people have heard about the 'morning-after' Pill, but fewer know about the post-coital IUD.

The post-coital Pill is in fact a special dose contraceptive Pill containing oestrogen and progestogen, taken within 72 hours of intercourse. The

MALE PILLS AND OTHER MALE METHODS

Probably the most intriguing possibilities for contraception lie in the development of a male Pill

Magazine surveys show that men have a variety of reactions to the idea of shouldering the responsibility of contraception by taking a pill every day.

Women, too, while wanting to shift the responsibility, question how dedicated men would be in taking it regularly. After all, it is not the man who gets pregnant if he forgets to take it.

A male Pill is actually more difficult to 'design' than the female Pill because there is no single event – like the release of the female egg – on which to work.

The most promising male Pill so far has come from China and was discovered by accident when it was noticed that in rural areas, where cotton-seed oil was used for cooking, the men had become infertile.

The first clinical trials on the plant extract gossypol, responsible for the infertility, started in China in 1972 and were reported six years later. The results were very encouraging, the effectiveness was nearly 100 per cent and there were few side-effects.

Further research carried out by the World Health Organization (but which has been abandoned) showed that side-effects were more common than originally thought, and included a feeling of weakness, digestive problems and loss of sex drive.

The conclusion seems to be that gossypol itself will not be the male Pill of the future, but something similar may be developed instead.

Other male Pills could be developed from existing drugs, such as one used for hypertension and at present on trial in Israel. This particular drug acts as an 'ejaculation inhibitor'.

fitting of a coil within five days after intercourse is the alternative.

STERILIZATION

Female sterilization and male vasectomy are permanent methods of birth control. They involve operations that close the Fallopian tubes in a woman, and the tubes sperm travels through in a man.

Sterilization was once a last resort chosen by couples who had many children.

THE PSYCHOLOGY OF SEDUCTION

Seduction is like a game of chess – it is all a question of strategy. There are moves, countermoves and, eventually, one of the players surrenders

The need for sex is a powerful force within us – as strong, some say, as the need to breathe and to eat. But unlike eating and breathing it is not so easy to satisfy. It involves the playing of a fairly complex game – the choosing of a partner and a certain ritualized courtship, which is where the art of seduction comes in.

Seduction has one ultimate goal – to have sex with the chosen partner. This can only be achieved by accomplishing a series of mini-goals such as selecting the right opportunity, choosing an available partner, getting them interested, sustaining their interest, introducing the idea of sex and finally – and for the would-be seducer, more importantly – making them willing to have intercourse.

WHY SEDUCTION?

We seek out sexual partners because most of us find sex enjoyable. In the long-term, a stable sexual relationship creates the next generation but this is usually the furthest thing from one's mind at the moment of seduction. We want sexual partners because it is fun, because it is exciting and because it is physically rewarding. When the seduction extends beyond a 'one-night-stand' there is stability, companionship and love – and these are important human needs.

SET UP THE BOARD
Good options for arousing excitement

■ Dances

■ Pop concerts

■ Religious meetings

■ Physical sports

■ Moments of danger – roller-coasters, big wheels, helterskelters

---

Research has shown that lonely people, and ones who actively shun human companionship, often have intense dreams about being with other people. It appears that when people are deprived of sexual outlets, erotic dreams and fantasies abound.

The way in which we seek out sexual partners is significant. For some people the thrill of seduction is all in the 'chase', not the eventual conquest. They love the electricity generated by wanting someone and pursuing them – and the rougher the pursuit, the better. Such lovers tend to be fairly self-confident. They believe in themselves, in their charms, and in the likelihood of success. Almost certainly, their confidence has an effect on the outcome.

Eye contact is strong and the pose open and intimate, with arms and bodies tantalizingly close

People who regard themselves as unattractive to the opposite sex encounter much greater difficulty. They have to believe in themselves first, and then they have to convince the object of their desires to

PLANNING YOUR STRATEGY
Ask yourself

■ Is he/she available? (body language)

■ Is he/she very attractive? (private rating scale)

■ Would you make a good match? (private rating scale)

■ Is he/she interested in you? (verbal and non-verbal clues)

believe in them. What tends to happen is that people use a 'secret ranking' of sexual attractiveness, rating themselves on this scale as well as rating potential partners. Unconsciously we seek out partners of similar rank.

Most of us believe that we would be wasting our time approaching very attractive partners as we think that they would almost certainly reject us.

Seduction is a question of looking the part as well as saying and doing the right things

Instead, we seek out those who are just about as attractive as we are, and endeavour to strike up a conversation or, at the very least, establish some eye contact with the object of our desire.

Two of the main points about starting a sexual

OPENING GAMBIT
Gaining his/her attention

■ Find an interesting topic

■ Make some intimate revelations about yourself – show that you are psychologically healthy

■ Elicit some intimate revelations

■ Flatter him/her by listening attentively to answers – always a winning move

encounter are the choice of the appropriate opportunity and the right person to approach. The right person is usually a matter of instinct, once the subconscious rating has been done. The right moment is often trickier.

Some situations are not suitable for sexual advances – the place is wrong, the time is wrong, sex is not 'in the air'. But those that are suitable have two features in common. They increase a person's arousal – although not necessarily sexual – and preferably both partners' excitement.

For this reason, any occasion that increases physical excitement can be a useful preliminary to sexual encounters. People go to dances, not only because they are good places to meet willing partners, but also because the physical exercise of dancing increases arousal.

Pop concerts, and even intense religious meetings like those of Billy Graham, often arouse people in such a way that they are more willing to accept sexual advances. Some practised seducers attend such meetings because of this very fact. They know from experience that they will meet partners who are easier to seduce because of their heightened state of arousal and excitement.

Strangely, even the excitement generated by danger can have this effect. Researchers have found that men walking over an alarmingly high bridge are more likely to make sexual advances to a pretty girl that they meet halfway across the bridge than they would normally.

READING THE CUES

Another thing to get right is the decision over who looks interested and available. The various ways of deciding this usually come down to very crude and unreliable types of judgements based on what someone is wearing, or whether they smoke or not. (Surveys show that women who smoke are more likely to be promiscuous, too.)

Aside from such hazy clues the most instructive signs come from a careful reading of body language – the non-verbal cues that we give out in our behaviour.

Body language is often a more reliable indicator of how a person feels about you than actual spoken language, probably because it occurs naturally, without involving conscious thought.

For example, we can stand in what are known as 'open postures' or 'closed postures'. In a closed posture a person might stand with their arms folded across their body. This indicates that they are not

---

THE MID-GAME

■ Flirt with your partner – get him/ her interested and sexually aroused

■ Establish that you are desirable, and desired – and will need to be wooed

■ Play hard-to-get – but not too hard – keep his/her interest

■ Show that you are 'gettable' sometimes – that the chase will be worth it

---

interested in talking to, or getting to know, the people who are around and are trying to shut them out.

An open posture is one where the person sits or stands in a way that displays himself or herself with more effect, for example, leaning back with one arm draped along the back of the chair or standing aggressively with hands on hips. A person sitting or standing in an open posture is more available than someone who adopts a closed one.

Other clues about availability are indicated by the eyes. Gazing wide-eyed at another person can often mean strong liking and interest.

THE DISCLOSURE GAME

Once the right place and an available person have been selected these are other elements that come into play. For example, you have to make it clear that you are a normal, psychologically healthy person or your intended partner is likely to back away from you.

To achieve this, it is necessary to engage in what psychologists call self-disclosure and make some appropriate revelations about your feelings and emotions. These help the other person to realize that you are an open person with a mature approach to life who trusts them with your feelings.

Men usually take the lead in this. They ask women direct questions that encourage them to make personal disclosures. This may be because women are expected to reveal more about themselves and so have to do it more to appear normal, or it may be because men are afraid to do it and are generally less open about their feelings. However, a person who does not self-disclose properly, and does not give the other person a chance to do so also, is not going to get anywhere.

SUSTAINING INTEREST

While assessments about someone's availability can be instantaneous – based on snap judgements about very tiny cues such as gestures and tones of voice – taking availability to the point of seduction is a much more complex affair. For a start, when you talk to a person who is available, that person may change his or her mind – perhaps you bored them when you opened your mouth.

Alternatively, someone who was not interested can become interested if you hit on the right things to talk about.

It is important to be sensitive to the signs of rejection or acceptance as things progress. Seduction is a game involving two people and no fixed rules. The only reassuring factor for the would-be seducer is that most people do enjoy having sex, so the odds are not entirely against you if you learn how to play the game.

PLOYS PEOPLE USE

Because seduction in humans can be a lengthy affair, the problem of sustaining interest up to the critical moment has to be sorted out. There is a variety of ploys that are commonly used by both

---

THE END-GAME

■ Talk about sex in the abstract – test reactions in a non-committal way

■ Check that all non-verbal cues are positive – behaviour, body language

■ Check that all verbal cues are positive

■ Discuss sex more intimately

■ Move closer and prepare for final yielding

---

partners to achieve this, usually involving a mixture of flirtation and playing hard-to-get.

PLAYING HARD-TO-GET

Flirtation serves to keep the partner aroused and excited but has a side-benefit as well. It can be used to indicate that you are available to others also and consequently need fairly serious wooing. That in itself can be exciting for both partners as long as it is not done to the extreme where it becomes threatening to the developing relationship.

After all the preliminaries have been dispensed with, and the game played successfully by both partners, it is time to reap the rewards

Unavailability is a time-tested part of the seduction game. It seems to sustain a partner's interest up to a point. Being too readily available can be as off-putting as being completely unavailable.

This is an area which has been researched very thoroughly and it seems that the following general rules apply. First, men fear rejection by attractive partners and anything to reassure them that they are unlikely to be rejected – even if they are not accepted outright either – is helpful. Thus, a woman who wants to play hard-to-get must manage to convey the message that she is 'gettable' and that she likes the particular man who is chasing at the moment.

Second, any woman who is generally regarded as hard-to-get is not attractive to most men. Once again, there has to be some evidence that the chase could be rewarding ultimately.

Third, the best strategy is not to play hard-to-get all the time with the chosen chaser, but to relax the hardness a bit so that hope is sustained.

OTHER SIGNS

There are other signs that carry important messages, as well. For example, people do us favours when they like us, so a request for someone to do a small favour is a good quick way of assessing their feelings towards us. Also it is advisable to assess the willingness of a partner to talk about sex in the abstract before making any definite moves.

People typically start to discuss sexual matters in a general, light and uncommitted way during their self-disclosures to assess the partner's willingness to contemplate such things.

CHECKMATE

- Was it pleasurable for you?

- Did you convey your pleasure? (verbal and non-verbal cues)

- Did he/she enjoy it?

- If responses are positive, show interest in meeting again

- Convey your availability

- Make practical arrangements – how, when, where

APHRODISIACS

*Oysters are an enduring and ever-popular
aphrodisiac, while eating ground rhino horn
or a wolf's penis has been in and out of
fashion. Do these old methods work, or will
20th-century science provide the elixir of love?*

More than 900 supposed arousers of sexual desire, known as aphrodisiacs, have been recorded, yet it seems that only some of them have stood the test of time. Indeed, a list of all aphrodisiacs would also be a testament to the gullibility of man in his desperate bid to discover the fabled elixir of love.

All manner of concoctions have been dreamed up and consumed over the centuries – the testes of an ass, the intestines of birds, fresh semen, menstrual

blood, the penis of a wolf, hedgehog and musk – as well as onions, wild cabbage, pineapple and nettle seed.

One stimulant highly esteemed in Mediterranean countries since Biblical times is the root of the mandrake plant (*Mandragora officinarum*).

While the mandrake's powers as an aphrodisiac have now fallen somewhat into disrepute, it used to be thought that the more the root resembled the human form – especially if it had appendages that looked like testes – the more prized and expensive it was.

It was very fashionable to use as aphrodisiacs any organic matter – animal or vegetable – that resembled the genitals of a man or woman. Hence, beans, bananas, cucumbers and oysters were reputed to be powerful love stimulants.

Even potatoes, when they were brought from South America to Europe by the Spanish in the 17th century, were thought to have aphrodisiac properties.

Erotic writers from Greece and Rome laid great store by love stimulants, especially a brew made with 'satyrion' – a substance derived from the wild woodland orchid. It is said that Hercules drank such a brew and then proceeded to deflower the 50 daughters of his hostess.

Arabs, Hindus and Chinese have always excelled in the art of love and their erotic manuals are rich in aphrodisiac recipes.

POWERFUL PROPERTIES?

Many people today reject the idea of aphrodisiacs altogether, saying either that they do not exist or else that there is no scientific proof that they work.

Such a view may very well be right in a great many cases. But, there is also evidence that certain substances, in particular some foods, are endowed with properties that give one a sense of well-being that may enhance sexual desire. Are these aphrodisiacs?

One thing is certain – aphrodisiacs are much

more likely to work if you think they will. And, for those of us who are willing to keep an open mind as to their 'powers', there is nothing to stop any of us trying a few out.

Fortunately, foods that are claimed to be aphrodisiacs are not all rare delicacies imported at great expense from exotic eastern islands – or indeed, the sort of ingredients you would be more likely to find in a witch's cauldron. Often they are widely available everyday substances such as honey.

It should be noted, however, that the ingredients for the cookery of love are not designed to cure impotency or frigidity, but are for people who want to extend their sexual enjoyment – even if this is simply by a little light-hearted experimentation.

Love dishes – even their preparation and presentation – may serve to brighten any sex life, however full.

But aphrodisiacs are not medicines. Treatment for a sex life in disarray requires a different remedy, such as more sleep, less anxiety, vitamins or perhaps counselling.

FOUR FOODS OF LOVE

The tradition of the ages is that if you eat well you perform well – and choice of food may be all-important. It has been said that the four best aphrodisiac ingredients are garlic, honey, anchovies and wheatgerm – all quality stuff.

Giving strength and stamina, garlic is claimed to have antiseptic and antibiotic properties which clean the blood and tone of the body. It can be off-putting on the breath though.

And American scientists recently made the curious discovery that the main constituent of garlic's odorous and volatile oil is the same as one of the chemicals secreted by a woman when she is sexually aroused.

An instant source of energy, honey is a good all-round food for everyone. In the illustrations of such erotic books as *The Perfumed Garden* and *The Kama Sutra*, there are always sweetmeats made from honey and spices – essential fare for lovers. Honey is still used today in the widely available love-boost pills.

Like most other seafoods, anchovies are especially rich in phosphorus, salt and many of the trace elements and minerals which our bodies constantly need. Oysters are the best-known seafood aphrodisiac – because they resemble the open female sex organ – but anchovies surpass them in quality.

Wheatgerm, present in wholemeal bread, is the richest source of Vitamin E on this planet. Called the 'fertility vitamin', a deficiency of it leads to sterility, impotence or other sexual problems. So stock up on Vitamin E.

No-one disputes the vitamin's essential contribution to health and vitality, but its qualities as an aphrodisiac are still a matter of debate.

ALCOHOL AND SEX

Alcohol has long been considered an aphrodisiac. In small amounts it can reduce anxiety and lessen inhibitions. Consequently sexual overtures and encounters are easier. The quantity, however, is critical because in increasing doses alcohol has the opposite effect, causing a slowing down of all nerve motor responses and temporary sexual incapacity. With chronic alcohol use sexual performance can be permanently impaired.

The concentration of alcohol in the blood depends on a variety of factors, including the amount and strength of the alcohol taken, the length of time spent drinking the presence or absence of food in the stomach and the age, sex, weight and particular metabolism of the drinker.

2 measures *Relaxation, feeling of social inhibitions, mild arousal.*
Sexual response *Increased blood flow, which can facilitate erection.*

4 measures *Speech slurred, some difficulty in co-ordinating movements, increased sexual aggression.*
Sexual response *Affects centres in brain that control orgasm, necessitating more stimulation for orgasm.*

6 measures *Movements awkward, staggering, exaggerated emotions.*
Sexual response *Many women find orgasm more difficult. May be more difficult in men too.*

8 measures *Thoughts incoherent, movements uncontrolled.*
Sexual response *Increasingly difficult to maintain erection and orgasm often impossible.*

SPICE IT UP

The subtle effect of aphrodisiac ingredients should never be underestimated – each person has his or her own preferences. So if one food, herb or spice does not turn you or your partner on, then try another one – but do not expect instant wonders.

You may choose caraway, a widespread ingredient in love potions since the days of Ancient Egypt, or coriander.

But beware of chillies – the right amount may release more passion than you expect, while too much might roast your passion altogether.

Chilli pepper sauce is regularly used as a companion to oysters – it is also an ingredient in several erection creams for men.

APHRODISIAC BATHS

A warm bath, scented with aromatic oils, may work wonders for your sex life. Remember to run the bath before adding the essential oils, as they should float on top of the water.

The bath should be reasonably hot, so that the steam rises. This allows you to inhale the fragrance captured in the moist air. The hot water will also bring a flush to your skin. When you emerge from the water, the oil will cling to your skin without leaving an oily residue.

A glass of wine will further relax you and help put you in the mood for lovemaking.

Essential oils with aphrodisiac qualities include

Black pepper   *Orange blossom*
Cardamon   *Patchouli*
Clary sage   *Rose*
Jasmine   *Sandalwood*
Juniper   *Ylang ylang*

For your man
2 drops of black pepper
5 drops of clary sage
2 drops of ylang ylang
5 drops of sandalwood

For your woman
3 drops of patchouli
2 drops of ylang ylang
2 drops of orange blossom
5 drops of sandalwood

For you together
3 drops of jasmine
3 drops of rose
7 drops of sandalwood

Another excellent love stimulant is one of the most versatile of all hot spices – ginger. Eaten at the end of a meal in a crystalized or chocolate form, ginger has the reputation of stirring one up sexually.

CHANGE WITH THE SEASONS

Spices are at their best on cold, dark winter days, whereas the more subtle repertoire of aphrodisiac herbs are most efficient on warm, light summer days. And such herbs must be fresh. Dried herbs have little or no effect at all.

Sweet basil is one of the most seasonal of love's herbs – it must be extremely fresh, and if its taste or smell arouse no excitement in you, then it is not for you.

You may have, however, a particular liking for the French drink, pastis, or the Greek, ouzo, in which case you should try aniseed in your food.

And if you are partial to mint, you may find its coolness arouses the passions on a hot summer's day. Various other herbs, such as parsley, tarragon and lovage, and foods such as celery, nuts, watercress and asparagus, all have reputations as love foods.

The only way to discover if any of them increase your sexual desires or improve your sex life is to try them out.

THE DANGERS OF SPANISH FLY

A 19-year-old university student was having trouble seducing the girl he was dating and so sought the advice of a friend. One day out of the blue, his older friend slipped him a package of white crystals saying it was a famous old love stimulant called Spanish Fly which was known to turn on men and women.

Later that evening the student emptied the contents of the package into his girlfriend's coffee and waited to see how she would respond. She died an hour later from severe internal bleeding. He was sentenced to five years for manslaughter.

Such a tragedy highlights the ignorance many people have about aphrodisiac drugs and other love potions. Spanish Fly is the dried extract of the bodies of dead green blister beetles (*Lyatta vesicatoria*) which live in southern Europe. If smeared on to the testes of unwilling horses or bulls, it makes them so uncomfortable they have to mate.

Taken internally it irritates all the mucous membranes, especially the urethra. Whether a man has his thoughts on sex or not, he usually gets an erection, with an itch in his urethra that needs scratching. Women get the same urethral itch. But more than a minute amount is deadly.

SEXY DRINKS

Alcohol is a mild but much abused aphrodisiac. Small quantities have a subtle effect because they remove inhibitions and increase the flow of blood through the peripheral blood vessels such as those in the penis.

For most men, any more than a pint or so of beer – or a couple of glasses of wine – and the sedative effect of alcohol begins to dominate the stimulating effect. The optimum dose for a woman is thought to be less, probably because of her smaller body weight – about one and a half glasses of wine.

White wine is normally considered better than red, although the better the quality of either, the better the potential aphrodisiac effect.

As a general rule, the least acid wines such as claret make the best aphrodisiacs. Many people would say that champagne is probably the best drink to arouse the passions, and increase the sex drive. This may be true, but the effect will not last as long as a good claret.

Green Chartreuse and tequila are both high up on the alcoholic aphrodisiac list – green Chartreuse, for example, is said to contain essential oils that slightly irritate the bladder and the pelvic region.

RHINO HORN

'Horny' is a word from the aphrodisiac language, derived from the use of the rhinoceros horn as a sex stimulant. Ground into a fine powder and drunk as a potion, rhino horn irritates the urethra, in the same way that Spanish Fly does.

But its effect is only slight, while its cost is very high – not only to purchase, but also because several species of rhinoceros are threatened with extinction as a direct result of the aphrodisiac trade.

Cocaine is reputed to be a useful sex stimulant in that it prolongs intercourse, but the anaesthetic effects reduce feeling and expressions of love.

Cannabis loosens inhibitions in a similar way to alcohol. A very popular aphrodisiac for centuries, the oil of cannabis is, by reputation, the source of the most exquisite sexual sensations.

PERFUMES

It seems strange that if our natural body chemicals can act as sexual attractants that we should spend so much time and money washing them off and covering them up with cosmetics – especially as most perfumes contain extracts from the sex glands of animals such as the musk deer and the civet.

But there is no doubt that scent and perfume are a turn-on for many people. Perhaps it is because they suggest cleanliness, but most probably because we associate perfumes with our earliest sexual encounter. This is reinforced by advertising that suggests that cosmetics equal sexual success.

Yet the power of aromatic substances as seducers has long been recognized.

SEXUAL TURN-ONS

In some senses of the word aphrodisiacs need not be substances which are eaten or drunk. To some, money and power are the most potent aphrodisiacs.

Clothes are an obvious sexual device which can be used to announce sexual availability. Some women are turned on by the sight of a man in tight trousers, or a chunky sweater, while black stockings, skin-tight sweaters and leather trousers may have aphrodisiac effects on some men.

Cosmetics, too, have stimulant qualities – lipstick, blusher, mascara, eye-shadows, bath oil and perfume all have alluring properties.

The whole range of sexual preferences have their own particular 'activators'. Some find taboos exciting, while in certain cultures scarring of the skin is a turn-on. To others, the very thought of leather, whips and any of the other sado-masochism equipment is enough to stimulate them.

Then there are the visual foods for sexual stimulation – the hard and soft pornography books, films, magazines and videos.

Mechanical aids, such as 'french ticklers' to stimulate the clitoris, penile rings to maintain erections and vibrators to augment arousal, all may achieve the desired result without the consumption of any substances.

According to a study reported in a journal of sexual medicine, self-hypnosis has an 86 per cent success rate in relieving impotency.

PROMISCUITY

*Promiscuous sex can be born of despair, or of
youthful experimentation. We recommend
the use of the sheath at all times in casual sex*

The last few decades have seen an astonishing increase in sexually permissive attitudes in the West. More widely available contraception and more explicit discussion of sexual matters in the media have been accompanied by a marked increase in pre-marital and extra-marital sex. And as several studies show, people in general feel far less guilty about sex outside marriage than they did in the past from a moralistic point of view, although the fear of catching AIDS is now a very real deterrent.

To say that people are more sexually experienced is not, however, to say that they are necessarily more promiscuous. Two separate studies conducted in Britain in 1983 (by Dr Bury) and 1984 (by Dr Tobin) showed that more teenagers had sexual intercourse than 20 to 30 years ago, but they were no more likely to have 'casual' sex than they were in the past.

Promiscuity can best be defined as fairly frequent, casual sex, and distinguished from 'standard' sex in that it is relatively indiscriminate. It can take place without love and even without friendship. Its goal lies either in the sexual release or in the notching up of a new conquest, not in the beginning of a serious relationship.

A PASSING PHASE
Many young people go through a promiscuous phase in their lives, a time when they experiment with a number of different partners. Sexual expression is new to them, and there is so much to learn.

But in the normal course of events, as adolescents grow into young men and women, they begin to look for more stable and longer-lasting relationships.

Only a small minority of people choose to remain promiscuous throughout their adult lives, and since the outbreak of AIDS, this number is diminishing steadily. In one study that was conducted on the sexual behaviour of young people, it was found that those who were promiscuous at 18 were just as likely to have settled down with one partner seven years later as those who were 'monogamous' at 18. It seems that promiscuity as a young adult has no effect either on the degree of fidelity within later relationships or on subsequent marriage.

In the transition period between promiscuity and fidelity people may practise what is known as 'serial monogamy' – several partners but only one at a time. A 'stable' relationship may be counted in weeks rather than years.

FEAR OF COMMITMENT
Relationships take time to establish. If they are to succeed, they demand a degree of caring and commitment from each partner and a mutual appreciation of each other's qualities. It is often the person who is unable to make this sort of commitment, either because they are too young, too bruised emotionally or too anxious about proving something about themselves, who is likely to behave in a promiscuous fashion.

Before the onslaught of AIDS, promiscuous sex used to be an easy option. It avoided the necessity

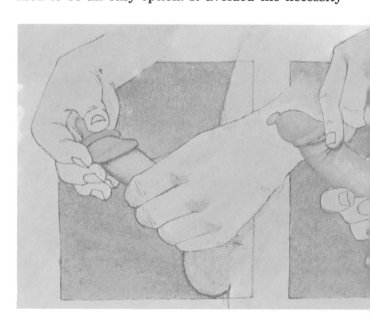

of seeing one's partner as someone with needs and feelings for which one may have to take some responsibility. Even if the sex turned out to be good, there was often little interest in arranging a further encounter in case this resulted in some level of commitment, however small. It was as if novelty and anonymity were all-important.

In promiscuous sex there is a refusal to allow either your own or your partner's emotions to enter into the activity lest they upset the fantasy.

STRAIGHTFORWARD SEX
The reasons for promiscuous behaviour are as varied as the people who do it. For some people, it may simply be the search for sexual experience and confidence.

For others, the attraction lies in the excitement of discovering different people's bodies and pleasures. And for still others, promiscuity affords them a means of satisfying their strong sexual urges.

Sometimes, however, motives are more complex and unconscious, and promiscuous behaviour can then result in confusion and despondency.

There are those, for example, who because of unhappy experiences in childhood are searching for the affection they feel they missed. Sex affords them a temporary release from loneliness, a sense of being close to another human being, but it is never enough. They turn from one partner to another, but the encounters just reinforce their basic feeling of emptiness.

Of all activities, promiscuous sex is one of the least likely to provide the kind of reassurance unhappy people need and may well leave them feeling even more lost and unloved.

This is most serious with young people who have been sexually abused as children and grow up believing that promiscuous sex is all that they are entitled to. Their guilt is such that they feel 'dirty', unlovable, and so they form 'dirty', unloving sexual relationships as a result.

What they need is not further meaningless sex, but the opportunity to talk openly with someone they can trust and who can help them regain their self-esteem.

TO FORGET
Among older people, the motives for bouts of promiscuity may be different. Occasionally quite conservative people who have always been 'monogamous' find themselves seeking comfort in a stranger's arms. It may be that something drastic has happened in their lives, such as bereavement or divorce, an upheaval which has left them aching for solace or a chance to forget.

Often, apparently strong and stable people reach a point where they suddenly feel unable to handle emotions and cannot bear to be alone. They need to be reassured that someone can care about them, even if only for a night.

FOR A CHANGE
In a lighter vein, a promiscuous relationship may simply occur because the opportunity presents itself, perhaps away on a business trip or on holiday.

At times people feel 'stuck in a rut' and want to do something radically different to break out of it. For them a short promiscuous phase may herald changes in different directions.

THE DANGERS
But there are always the sadder cases of those men or women who embark on an endless succession of sexual encounters, not because it brings them pleasure, but because they are anxious about their own sexuality and popularity with the opposite sex.

By parading a line of conquests they are hoping to prove their masculinity or femininity to the world, but the world remains unimpressed. And the fact that they just keep on at it seems to indicate that they do not even manage to convince themselves.

Such anxieties about sexuality are far better sorted out with the help of a trained counsellor or therapist or within the context of a loving relationship.

In the light of the AIDS outbreak we strongly advise anyone who indulges in promiscuous behaviour to think carefully about the consequences. If a complete change to monogamy seems too radical, or if you are between relationships, it is worth learning about safer sex methods. Using a sheath is the best method for avoiding disease, although it is by no means foolproof.

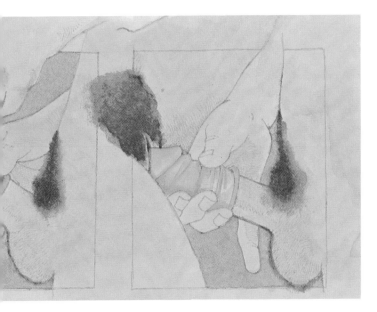

*The correct way to use a sheath is to **1)** Squeeze out the air and place it on the penis tip **2)** Unroll it carefully with both hands **3)** When withdrawing hold it firmly to ensure no sperm escapes*

CHAPTER FOUR

UNDERSTANDING INTIMACY

ORGASM

Orgasms come in one-person sizes. No two are the same. But research reveals some fascinating findings about what you can expect to enjoy. Can men have multiple orgasms? Discover ways to increase your own – and your lover's – pleasure

The overwhelming sense of release – both physical and emotional – that occurs during erotic arousal is an orgasm.

It is not, however, the same for men and women. In men an erection is easy to see and at ejaculation the release of semen is hard to miss. But in women everything is more subtle and can even be missed entirely, if only because some women have few outwards signs of anything happening.

MULTIPLE ORGASMS

On the principle that if something is good then more of it must be better, many people are rather preoccupied with the idea of multiple orgasms.

Most women are capable of having several orgasms one after the other but many say that one is quite enough and that they feel perfectly satisfied and have no need for more. Some women can have twenty or more orgasms one after the other but between one and three is the most common number.

How many a woman has depends on many factors including her early sexual experiences, her level of sexual inhibitions, her emotional involvement with her lover, her partner's ability and willingness to continue stimulating her and, of course, her own desire to have more. Also, some women are more sexually responsive than others just as some are more ticklish than others.

A small percentage have several orgasms all the time, and a few more experience them from time to time, especially when they are highly aroused. Some women claim that their first orgasm is the best, and others say that they build up their best sensations as they have more orgasms one after the other.

MULTIPLE FOR MEN

There is little doubt that preadolescent boys and some young men can have repeated orgasms, but few men can over the age of 30. Between 8 and 15 per cent of younger men have experienced multiple

orgasms. However – and this may be surprising – there is increasing evidence that multiple orgasms for older men could become the norm if they wanted them to.

At the moment, it is commonly thought that ejaculation and orgasm are the same thing, or at least are inextricably linked. But this is not so.

Evidence for this comes from part of the Chinese Taoist tradition which states that prolonged intercourse is the ideal. Realizing that most men would become bored with this prolonged lovemaking if they were not able to experience orgasm, Taoist teaching shows a man how he can separate orgasm from ejaculation. This might seem impossible to achieve, but with practice it can be done.

When a man is about to come the muscles in the pelvis and the legs are usually very tense. If he consciously relaxes the muscles and lets the tension go, the sensations become very intense. He can now allow himself to feel a deep throbbing that approaches orgasm – it is an orgasm without ejaculation. The secret is to be able to recognise the 'I am beginning to come' sensations and to stop them there.

Men in oriental cultures, and indeed some in the West who prefer not to ejaculate every time they have intercourse, can train themselves in this type of intercourse.

To learn how to have better orgasms, it is necessary to understand what exactly happens during the sexual arousal that leads up to orgasm.

MEN AND SEX

For a man, arousal usually starts in his mind. He is 'turned on' by something erotic either in reality or fantasy. This mental change sends nerve impulses

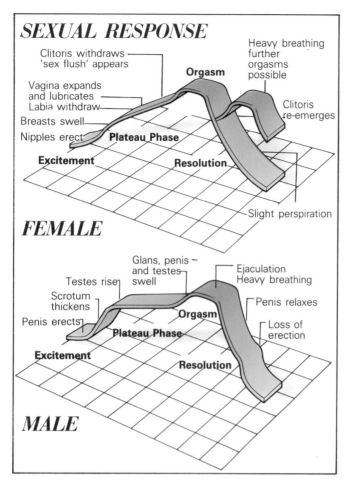

SEXUAL RESPONSE

FEMALE

Clitoris withdraws 'sex flush' appears

Vagina expands and lubricates
Labia withdraw
Breasts swell
Nipples erect

Plateau Phase

Excitement

Orgasm

Heavy breathing further orgasms possible

Clitoris re-emerges

Resolution

Slight perspiration

MALE

Testes rise
Scrotum thickens
Penis erects

Glans, penis and testes swell

Plateau Phase

Orgasm

Ejaculation
Heavy breathing

Penis relaxes

Loss of erection

Excitement

Resolution

THE POINT OF NO RETURN

The next stage is the orgasm itself. At this stage the intensity of sexual arousal is so high that the man has to come off, or ejaculate.

Surges of nerve impulses run back and forth from his nervous system to his genitals. The passages that run from the testicles to the penis contract, along with pelvic muscles, to squirt semen out at the end of his penis. Once an orgasm is near and the man has passed the point of no return, there is nothing he can do to stop it – it takes him over.

At ejaculation a small quantity of semen shoots out of the penis, often for some distance.

This is associated with a pleasant sensation deep in the pelvis as the prostate gland discharges its contents. A series of four or five contractions follows with a gap of just under a second between.

Each contraction produces a smaller volume of semen until the tubes carrying the semen are empty. When the contractions stop, the man relaxes. His erect penis returns to his normal size and he feels relaxed and even sleepy.

The amount of semen a man ejaculates depends upon how recently he last ejaculated and implies nothing about his virility. Each ejaculation, about a teaspoonful, contains millions of sperm, many of which could make a woman pregnant. There is no way of judging the quality of semen by its appearance or its volume and the colour and consistency vary depending on the time since his last ejaculation.

Once the man has ejaculated, it may take several hours before he can be aroused again. The time between ejaculation and the next erection is called the resolution period. Younger men are arousable again sooner than older men.

The male cycle from excitement to ejaculation can be achieved very quickly, especially in teen-

down his spinal cord to his genitals. In response, the spongy tissue of the penis becomes filled with blood, causing it to stiffen. It changes from the limp, downward-hanging organ it usually is to a protruding rod-like one – the penis has become erect.

OTHER CHANGES

During this time, several bodily changes occur. The man's breathing quickens, his pupils enlarge, his blood pressure rises, his heartbeat quickens, his nostrils flare, his muscles tense, he sweats a little and he feels sexually excited.

Appropriately, this is called the excitement phase of his sexual response. As well as his penis becoming erect, his scrotum, the pouch containing his testes, becomes tenser and thicker and the testes themselves are drawn up tightly against the body.

GOING FURTHER

It is possible for all these changes to occur and for the man to return to his normal pre-excitement phase within minutes. But most men will go further by either masturbating or by having sex.

The penis now swells even more and its tip, the glans, becomes purplish blue and the contents of the scrotum increase in size. This is the plateau phase and it is more difficult to return to normal from this than from the earlier excitement phase.

WHAT DO ORGASMS FEEL LIKE?

What is common in all the descriptions people give is the climactic and explosive release of pent-up sexual emotions, the physiological changes, and the subsequent sense of relief and calm.

Most women describe an orgasm as something like an 'explosive sneeze' which overwhelms them. The variations on this are vast with some women describing exquisite genital sensations and others talking about whole-body experience.

For men the sensations are usually more closely tied to the genitals. Some describe a bursting powerful energy in the penis which has a hot core of demanding pleasure. The overwhelming surge of orgasm leads to an explosive draining of the body.

agers and young men who can become aroused and ejaculate in a few minutes.

WOMEN AND SEX
In many ways the body-changes that occur in a woman are very similar to those in a man. But the whole cycle usually takes longer to get going, lasts longer and is capable of near-instant repetition – which a man's is not. However, some women say that depending on the level of their emotional involvement and mood they can become aroused and have an orgasm very quickly indeed.

BUILD UP
Like men, a woman starts off with the excitement phase. During this phase her nipples erect, her breasts swell and the veins in her breast skin become more easily visible. The skin of the whole body usually becomes slightly dusky because of an increased blood flow and there may be a sex flush – a faint measles-like rash over the stomach, chest and neck. This rash disappears at orgasm.

During the excitement phase the woman's genitals become engorged with blood. The inner lips of her vulva, the labia minora, and clitoris swell and become darker in colour. As the clitoris is stimulated it becomes erect – like a miniature penis.

READY TO COME
If stimulation is continued the 'plateau' phase is attained. Here, the shaft and the tip of the clitoris go back under the protective foreskin. This makes it appear that the clitoris has disappeared but the tip and the shaft reappear if stimulation stops. After orgasm has occurred, only about ten to fifteen seconds are required for the clitoris to return to its resting position and size.

The outer lips, the labia majora, swell and pull back so as to open up the vulva a little. The vaginal walls start to 'sweat' and the fluid produced lubricates them. This secretion appears at the vaginal opening in some women. The woman feels moist inside and her sexual tension grows. The vagina now relaxes and becomes enlarged or 'tented' at its top end. The womb is pulled upwards and makes the vaginal cavity larger still.

MUSCLE TWITCHES
Further breast-swelling occurs, the areolae round the nipples swell so much that sometimes the nipples seem to disappear. The woman may begin to twitch all over her body. Sometimes the twitching starts in a toe or a leg, or her stomach muscles may give fluttering twitches. Her pulse rate and breathing speed up and she is ready for orgasm.

FEMALE ORGASM
No two women experience an orgasm in exactly the same way and feelings and reactions vary. But as she has one, her body arches, her muscles tense, her face may draw into a grimace and her vagina and uterus contract rhythmically along with some of her pelvic muscles. Her body may be thrown into spasms of violent contractions or she may sense very little. Some women scream, cry out, moan, gasp or bite their lips as they have an orgasm. The response depends entirely on the personality and experience of the woman. Once the intense contractions of the vagina and uterus are over, the woman returns to her plateau phase and may be able to have another orgasm very soon.

MYTHS ABOUT ORGASM

■ **Women do not ejaculate at orgasm** *They can do, but it is not common. US researchers have found that some women, especially if the G spot is stimulated, produce fluid from the urinary passage just like men do at ejaculation. The fluid is not urine and on testing is found to be just like prostatic fluid in its content.*

■ **Simultaneous orgasms are best** *No they are not necessarily – although they can be very pleasant for some couples. Most find that the effort involved is not worth while and it makes them both too self-conscious about their level of sexual arousal.*

■ **A woman who has only one orgasm has a problem** *No she does not – she may in fact even have more pleasure out of her single orgasm than does a multi-orgasmic woman out of numerous ones. Some multi-orgasmic women are difficult to please, because they seem insatiable. For many men having their woman experience one shattering orgasm can be the best.*

■ **As men and women get older they want to have fewer orgasms** *Although there is a tendency for this to be true it is by no means universally so. Certainly most women in their 80s and 90s have fewer sexual outlets than those in their 20s and 30s. But some people stay highly active all through their lives.*

■ **Orgasms are essential if a couple are to feel sexually fulfilled** *This is a harmful myth and is probably untrue as millions of happily married, non-orgasmic women can tell.*

■ **Genital stimulation is the only way to produce orgasms** *This is mainly true for men but not for women who can come off using all kinds of non-genital stimulation. Some women can have an orgasm by fantasy alone and certainly other parts of their bodies, when stimulated, can bring them to orgasm.*

■ **Women after the menopause stop having orgasms** *Not true, many women, once the chances of unwanted conception are removed, are more sexually at ease and enjoy sex more, not less.*

HAVE I HAD AN ORGASM?

Strange though it may seem, some women do not even know if they have had an orgasm and some who undoubtedly are doing so deny it fervently. They do this because they are unconsciously playing tricks on themselves as a result of inhibition and thoughts that sex is 'dirty'.

PROBLEMS WITH ORGASMS

For many reasons, women have more problems with having or enjoying orgasms than do men.

The first step along the journey to having orgasms at all, or to having better ones, is for her to recognize that her sexuality is something she possesses herself. It is not something that is done to her. If she is not able to do so she needs at least to accept the sexual aspects of her body and mind.

LEARNING ABOUT YOUR BODY

To learn about her sexuality, she may like to act out a sexual fantasy. She could, perhaps, try a stripper exercise in front of a long mirror, pretending it is a male audience. Instead of being unimpressed at the sight of her body she should try to pose and move erotically, stroking and admiring herself rather than giving way to feelings that she is being dirty or bad. She can finish, by opening her legs and vulva, stimulating it and watching the swelling and change of colour as it congests with arousal.

Some women who think they are unarousable or aroused only with difficulty have never watched this response of their vulva to stimulation and are often surprised at how quick and vigorous it is. If she does not normally stimulate her vulva by hand to masturbate she should practise doing so, and hopefully learn to achieve an orgasm in this way. If she can masturbate 'normally' but takes much longer than a few minutes to reach orgasm she could practise frequently.

Some women are vastly encouraged in all this if they can discuss it with a trusted woman friend, or if they read some books devoted to female masturbation, or look at magazines or videos showing women touching their vulvas. This helps to overcome the tendency to believe unconsciously that she is the only woman who wants to touch her genitals.

Some women have been made to feel so bad about touching themselves that it makes them so tense that they cannot have an orgasm. Such women can often succeed using a vibrator. Most are designed to be applied to the vulva or to be inserted into the vagina. Provided that they want to succeed, most women can have an orgasm using a vibrator.

USING A VIBRATOR

In a woman who has not had orgasms, or at least not consciously, earlier, the quality of the orgasms usually improves rapidly and the time to orgasm becomes shorter. After a time, as they become more skilful, most women discover they can get more precise stimulation using their fingers, and so tend to use the vibrator less. A vibrator is a good learning

Rear entry positions are exciting for many women as they say that they feel totally vulnerable and exceptionally abandoned

device and most women who use one do not – in the long run – become addicted to it.

INVOLVING YOUR PARTNER

Although problems with orgasm are best discussed with your partner from the outset, it may be that you feel embarrassed about telling your lover. And it is true that some men become hostile over their women masturbating themselves, especially if they use a vibrator, seeing it all as criticism of their masculine capacity to satisfy them. Of course, this type of response is unlikely to help.

Men should be very encouraging to partners and help them by buying erotic literature or a vibrator if the woman is too shy to do so.

Once the woman feels more confident about her own sexuality, and feels she can cope with the pres-ence of her partner, he can then become involved and help her. She should try to enjoy 'showing-off' and to notice and enjoy her partner's signs of arousal in response to her display. He can help, at first, by stroking her and using words of encouragement.

ORGASMS AND INTERCOURSE

To most men intercourse is about having orgasms. And women have been led to believe, almost, that there is something wrong unless they have multiple orgasms during intercourse. Also, many men believe that if a woman really loves him she will have an orgasm during penetration.

However, according to a recent survey of 15,000 women only about half reach orgasm during inter-course, probably after at least some foreplay, but only one in seven do so every time they make love this way. Almost all men in the survey said that it was important for them (the men) to reach orgasm during intercourse but only two thirds of wives said it was important for them (the women).

Many women are quite happy to have inter-course time after time without having an orgasm – much to the frustration and sometimes the annoy-ance of their partner. To such a woman, having an orgasm is unduly goal-centred and 'typically male' whereas, to her, the cuddling, kissing and the all-over body sensations may be quite enough.

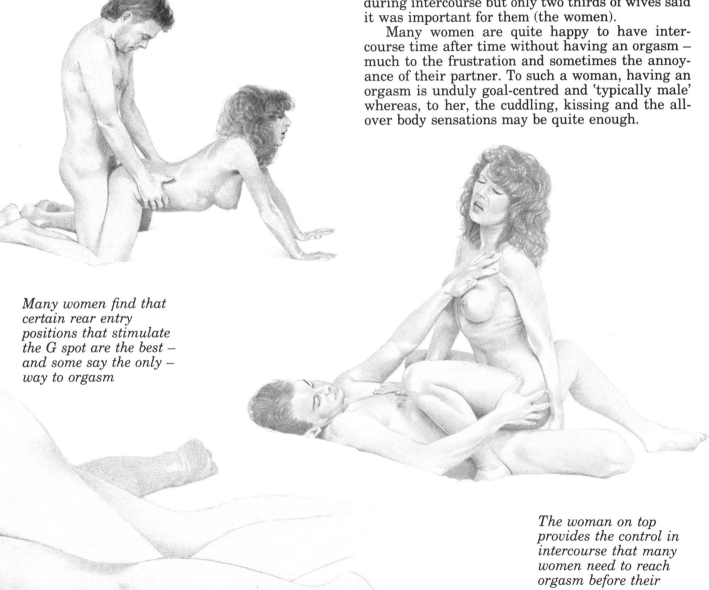

Many women find that certain rear entry positions that stimulate the G spot are the best – and some say the only – way to orgasm

The woman on top provides the control in intercourse that many women need to reach orgasm before their partner

WHAT TURNS WOMEN ON

Women are not unappreciative of classic male beauty, but it takes more to excite them than just rugged good looks. Personality, reliability, sensitivity, and humour all have the power to turn women on

In the process of sexual arousal, cultural expectations have a large role to play. What turns a European woman on is very different from what turns a Ghanaian woman on. So a man with saucer-shaped lips, a large nose-ring or all-over body tatooing might have women swooning adoringly at his feet, only to have women swooning for very different reasons if he ventured out of his society.

EVOLUTION AND BODY STRUCTURE

But universal factors involving the different ways in which men and women have evolved are also very important. In this case, sexual attraction is based primarily on the differences between men and women.

It may be that because men were originally hunters, they needed to develop taller bodies, which were more muscular and had larger feet and hands than women. Because women were childbearers and rearers, they evolved a broader pelvis, large breasts, a greater gap between the thighs and a higher proportion of body fat to men.

All of these identifying features are likely to be seen as sexy by members of the opposite sex because they accentuate and typify the differences between men and women. And their exaggeration, for example broad shoulders in a man and large breasts in a woman, may be seen as even sexier.

FINDING A MATE

Since women's involvement with reproduction is so much more extensive than men's, they approach sex

While rippling muscles may not be a primary turn-on for women, some anthropologists believe that women value strength in a man for what it denotes – his ability to fend for and protect his family

and therefore sexual arousal in a different way.

While a man could theoretically impregnate hundreds of women during a nine-month period, a

woman can only be impregnated once and carry the child or children to term. And her criteria for choosing a partner, even if she has no intention of having children with that person, is influenced by generations of women before her.

Anthropologists argue that because of their evolutionary history, women are naturally more choosy than men and more hesitant in encounters. They are necessarily less easily turned on, because they are so much more at risk from making a bad choice. Before they select a mate, they have to make sure that he is reliable, that he could comfort and provide and stay around for nine months and beyond.

SEX AND AGE

Women do not have to be attracted only to young men, since a man's ability to reproduce does not diminish with age the way a woman's does. So whereas men are more likely to be turned on by young women who are capable of bearing healthy children, women can be attracted by a wider range of ages.

And a woman's own age makes a difference. Girls are likely to be turned on by quite different criteria from their older sister or their mothers.

An experienced teenager may well be flattered

A smile rates high on the list of female turn-ons

by the attention of an older man. A mother with tiny children could be turned on by a man who sees her as a woman rather than simply a mother-figure. An ambitious career woman might succumb to the offers of help – professional and otherwise – from a male colleague further up the ladder.

INNER QUALITIES

Physical appearance is not of primary importance either. Instead, women look out for reliability, faithfulness, status, prowess and the ability to accumulate wealth.

Women tend to respond sexually not to instant cues but to atmosphere – all those signals that show warmth, intimacy and absence of danger, such as attentiveness, a soothing voice and touching.

Women are not attracted specifically to male genitals the way a man might be by the sight of a woman's breasts. Instead, they are attracted to a particular kind of juxtaposition of qualities.

STATUS SYMBOLS

When men are asked to rate women according to desirability and attractiveness, there is a high degree of agreement among them. Women, on the other hand, have relatively idiosyncratic criteria for assessing men. For example, they tend to like what a man's body symbolizes – power, protection, or comfort – rather than what it looks like.

They may be impressed by a man's skill and prowess at work or in sporting activities, but they are seldom excited by the mere sight of a hairy chest

or a display of huge bulging muscles.

WOMEN AND PORNOGRAPHY

In a number of studies conducted during the seventies aimed at discovering whether women were turned on by pornographic videos, it was found that their arousal was greatest when the film included a sequence of activity between a man and a woman involving a slowly developing relationship. The sexual act on its own was not enough – although it was for men.

Donald Symons in his book *The Evolution of Human Sexuality* suggests that for a woman imagination is very important. She needs to be able to project herself into the situation – to identify with the woman on the screen and to gradually become involved with the man in order to become highly aroused.

Again, this difference may be cultural – women are not brought up to think of sex in the same way men do – or it may be a matter of perceptions. There is some evidence that women simply do not recognize signs of physiological arousal in themselves, although they are indeed aroused.

Another possibility is that women are reluctant to admit arousal and so subconsciously repress it. Instruments measuring vaginal lubrication have shown levels of response of which the women themselves were not consciously aware.

FEMALE TURN-ONS

It is less easy to assess psycho-sexual triggers for women than for men, because the physiological signs of female arousal are more subtle. A slight moistening of the vagina presents a much more difficult gauge of arousal than a male erection. The majority of studies that have been done have relied more on questionnaire than objective measurements, but have nevertheless come up with some interesting results.

A 1983 MORI poll found that looks were thought to be important by only 23 per cent of women compared to 40 per cent of men. Faithfulness and personality were rated as more important than looks by most women.

Women also tended to be aroused by men who were assertive and competent at what they were doing. So in an experiment in which men helped blindfolded women to find their way through a maze, the women were more attracted to their partner if he was successful in helping them reach the end of the maze. Also, they liked being physically guided – actually touched – rather than simply talked through it.

BODY POSTURE

Women who like confident, assertive men will be more likely to be turned on by men who sit with their legs apart, since this is the gesture of the sexually assertive male.

Sexual excitement or prolonged sexual interest automatically results in the tightening of the stomach muscles, and a woman is likely to respond instinctively to this in a man. She will be turned on by a man with a flat stomach because it shows he is interested in her – and women like attentive men.

The physical characteristics which women do seem to desire in men are quite different from those suggested by the stereotype of a masculine man. Sexual surprise, such as finding 'feminine' characteristics in a man – long eyelashes, soft hair on strong arms – excites them more than rippling biceps and a strong jaw.

In their book *Love's Mysteries*, G. Wilson and D. Nias define the sort of man who turns a woman on – in looks, five to six inches taller than them, with small buttocks, a flat stomach, slim and with a good complexion. In character, they go for men who are assertive and dominant.

WOMAN TALK

Men who try to get on with women and tune into their conversation are also more likely to turn a woman on to them.

A 1978 study compared men who are successful and unsuccessful at dating women. The successful ones were more fluent in saying the right thing and in joining in more quickly, and they agreed with the women more.

Their non-verbal behaviour was also different – they smiled and nodded more than their less-successful counterparts.

SOCIAL CONDITIONING

Because women tend not to see too many male nude bodies as they grow up, and because they are not assailed daily by a host of male pinups in their newspapers, they are not tuned into men's bodies as symbols of sexual desirability the way men are to women.

Their unfamiliarity makes them uncomfortable with men's bodies in the abstract and lessens their sexual responses to them.

Instead, women are more likely to react to a man's clothes and his 'props'. They might deduce from a man's sports bag, for example, that he is probably athletic, fairly healthy and fit, and probably also an active lover.

SEXUAL DISPLAYS

While women can wear clinging dresses or plunging necklines to attract their mates, men have fewer options in terms of clothing. One that has become fairly widespread is the wearing of tight jeans. These hold the penis in place in an upright – and therefore seemingly erect – position.

What women respond to is not the overt sexual symbolism of the tight crotch, but rather the nudge that the sight of the jeans gives them to make them start thinking about sex.

WHAT TURNS MEN ON

Brought up to appreciate the female form, men set a high premium on a woman's appearance. But what do they look for, and what turns them on?

Every time you walk into a room or down the street, you transmit a series of signals. These signals vary, depending on your sex, cultural background, mood, appearance and age – and also your intentions at the time.

When you go for a job interview, you probably encourage the interviewer to feel well-disposed to you. You smile a lot, talk in well-modulated tones, and look him or her straight in the eye. Equally, when you are trying to turn someone on sexually, you consciously or unconsciously adopt patterns of behaviour designed to attract and impress.

GENDER DIFFERENCES

There are some differences between the sexes as to what turns each of them on, and some areas of overlap. Generally, appearance is a very important aspect for both men and women. Partly because of the stereotyped view that attractive people are warm, sociable, interesting and kind, good looks are rated very highly as an initial sexual turn-on.

Men are more likely to be turned on by physical features and appearances, setting a higher premium on those characteristics associated with good looks than women do. A British survey conducted in 1985 found that looks were rated highly by 40 per cent of men, compared with 23 per cent of women.

But research on masculinity and femininity shows that, in addition to looks, men are attracted to women with traditional qualities of warmth, sympathy, kindness, gentleness and cheerfulness. Women, instead, are attracted to men who are assertive, independent and self-reliant.

LOOKS OR PERSONALITY?

In an earlier survey in 1972, men listed the traits most likely to attract them to a woman in the following order:

A woman's waist tends to be much narrower than a man's and women have accentuated this difference – even by surgically removing the lower ribs

DID YOU KNOW?

Our vision turns us on in an unexpected way, through the effect of sunlight on the pineal gland, which is located in a part of the brain behind the eyes.

If you feel very sexy after basking in the sun, it is partly because sunlight acts on this gland to reduce production of the hormone melatonin, an inhibitor of sexual activity. More babies are conceived during the summer – the season of longer sunshine – than during the winter months.

1 Physical attractiveness
2 Erotic ability (sexiness)
3 Affectional ability (warmth and understanding).
Domestic ability was less sought-after and came further down the list.

In the western world, there is fairly widespread agreement as to what constitutes feminine beauty. Miss World, for example, is usually 21 years old 5′ 8″ tall and measures 35″–24″–35″.

But when two people are trying to attract each other, very different factors come into play. Extrovert men, for example, are more likely to be turned on by women with large breasts, while introverts, prefer women with small breasts.

The reasons for this are speculative. One suggestion is that extrovert men actually relish the attention which their big-breasted partners evoke, while introverts would prefer to be unobtrusive.

HANDS OFF

Unless we are accidentally thrown against someone, for example in a crowded train, we never touch one another until we have carefully read the signals.

Our brains are constantly assessing the hundreds of separate signals coming to us from the details of the other person's shape, size, smell, posture, movements, colour, sound and expression. These are translated in a fraction of a second and the brain lets us know whether it is acceptable to make further approaches.

MALE TURN-ONS

Women wearing stockings has traditionally been one of the great male turn-ons. Stockings cover most of the leg, with the tantalizing exception of the part of the leg which is nearest to the 'forbidden' genitals. And lacy stockings which both conceal and reveal are highly erotic.

LEGS

Long legs are in themselves powerful attractants to men. The transformation of a girl's legs into the shapely legs of a woman signifies that she has attained physical, and therefore also sexual maturity. Wearing high-heeled shoes or skin-tight ski pants accentuates the length and shape of the leg and also emphasizes its allure.

With the advent of trousers for women, sitting with legs apart is seen as more of a challenge than a turn-on. But sitting with legs pressed tightly against one another or crossed so vigorously that the thighs are squeezed together may reveal that a woman has sex very much on her mind.

The woman who tries to protect her genitals very obviously draws as much attention to them as the one who exposes them to view. Consequently, a skirt riding up and then being pulled down again is a turn-on, enhancing the sexuality of the situation. If the skirt had just been left, it might only have momentarily diverted the man. But the woman's effort to correct its positioning shows she realizes its potential significance. It may also emphasize her vulnerability.

BUTTOCKS

Women's buttocks also offer a powerful erotic signal to a man. More pronounced in women than in men, buttocks are the equivalent to the sexual swellings of other species when they are 'on heat' – except that in humans the swelling is permanent.

BREASTS

A woman's breasts are the most obvious sexual turn-on for men. They may remind men of the warmth and security of the mother's nurturing, or perhaps the fascination they hold is more straightforward than that. They are the most obvious bodily 'label' of her sex and are sensitive, erogenous zones. Nipples become erect when the woman is aroused and rarely lie.

If a man prefers to play the 'dominant father' role in a relationship, he is more likely to be turned on by the little girl look of small breasts. If he prefers older, more mature women, he will probably go for larger breasts.

THE WAIST

The woman's characteristic narrow waist also highlights her breasts. Historically, bodices and corsets drew in the waist and accentuated the breast. In Tudor times, the breasts were sometimes even left exposed above a tight, restrictive bodice. Today, tight belts create a similar effect.

SHOULDERS

A woman's shoulders, like her breasts, are an echo of the basic buttock shape which, in our early ancestors, was the most erotic part of the body.

Many men find exposed shoulders tantalizing which explains why off-the-shoulder dresses are popular for evening wear as sexual appetizers.

LIPS

Psychologists suggest that many men subconsciously connect fleshy lips with fleshy vaginal labia, a factor which may have been behind the

Men's bodies are typically angular and broad-shouldered, with the torso forming a triangle. Women's bodies instead are often valued for their curves, with breasts, buttocks, shoulders, even knees forming a series of sumptuous circles

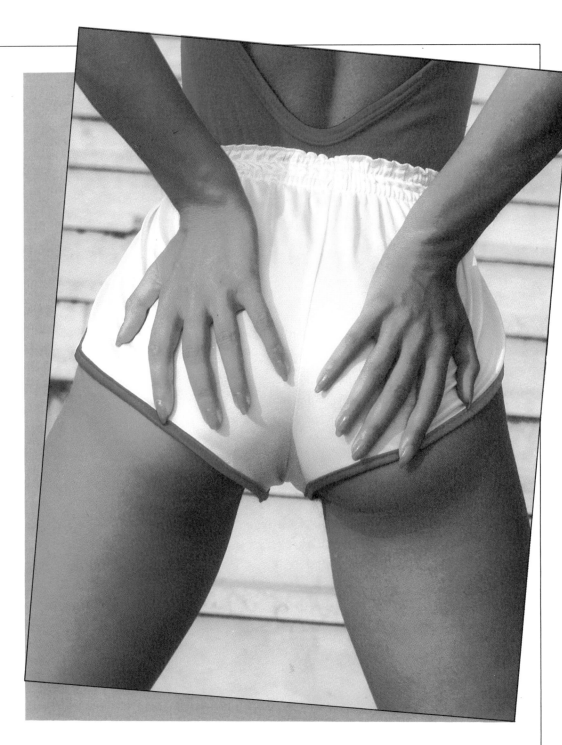

growth and popularity of lipstick. Thick, pouting lips, particularly when they are painted red, echo the flushing of the labia during the advanced stages of sexual arousal, when they are engorged with blood.

BODY SHAPE

Men are more likely to be turned on by a slender young girl's shape than by the more rounded, maternal silhouette except in certain cultures where motherhood is considered to be erotic. The slimmer version tends to remind them of the woman they mooned over, stared at, touched, kissed and fell in love with, although it may be the fuller, more

rounded, more maternal woman who they will spend years making love to in reality.

EYES

The eyes are also powerful accessories to sexual attraction, for both men and women. Under the influence of strong, pleasant emotions, our pupils dilate to an unusual degree so that the small spot in the centre of the eye becomes a great black disc. Unconsciously, this transmits a powerful signal to the person you are with. On first encounter, the holding of a glance slightly longer than is usual can make an impact. Alternatively, a demure dropping of the eyes also indicates interest.

LEARNING TO TOUCH

Touching is for lovers. It is the way we explore each other's bodies, discovering the areas which thrill and excite, turning lovemaking into a completely sensual experience

Touch is the sense that registers heat and cold, pain and pressure. But as every lover knows, it is far more than this. Through touch we communicate our feelings, we give and receive pleasure, and express our needs and desires.

But although touch is a natural sense, its full expression does not always come naturally. It may be something we need to re-learn if our lovemaking has gradually become more and more focused on intercourse alone.

THE TOUCH SEQUENCE

The exact progress of every sexual relationship is individual. But research has shown that however long we take to get to sex, there is a set sequence that we follow.

At first the erogenous zones are no-go areas which it would be inappropriate – even offensive – to touch. We move from hand-touching through embracing, kissing and caressing to genital contact and sexual intercourse.

The 'arrival' at sexual intercourse does not mean that the other stages in the touch sequence are no longer important. But in any long-term relationship there will be times when we lose touch with touch. Taking a step back in the sequence can be a step forward in lovemaking.

For stroking, caressing, fondling, holding and kissing are all part of the recipe for making love. They are the ingredients that turn sex into a mutually satisfying sensual and emotional experience.

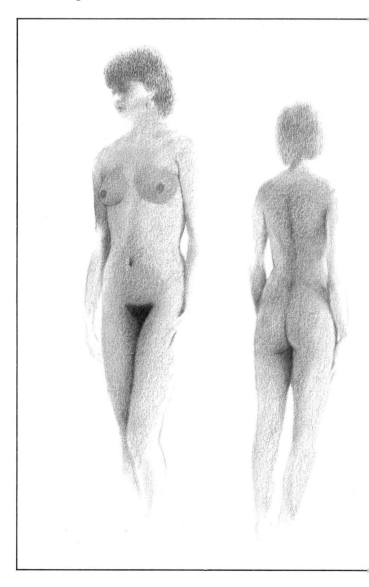

Our artist has interpreted scientific research to show the graduation of erogenous zones to maximum sensitivity

SENSUAL MASSAGE

Between lovers, sensual massage is an erotic, very intimate laying of hands on skin. Sometimes it may be part of the prelude to lovemaking, while at other times, it is a form of lovemaking in itself.

A SENSUAL SHARING

The secret of massage is that one partner can be completely passive, while the other makes all the decisions and is the pleasure-giver. A heady sensation for either partner, it can provide even greater feelings of closeness and give yet more complex exchanges of lovemaking.

You can refine the basic art of massage in order to learn more about your partner's body. For example, take it in turns to select small sections of each other's bodies, and rate your partner's reactions.

You could try a gentle, exploratory massage, using oils, essences, creams – anything that will make the experience more intensely sensual.

Sensual massage will help you to learn how to release and to enjoy both your own and your partner's body by relaxing tight muscles and, possibly, pent-up emotions. As it is often a preliminary to more direct sexual stimulation, avoid touching the genitals and breasts until your partner is totally relaxed. This relaxation is not going to make you passive or sleepy, but will leave you refreshed and full of energy from this highly sensuous experience.

Massage is the rhythmical application of pressure on the body using the hands, thumbs and fingers. Blood and lymph vessels – the body's drainage channels – run through the muscles and as the muscles relax, the gentle pressure of the

DISCOVERING THE PLEASURE ZONES

When you map your lover's body with hands or mouth you soon discover which areas are the most sensitive and provoke a sexual response.

Generally, women are more responsive to touch than are men as their pleasure zones extend over more of the body. But everyone, everywhere finds the mouth, the genitals and the anal area sexually sensitive, and stimulation of them may lead to an orgasm in some people.

But if you explore further you will find that the breasts, especially the nipples, the buttocks and earlobes, the inner arms and legs and the nape of the neck are all sensitive to touch and can be used to heighten sensuality during lovemaking. Some women may be brought to orgasm by this stimulation alone.

But during sex the whole body can respond to arousal. People may have different preferences and it helps to talk freely about them to your partner. Perhaps you can discover your own unique areas of pleasure. Licking or sucking the toes or rubbing the small of the back, caressing the contours of the hips or gently stroking the soft down on the back of the neck may well be exciting to you.

 Highly erogenous

 Moderately erogenous

 Erogenous

TECHNIQUES OF MASSAGE

The massages shown on the following pages give a maximum of sensual relaxation without too much time or effort. Some of the following techniques are used, but there is no reason why you should not experiment. The ideas, of course, are for both partners – the masseur, or masseuse, and the massee – should have an interesting and pleasurable experience.

Effleurage is the most important stroke and should always precede all the other movements on each area and be used to finish and relax the muscles you have been working on. Apply the pressure by leaning your body weight behind each upward stroke and then slide your hands lightly back down to your starting point before starting the cycle all over again.

Kneading uses just the same action as working on dough. Keeping your hands in a relaxed curve, pick up and roll the areas of soft tissue over the bone as smoothly and rhythmically as you can manage.

Petrissage is a small circular movement made with the balls of the thumbs or fingers, particularly effective on the back moving up from the spine's base. Work only on the muscles on either side of the spine and not over the spine itelf. Make a few outward circling

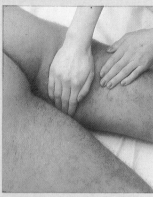

Kneading

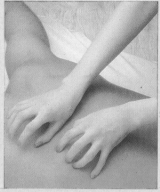

Tapotement

Hacking

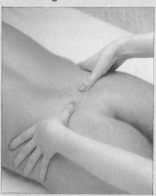

Petrissage

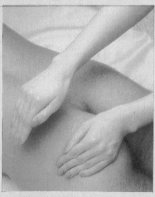

Cupping

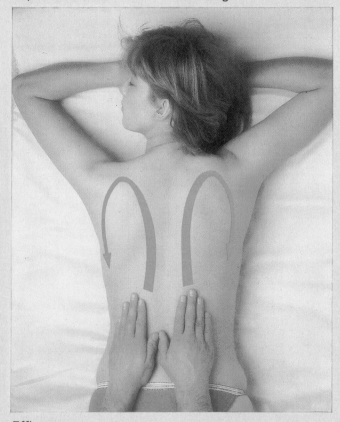

Effleurage

movements and then slide your thumbs up an inch or so and then circle again and so on.

Tapotement is a quick, light tapping movement made with the fingertips, like drumming your fingers impatiently on a table.

Hacking is a light, quick flicking movement made with the outer edge of the hands. Let your fingers become quite relaxed so that they flap together as your hands come down on the body of your partner.

Cupping is a light, quick movement using alternate hands. Cup your hands, keeping the fingers together and your thumbs tucked in. As the cupped hands hit the body they should produce a hollow popping sound.

massage helps stimulate the circulation and clear away toxins. It is important, therefore, that all the long strokes, called effleurage, apply the pressure towards the heart. It is also important not to lose contact with the body, so you should apply the pressure upwards and then lightly drag your hands back down.

KEEPING A RHYTHM

The essence of a good massage is rhythm. The long strokes should be like the ebb and flow of the sea washing against the shore. Do not try to hurry a massage. Keep the movements steady and slow. Jerky movements will leave your partner feeling edgy and uncomfortable.

How much pressure you apply is a matter of preference. Most people like to feel some weight behind each upward stroke without it being too fierce or rough, while others prefer a lighter touch. Generally, though, try to put your body weight behind your strokes rather than just using your arms and shoulders. This makes it possible for you to lean well into the upward strokes.

OILS AND TALC

It is important that your hands slide easily over the skin, so use a light application of talc to the palms of the hands or use an oil. Some people do not like talc as it can dry the skin, but an oil will leave skin feeling wonderfully soft and smooth. Do not use hand cream or body lotion as this will disappear into the skin too quickly and the skin could become sore when you rub.

Baby oil is an ideally textured oil but some people are put off by the scent. However, there are precious oils and balms, herbal and flower essences that have all been used with massage for their beneficial effects.

There are some specially prepared massage oils available or you can buy your own base and blend your own fragrances. But be careful when adding chemical, as opposed to natural, essences as some people are particularly allergic to synthetic products.

MASSAGING THE ABDOMEN

1 *Begin with one-handed effleurage, sweeping around clockwise. The abdomen must not be massaged anti-clockwise*
2 *Now knead the abdominal area gently, again moving the hand clockwise. Keep the other hand in contact with the body by resting gently on the skin*
3 *Finish with two-handed effleurage.*

LOOSENING THE NECK

4 *Begin by stroking up the back of the neck*
5 *Then carefully work your fingers around the base of the skull*
6 *Knead one side of the neck then the other, and lastly, lift the head so the chin touches the chest and lower it to the floor gently*

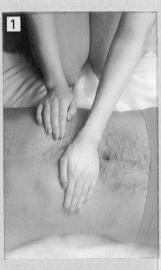

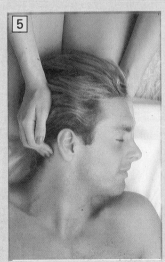

Sandalwood is well known for its relaxing properties while lemon balm is lightly refreshing. Almond oil is a good plain unscented oil and is available from most chemists' shops.

USING OILS

Always apply the oil to your hands first and then lightly distribute it over the area of the body you are going to massage. Do not use too much oil as your hands will slip and it will be difficult to work all the oil into the skin. It is a good idea to place a towel under your partner to prevent any excess oil marking the floor or bed coverings underneath.

WHEN AND WHERE TO MASSAGE

You can massage your partner on the bed or on the floor. The floor will provide a firmer resistance to your pressure and will allow you more freedom of movement. Placing cushions or pillows under your partner makes it more comfortable. A pillow placed under the stomach when lying face down or under the thighs when lying face up helps release the lower back.

Make sure, too, that you are comfortable giving the massage. You can place a pillow under your knees while you are kneeling. Try to keep close to your partner so that you do not have to stretch out too far and strain a muscle.

Ensure that the room is really warm so that neither of you feels cold. It is a good idea to cover the parts of the body which you are not working on. Also, warm your hands and remove any rings. Soft lighting and background music also help you feel more relaxed.

TIME AND TOUCH

Allow plenty of time to massage each other so that you do not feel hurried. Take the telephone off the hook. You need not go through a full sequence every time, but choose just one area which seems particularly tense or which seems particularly pleasurable. You can take ten minutes or an hour or two. Let your partner unwind and talk about what feels pleasant, or just allow the sensation of touch to find its own way.

Throughout these exercises the emphasis must be on sensual delight – on the joy of discovering your own and your partner's response to touch. Vary the strokes, the roughness or gentleness of your pressure.

AN INTIMATE JOURNEY

Go on a more intimate journey around the body – kissing and stroking the back, shoulders, limbs and face, touching buttocks, breasts, genitals. Use whatever accessories please you both – feathers, silk, velvet, fur, wool. Consider the application of differently textured brushes, the shock of an ice cube, or the comfort of a bowl full of warmed – but not hot – aromatic oil.

WHEN NOT TO MASSAGE

There are times or conditions when massage can be harmful. If any of the following are present, do not massage. If in doubt, check with your doctor.

■ *Cardio-vascular troubles including thrombosis, phlebitis, angina pectoris, hypertension (high blood pressure) and prominent varicose veins (locally).*
■ *Contagious or infectious skin diseases*
■ *During pregnancy do not massage over the abdomen*
■ *Where there are areas of unexplained inflammation or pain*
■ *Any condition being treated unless the doctor has agreed*
■ *Do not massage over sore, tender or wounded areas*

TAKING TURNS

Take it in turns to be massager and massaged. Touch everywhere, and then let each other know what pleases you most and least. Above all, learn to relax. Put out of your mind any notion that these activities have purpose beyond the simple pleasure of touching your partner's body.

Then progress by concentrating on just one part of the body – the face, perhaps, a terrain alive with erotic responses, or the genitals. You may find it unbearable to be this aroused without making love.

Remember that massage should be highly pleasurable and not hurt. The more you practise the more proficient you will become. It is also important that partners should learn to massage each other, as this will not only allow you to learn what feels good on yourself but also shares the giving and receiving of pleasure.

There are other times when you can make love so do not rush hastily into sex. A massage will bring you closer together in ways different to the passionate intimacy of the act of love itself. And if you are using massage as a prelude to sex, take your time – the relaxation and the sensuality it creates will only heighten the feelings and pleasures you will both eventually experience.

INTIMATE TOUCHING

Sexual contact does not only mean touching breasts or penis, it is also stroking a shoulder or kissing an eyelid.

Sexuality needs sensuality – sensual pleasure enhances sexual performance. You will find that sex can become more intimate when sensuous touching is emphasized.

GETTING READY

Prepare for a lovemaking session as for an event. Make sure that you and your partner are relaxed, as though you are taking time out of your routine for something special.

Begin by kissing, caressing, cuddling. The mouth, lips and tongue are easily aroused, but many people find it just as exciting to be kissed on the ears and neck.

SECRET SPOTS

Next explore every area of the body – the feet, behind the knees, the inside of the thighs, the shoulders, the back – stroking, kneading, kissing or licking as you go. If you find a particularly sensitive zone, linger there, lovingly. Do not forget to tell your partner what you like or what you discover you like. You are charting your partner's body. The more you get to know that body, the better your lovemaking will be.

BREASTS AND NIPPLES

After caressing the moderately erogenous zones, at some point attention will turn to more highly charged erotic centres. A man will probably move to the woman's breasts. It is best to start with a gentle approach such as kissing, stroking or sucking as many women complain that men are too rough with their breasts. Later, though, if the woman likes it, the man can be more firm and squeeze, tweak and gently bite the breasts and nipples.

The nipples will harden when a woman is highly aroused, and squeezing them can be very exciting. But sometimes, at different points of the menstrual cycle, the woman's breasts may be more tender than usual – do not assume you always know what your partner wants. Never be afraid to ask. Many men also have sensitive nipples and like them sucked, squeezed or gently nibbled.

BUTTOCKS

Buttocks are sensitive in both men and women. Some people respond to gentle stroking, while others like a more vigorous kneading. But most people, even those who enjoy rougher sexual movements, do not like to be hurt. Be very careful not to make a cry of pleasure turn into a cry of pain.

Be especially careful if you are touching the anal area, but do not be afraid to explore. The area

RELAXING THE BACK

The first thing to do to the back is to use effleurage, sweeping up from the base of the spine to the shoulders. 7 Then use petrissage on either side of the spine, starting at the base and moving up. 8 Next knead the fleshy part between the shoulders and the sides of the neck. 9 Then stroke around each shoulder blade in turn, using both hands. 10 Now use petrissage on the shoulder blades, one at a time, using one hand. 11 Stroke the side of the body from the armpit to the waist, doing first one then the other side.

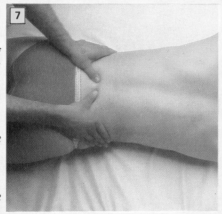

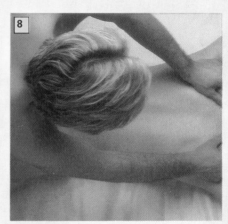

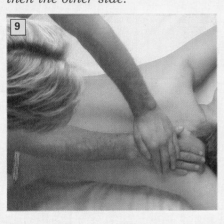

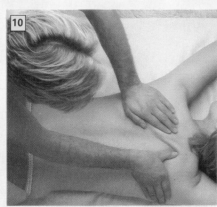

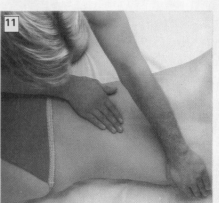

around the anus and between the sex organs and the anus – call the perineum – is richly supplied with pleasure-sensitive nerves. Some people find it very exciting to have this area stroked, gently rubbed or squeezed. When really aroused or close to orgasm, the tip of a finger placed in the anus can give extremely sensuous feelings.

When you are both ready, the man's hand may travel down to the vaginal area and start to caress the vulva. If not already moist you can apply KY jelly or saliva.

EXPLORING DEEPER

The clitoris is highly sensitive, and capable of producing orgasms without penetration of the vagina. But because it is so tender it can be ticklish too. Try firm, definite, rhythmic strokes rather than fluttery ones. Men often insert one or two fingers into the vagina to stimulate it before penetration. Be slow and deliberate. Explore the vagina and perhaps, if you can, caress the cervix.

For the woman caressing the man's penis, the key to pleasurable touch is, for most men, to be firm and unhurried. Allow the fingers to circle the tip, then gradually move the hand down, gently holding the penis, between thumb and fingers so that it is enclosed. Rub it gently at first, then harder. You may find that a lubricating cream will help. But while concentrating on the penis, do not neglect the rest of the area.

Try gently cupping the testicles in a hand and find the tender place underneath them. Some men find this exploration and caressing of the testicles and scrotum unbearably erotic.

ORGASM

For some couples, it is perfectly natural for the man to have an orgasm manually instead of during intercourse. Others prefer to bring each other to orgasm with mouth, lips and tongue. Use them as you would your fingers and hands – to communicate, find pleasure points, stimulate, explore and arouse.

Despite the fact that large areas of the body are in contact during intercourse itself, remember to keep up your dedication to touch. All the erotic charges will now be heightened, so that a hand on the breasts or the buttocks, stroking the inside of a thigh, or travelling over waist or back, will greatly add to pleasure.

AFTER LOVE

And when intercourse is over do not think that lovemaking has finished. Continue to keep open the lines of communication by touch. It will feel different now – less urgent, more friendly. But it remains vital. A man or woman can feel betrayed if, at the moment when climax has been reached, the partner just rolls away.

Keep on stroking and touching, but remember that now the genitals of both sexes and a woman's breasts and nipples may be very sensitive to touch.

Avoid if possible these highly responsive erogenous zones and return to the area of the body where you began – the neck, the back, the arms.

Lying close together, either face-to-face or face-to-back nestled together like spoons provides the close body contact that gives a feeling of security and reassurance.

ANOTHER WAY TO ORGASM?

In recent years there has been much talk of the G spot – a kind of 'magic button' inside the vagina that can produce orgasm even if the clitoris is not stimulated. But what is it, and does it actually exist?

The existence of the G spot has not been proved conclusively and while more and more women are reported to be discovering the pleasure of G spot stimulation, others cannot confirm its existence.

During lovemaking most women, and many men, enjoy having their nipples licked and sucked

The body hug. Press breast to breast, stomach to stomach, pubis to pubis, with arms wrapped around each other. Closing your eyes will heighten the sensation of closeness

Above left: *Through touching, kissing and rubbing the clitoris, a woman can often reach orgasm quickly and easily. A man should learn to stimulate his partner to a stage when she is so aroused that she is ready and willing for intercourse to take place*

By kissing, licking, rubbing and pulling the penis – and the testicles – a woman can usually help a man achieve an erection with little difficulty

CHAPTER FIVE

SPECIALITY SEX

ADVANCED FOREPLAY

For most couples, there are times when intercourse can become routine and predictable. Used imaginatively, foreplay can open up some exciting variations

Good sex requires good foreplay. And advanced sex requires advanced foreplay. In fact, in advanced sex, foreplay can often take over from actual intercourse completely as the main source of excitement. But where does foreplay begin and ordinary social intercourse end?

The answer is, it does not. Foreplay does not begin at the bedroom door. Many fairly 'innocent' social activities can take on a special significance between lovers and potential lovers.

Striptease can be almost an art form, especially when it is performed in the comfort of your own home. The woman can use her body to arouse her partner to such a point that he is powerless to do anything other than join in

Most couples find that sharing a meal and bottle of wine is a natural prelude to lovemaking. Some lovers find that special foods do more than set the mood. Spicy foods to heat the blood, exotic food that recalls an especially amorous holiday or just a favourite meal as a special occasion can all serve to arouse a couple.

DANCE TOGETHER

Dancing close together is an art all of its own. A couple out dancing together can easily carry the sexual display element and arousal home with them. In the comfort of their own home, there is no reason to keep their clothes on.

Professional striptease artistes and go-go dancers of both sexes have long been objects of erotic

attention. And there is no reason why similar 'acts' cannot be staged privately, as a shared experience between lovers. While one partner dances – clothed or naked – the other can sit down as an audience. Nudity and dance movements often have a particularly sexual effect. And when both partners are naked, they may find dancing leading to making love to the music.

KISSING

Kisses come in all strengths and intensities, from the merest brush of a pair of dry lips to the full force of a passionate embrace.

FUR AND FEATHER

Many things can be used to stimulate the skin to sensual effect. Some people have specialized tastes for rubber, leather and PVC. But most people enjoy the warm and stimulating effects of fur and feathers.

Nudity – except for a fur coat – is exciting both for the wearer and the viewer. A stimulating session on the fur rug in front of the fire can be a fantasy come true. And fur lightly brushed over the surface of the skin can be extremely sensuous. You could try using a fur glove to stroke your partner.

Feathers can be used to stimulate the nipples, the palms of the hands, the soles of the feet and the surface of the skin generally, rather than the genitals directly.

Softer feathers have their uses too, especially if they are attached to the nozzle of a hairdryer. The stream of warm air, when the dryer is switched on, makes the feather flap to and fro.

SPIDER MASSAGE

Anticipation is one of the most powerful sexual stimulants. The idea that you are going to become excited or sexually aroused is exciting in itself.

What the French call *pattes d'araignée* – literally spider's feet – takes advantage of this fact. It is a light, almost tickling, massage using only the lightest touch of the tips of the fingers. With their eyes closed, the recipient has to concentrate to appreciate that they are being touched at all.

The aim is not actually to touch the skin at all, but only to touch the hairs above it. This gives the feeling of spider's feet.

ICE

Sex is usually concerned with warm things, but the thrilling cold of ice has a special place in foreplay, for it can have a stimulating shock effect.

Be careful not to use ice directly from a deep freeze. Supercooled ice sticks to any moist surface and can burn like a red-hot iron.

But normal ice, which is on the point of melting, leaves deliciously cool damp trails across the skin. Test the ice on your tongue before you begin.

Ice will certainly stimulate the nipples – a single touch will have them erect in seconds – and many find the touch of a cold cube on the genitals a turn-on too. For some women, having a cube of ice put into their vagina first, before having regular intercourse, can be a real turn-on for them.

WET SKIN

Blowing on wet skin automatically produces goose pimples. And the resulting tightening of the skin can often be highly arousing.

The best way to moisten the skin is with the tongue. And blowing on wet skin is often the natural aftermath of a tongue bath – where one partner licks the other over every inch of their body. But if you do not have that much saliva, baby lotion will do just as well.

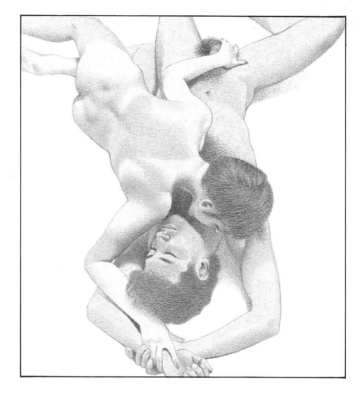

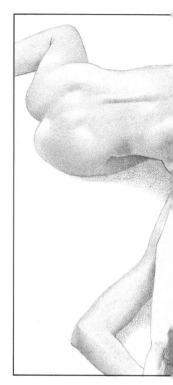

For him, slow masturbation can be a unique and mind-blowing experience, whether the man is restrained or not. It allows the woman to use her hands and mouth and her whole body in a tantalizing way to bring her partner to a truly memorable orgasm

A WORD OF CAUTION

But be very careful blowing around the ears. When stimulating the earlobes, breathe in instead of out, otherwise you will deafen your partner. And never blow or force air into the vagina of any other body orifice either. It can be extremely dangerous.

SLOW MASTURBATION

Slow masturbation is one of the specialized lovemaking techniques that benefits from one partner being totally passive.

Often it can be so exquisitely teasing that some couples enjoy it more if the passive partner is restrained slightly.

The idea is for the active partner to play the passive one like a musical instrument. They touch them, caress them, excite them, push them to the limit, then draw back – teasing them until they beg for more. The active partner raises the pitch until it is almost unbearable, then stops just short of gratification – until the time is right to continue.

FOR HIM

The woman can start by doing a slow striptease – but only down to her panties. Next, she treats him to the scents of her body by rubbing the perfumes of her armpits across his face. She can do the same with her breasts, limbs and torso.

She can even kneel on his shoulders and press her vulva against his face, with her panties still on.

After that, she can strip off completely.

Next, she can tease him with her body, offer it to him, then withdraw the offer when he gets within biting distance. Once he is sufficiently aroused, she should start caressing his body, lightly. She can blow on him, touch him lightly with her fingertips or nipples or brush him with her hair. Always she should move toward his genitals – but never actually touching.

When she finally arrives at his genitals, she should approach with caution – he will probably be dangerously close to ejaculation.

TO THE BRINK OF ORGASM

She can give him a direct genital kiss, but only for a few seconds. She can then stop and alternate between using her hands and her mouth, to gently brush along his penis.

With practice, she should be able to bring him to the brink of orgasm, then deny it. And every time his attention flags, she can turn her full attention back on him. But not for a moment should he be able to forget the feel of her.

There are two points that she should concentrate on – his mouth and his genitals. She should keep both of them constantly busy, but without triggering ejaculation. The methods of stimulation open to her are almost limitless.

Even trailing her hair across his body can be a turn-on. She can use her tongue, lips, hands, breath, nipples and vulva to keep him at fever pitch.

All his most sensitive areas in between should also receive some attention, never letting the rhythm slacken. If, by chance, his erection should subside she should concentrate her attention on stiffening his penis again – by whatever means gives him the fastest turn-on – before continuing the slow tease.

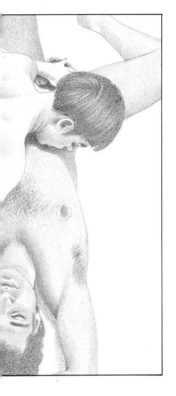

Next, the pace of the action needs to be increased. She can sit well up on his chest, if she is light enough not to restrict his breathing, with her buttocks against his chin and her feet hooked under his knees.

She can then take hold of the root of his penis with one hand. The other can be used to pull the foreskin back gently. With the thumb and finger, she can make quick, sharp strokes at around one per second, or slower. After about half a minute, she can give around a dozen or so fast strokes, then resume the former, slow rhythm.

These short strokes should be restricted if the man is dangerously close to ejaculation. The speed should slow down, the grip should slacken. But the woman should keep her man close to the brink of orgasm for as long as possible.

This may all sound terribly one-sided, but for a woman who usually takes the passive part in lovemaking, it can be a really exciting experience.

And the woman's hot vulva pressed against the chest-bone is an exhilarating sensation for both partners.

Most men cannot stand more than about ten minutes of this sort of treatment. If his penis goes limp the woman should arouse him – with hand or mouth – to ejaculation immediately.

AND VICE VERSA
This technique does not just work one way round. Both partners can enjoy the active and the passive role. When the man returns the treatment he has three points to concentrate on – the mouth, the breasts (especially the nipples), and the clitoris. Of course, if the man is heavier than the woman – as is usually the case – he should avoid sitting on her chest.

The woman's mouth and breasts should receive his attention first. Then, when stimulating the tip of her clitoris, he can pay close attention to her reactions.

MAKING THE MOST OF THE MOUTH
There are few men who do not enjoy fellatio – having their penis kissed and sucked. But there are plenty of advanced ways that this can be done.

Some men like the contrast between hot and cold that can be given by being sucked by a woman with ice cubes in her mouth. Others find ice cubes too hard and prefer the woman's mouth filled with cold yoghurt or some other creamy substance. For the woman putting soft fruit or wine into her mouth before she fellates her man can be a memorable experience as well.

Cunnilingus – or licking the vulva – can also benefit from the use of wine and foodstuffs.

Subtly flavoured fruits such as bananas, strawberries and figs are suitable. Slithering segments can be slid up just inside the vagina, then licked or sucked out again. Natural yoghurts – especially when chilled – can be used to bathe the whole area. When licked off and sucked from the nooks and crannies, they have their own special effect. And the flavours used to top ice creams can lend the vagina a playful, almost childish taste.

There is no need to be restricted, however. Almost anything you enjoy eating and drinking can be used.

LOVE GAMES

*Playing games can be fun – especially when
the aim of the game is to enjoy making love*

Almost all couples play some sort of love games, if only from time to time. These can be as different as simply having a private language so that they can communicate sexy things in public, to organized, formal sex games that involve dressing up or acting out various roles.

WHY PLAY SEX GAMES?

Many couples play sex games simply for the fun of them. It is a form of recreation – like playing tennis – and for the creative couple sex games add to the fun in their lives just as other hobbies and pastimes do.

Sex games can also be used as 'presents' to one another when they feel particularly loving, sad, depressed or just grateful. Playing a game that you know your lover enjoys can be a wonderful way of saying 'I love you'.

For the vast majority of people, however, sex games are used as enhancers to personalize sex and to increase their sexual repertoire.

After a few months together, most sexual relationships settle down to become fairly predictable and certainly, after a few years of marriage, many couples are keen to extend their range of activities together.

The next most common reason for playing sex games is to be able to fulfil, at least in part, a particular fantasy or dream that you have had. Within a longstanding and safe relationship one or other partner can declare his or her wishes and needs and know that they will be indulged and not ridiculed or put down. Most of us have at least some wishes and desires that are not being met at any one time and sex games can be a good way of defusing the tensions this can create.

ENLARGING HORIZONS

Games can also bring a couple together by enlarging their horizons – both for themselves and for one another. A man who previously thought his wife to be shy or prudish can totally change his mind about her once she declares her wishes to indulge in a particular game.

This is, of course, a major advantage to the whole

relationship. It helps protect it against attacks from outside – especially from members of the opposite sex.

If a couple's needs are all being met at home there is no need to look outside the relationship. This defuses many of the petty jealousies that so easily creep into even the best relationships. Most things that make sex more enjoyable for one or both partners should be acceptable in a loving relationship and gone along with wholeheartedly.

AGREEING THE RULES
Difficulty may arise when the wishes of one partner cause anxiety in the other. This can be a real

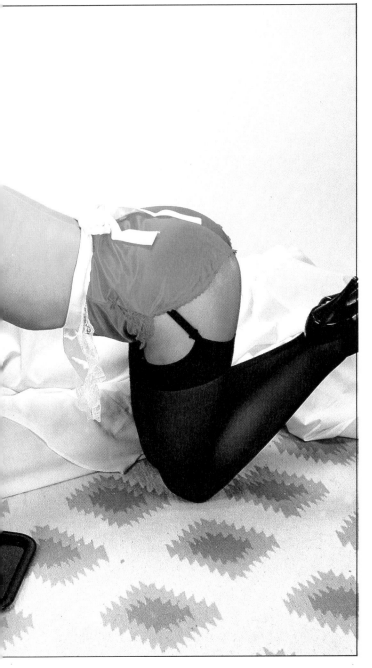

problem but need not be disastrous. Talking it over helps because it could be that the one making the objections has totally or partly misperceived what the needs of the other partner are.

Many people, for example, imagine that if they start experimenting with sex games it will escalate to a level at which they will not enjoy it or might be unable to cope. In reality the partner may well have not been thinking along such lines at all – the problem is largely an imagined one.

TAKING THE LEAD
While it is true that the most uninhibited of women, and younger women generally, are likely to be innovative, in most cases men take the lead in sex games. This happens partly because, as the operators in sexual matters, most men are expected by the woman to 'make things happen'.

This can, of course, lead to a situation in which the man stands to be rejected or put down as 'dirty' or 'perverted' for even thinking of playing games – and this can be a real problem in many relationships. Such men then indulge their wishes in fantasy during masturbation or intercourse or they may even seek fulfilment outside the partnership.

This kind of crisis need not occur. The answer is to find a way of indulging the needs in another, more acceptable, way. It is especially important to do this rather than make a big thing of it, because the very nature of sex enhancers such as sex games is that they change so rapidly.

A true perversion does not change – it is a fixed need each time a couple has sex. Unfortunately, in many relationships, what starts off as a fairly trivial request for a sex-enhancing game of some kinds gets blown up into a major battle because the unwilling partner thinks he or she will be stuck with having to play it for ever.

Most enhancers and sex games are transitory but in some couples, and especially with certain men, they are often replaced with another. This can lead to one partner becoming disenchanted with the endless variations and to long for 'normal' sex.

A lot of sex books and girlie magazines give the impression that if you are just having straight sex all the time you must be odd or plain boring, but this need not be the case at all. It all depends on the sexual personality of the individuals involved, and many couples stick to a very small repertoire of lovemaking techniques and positions which they have found please them both.

An obsession with endless sex enhancers is not, as might be expected, a sign of sexual 'togetherness' or of an uninhibited person, but rather the opposite. Very often such an individual is so intimidated by normal sex that to enjoy it he or she has to have

Dressing up to turn on your partner can be fun for both of you, and a sexy outfit need not be expensive if you use your imagination

'extras'. This kind of person needs professional help. Most of us, however, do not fall into this category – we simply enjoy a change from time to time.

COMMUNICATING SEXUAL NEEDS

A common complaint women have of men is that they are boring in bed. This can be a cruel irony because often the very same man has a rich fantasy life and would be willing to be much more adventurous if his woman made her needs known. Unfortunately, the woman who complains may be too shy to tell her man what she would most like.

A good game to overcome this is for each to take turns to write a short story outline for an X-rated film to give to the other to read. Such a scenario can give valuable clues as to what the other wants but cannot directly ask for. Also, a sensitive couple will discover what turns the other on when they are seeing films, videos or reading books or magazines.

GAMES PEOPLE PLAY

Many couples add to their pleasure of sex, and to their anticipation of what is to come, by playing sex games. There are endless possibilities and it is up to each couple to write their own rules. The only limitations are a joint desire to play them and imagination.

Research has shown that there are some games that are more popular than others, although the variations are enormous and can, if required, be adapted to every couple's desires.

TALK GAMES

Many couples, especially those who have been together for a long time or who are particularly in tune with one another, have a private language that refers to their sex life together. This usually includes terms of endearment for their sex organs or parts of them and, of course, pet names for themselves as individuals.

Many couples have a private way of saying that they want each other sexually and it can be exciting to have such a conversation in a public place such as a restaurant, on a bus or at a party.

SECRECY GAMES

These are an extension of the 'talk' game. Having a secret between you that no one else understands can be a great turn-on. A common form of the game is that in which the woman is naked under her dress when going to a party or public place. The best way to play this is for her to tell her man just as they are going into the place so that he has no time or opportunity to do anything about it. The tease of this can be almost unbearable for both – and the woman can later, apparently accidentally, open her legs when sitting opposite him so that he gets a tantalizing glimpse of her thighs and vulva, yet no one else knows what is happening.

Playing cards for sexual favours is certainly more fun than playing for financial stakes. Alternatively don a sexy outfit and dominate your partner with style – taking the lead can be fun once in a while

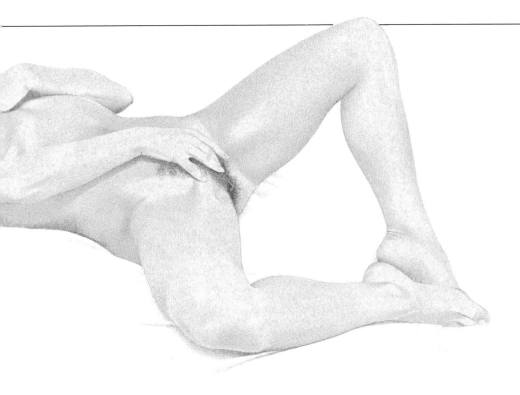

*Watching your partner masturbate to orgasm can be as exciting as making love, especially if that is the forfeit in a board game while (**below**) wearing something as simple as a white coat can turn your lovemaking into an exciting game of 'doctors and nurses' or 'sex therapist and patient'*

DANGER-OF-DISCOVERY SEX

Making love in public or semi-public places heightens excitement for some people from fear of discovery. Although making love in public is illegal, popular venues include deserted railway carriages between stations, in backs of cars and in the open air on beaches or fields in the country.

But this lovemaking need not go all the way to intercourse – masturbation is an alternative – or, like most sex games, it can be a prelude to intercourse back home.

BABY GAMES

Most of us play baby games far more than we realize. Even by cuddling up together and being vulnerable we are behaving rather like babies. Most people who really lose themselves in intercourse revert to babylike noises – and find this perfectly natural and enjoyable.

The baby games that some couples enjoy include making love on rubber sheets, the man breastfeeding (or pretending to if the woman is not lactating), the man being her baby as she mothers him, and bathing each other like babies.

CARD AND BOARD GAMES

'Adult' games are available from almost every sex shop, but it is cheaper and more fun to adapt any card or board game and use sexual favours as prizes – strip poker is an obvious example.

Use your imagination – the simplicity of snap or the intellectual battle of chess or backgammon can be turned into sexual delight. Snooker holds interesting possibilities and shooting aliens out of the sky with the home computer could become less monotonous if the loser pays a sexual penalty. This kind of game heightens excitement and bodes well for what is to come later.

If you park in a secluded spot, making love in the car can be a big turn-on, even if it is a trifle uncomfortable

A very enjoyable game involves giving one another love tokens. On these pieces of paper you write what you would most like to do, or have your partner do to you. Examples could be a weekend away in an hotel together, breakfast in bed, climaxing in the back row of the cinema, sex in the car and so on.

You arrange to play the game, by redeeming the tokens, on a particular day, weekend or any time that suits you both and build up your excitement by giving each other tokens in advance. Or you can put several in a container and ask your partner to choose.

A tantalizing variation is to send the tokens to your partner's place of work addressed to him or her privately.

DRESSING UP GAMES

Putting on sexy underwear itself is perhaps the commonest form of 'dressing up'. Many couples greatly enjoy sex if the woman is dressed in sexy undies, especially if they answer the man's (or the woman's) needs to fulfil a fantasy. Men who have fantasies of sexy, whore-like women will enjoy black stockings and black suspenders, while those who enjoy 'deflowering virgins' will go for a crispy white lace. Sexy underwear does not have to be tarty – it can be expensive and classy.

Doctors 'tell' people to undress and display the private parts of the body. Intimate 'examinations' of the genitals, including long, internal examinations are common forms of the game.

Nurse games are also fairly common. In this the woman is the nurse and tells the man what to do or carries out 'nursing procedures' on him.

SADO-MASOCHISTIC GAMES

Many couples play S and M games, even if it is in a rather tame way. These games, however, should always be played with caution.

Perhaps the commonest part of the game is smacking the woman's bottom before having sex. This 'punishes' the women in advance for their being so naughty as to want sex at all. Other couples 'fight' or wrestle one another before sex so that the woman ends up being overpowered by the man and 'forced' to open her legs.

In the 'slave' game the woman uses the man to do whatever she orders and once he has carried out a task she then rewards him with sex.

In the 'master' game the roles are reversed and the woman is the slave.

FETISHISM

*What kind of person is sexually turned on by
a pair of shoes, a woman's glove or even
rubber underwear? These fetishes are
surprisingly common and belong
predominantly to the world of men*

Most people have heard of a foot-fetish, and more and more there is talk of people who are 'into leather' or 'into kinky sex'. Sex boutiques throughout the world display clothing and other items that are supposed to be sexual turn-ons. All these, and many more, are what we think of as fetishes.

The term 'fetish' was originally used for religious or magic objects found in certain African and other non-western cultures. The meaning was apparently extended in 1888 by Dr Alfred Binet to refer to objects which could arouse intense sexual interest.

Various sexologists use the term with slightly different gradations of meaning, but traditionally it has included articles of clothing, certain parts of the body and sometimes even noises or odours. For example, some theorists explain the appeal of a singer's voice as a kind of sex fetish.

UNUSUAL PREOCCUPATIONS

The term fetish is applied when members of a society consider a particular sexual interest as unusual. No-one in Europe or the United States would regard a man who was sexually turned on by a woman's breasts as having a fetish. But in many societies in the world, breasts are not considered as erotic at all – only infants who gain nourishment from them are thought to have any special interest in them. In such societies, a grown man who was 'into breasts' would probably be considered unusual and expressions like fetishism would be completely appropriate to describe his interest.

More recently, a distinction has been made between a sexual interest in inanimate objects as opposed to body parts. Interest in the first is still referred to as fetishism, but interest in the second is often labelled as 'partialism'.

COMMON FETISHES

Practically any item could become a sexual fetish, although some, like long black opera gloves, are quite familiar examples and others, like women's hats, are among the rare examples.

A classic literary fetish is a fur coat, made famous by the German writer Leopold von Sacher-Masoch (from whose name comes the word 'masochism') in his book *Venus in Furs*. Here he writes about his fantasy of being dominated and whipped by a woman completely naked except for a fur coat. Interestingly enough, very few other people are reported as having similar fantasies.

Perhaps the most famous fetish material in modern times involves leather clothing, usually

A classic literary fetish is for fur and involves the fantasy of domination by a naked woman wearing a fur coat. But research has shown that fur fetishists are not 'into' masochism, but the feel of fur itself

black. At present this is often most associated with a subgroup of male homosexuals who tend to congregate in so-called 'leather bars'.

All the clothing such a fetishist might wear could well be made of black leather, right down to his underwear. The clothes tend to be custom-made and quite expensive. The general style approaches a motor-cycle uniform. Quite possibly this fashion was started by Marlon Brando in the 1953 film *The Wild Ones*. In it Brando wore a black leather jacket and played the part of a rebel. The film had an enormous cult following.

RUBBER

According to the British sociologist Maurice North, who examined fetishes in his book *The Other Fringe of Sex*, the most common material that constitutes a fetishistic interest is rubber. But this is difficult to gauge since rubber clothing generally has to be bought through firms that cater specifically for fetishists, whereas other types of clothing can be

picked up in ordinary shops.

The range of rubber items available is quite considerable, reflecting the fantasies of the consumers. One British firm offers, among other things, a nun's habit in black and white rubber.

SADO-MASOCHISM

Rubber fetishists in the English-speaking world tend to prefer black, but this is not necessarily true of fetishists from other countries. In West Germany, for example, the most popular items are rubberized versions of skirts and underwear in pastel shades.

Rubber and leather fetishisms are frequently accompanied by an interest in sado-masochism in various forms. Many rubber fetishists are devotees of what is called 'water sports' (or technically, urolagnia). That is, they are turned on by urine – either seeing someone urinate or urinating on someone or being urinated on.

For the most part, heterosexual fetishists would seem to have more difficulties finding partners and making contact with like-minded people than homosexual fetishists. Heterosexual fetishists might have to settle for fantasies and masturbation, although some do resort to working out their fantasies with other males in spite of the fact that they are not genuinely homosexual.

SATIN AND VELVET

The soft, frilly media fetishists have very different preoccupations. They are generally into lingerie or clothing made of velvet or fur and are rarely interested in sado-masochism despite von Sacher-Masoch's fantasy. Women's underpants are a common fetishistic object but surprisingly enough, bras seldom are.

Men who are into underpants fetishistically frequently want them to be soiled or stained with menstrual blood.

BOOTS AND HIGH-HEELED SHOES

One of the most famous fetishes is the shoe. The classic woman's shoe with stiletto heel is one such example. Whenever stilettos are in fashion, male shoe fetishists are known to walk around all day with an erection.

Boots are another classic fetishistic item both for heterosexuals and homosexuals. Very frequently shoe fetishists are also sado-masochists. Prostitutes who cater to sado-masochists often wear boots to indicate their willingness in this field.

A QUESTION OF FASHION

The same is true of stockings, although black mesh hose has traditionally been a fetishistic item. Corsets, garters and gloves used to be staples in the fetishist's wardrobe, but because of changes in fashion, these items are losing their historic place of importance.

Some glove or garter fetishists can still be found,

though. One case has been reported of a man who would steal women's gloves which he would slip over his penis and then masturbate.

Handkerchief fetishes seem to be common and are often associated with theft.

Fetishes can be quite idiosyncratic and any perusal of sex magazine 'want ads' will probably turn up interests that have not been mentioned here. And then there are still other fetishes which will not even appear in such advertisements; for example, pillows.

PARTS OF THE BODY

The classic partialisms usually involve breasts, feet and buttocks. In some African and Pacific island societies the labia minora have become a matter of intense sexual interest and they are stretched from childhood to be as long as possible.

Among the Tswana of southern Africa, an interest in elongated labia is so important in heterosexual relations that a woman might be abandoned by her husband if they are not long enough – after all, if they are too short what would he have to play with?

Hair festishists are sometimes reported. They may become a public nuisance because they are known to cut a lock off an unwitting person's head. There are even men who are tooth fetishists.

TINY FEET

The most famous of nationwide partialisms must be the former Chinese passion for bound feet. In traditional Chinese erotic paintings and drawings, women are usually shown naked except that they wear socks over tiny deformed feet.

The earliest reference to the practice of foot binding dates back to the 12th century, where it is said that an emperor two centuries before had his dancing girls bind their feet. From the court, the custom spread to the nobility and through the centuries even further down the social ladder until it became a general fashion for girls from respectable families that could afford to do so.

The most desirable feet were called 'Golden Lotus'. These were the smallest, no more than

7.5 cm (3 in) long. The 'Silver Lotus' was about 10 cm (4 in). Feet longer than this tended to be considered ridiculous and ugly, and comments about large feet ('goose foot', 'demon with large feet', and so on) were the ultimate insult for a girl.

DRESSING UP

Transvestism is an interest in dressing in clothing defined as appropriate only for members of the opposite sex. Some 'cisvestites' want to be dressed like little children, even as infants with nappies. More commonly, inappropriate adult styles are worn, including such things as Nazi uniforms, cowboy outfits and in the male homosexual world of northern Europe and America, motorcylist garb.

The Chinese obsession with tiny feet lasted from the 10th century until the early 1900s. By the time girls were adults, they were virtually crippled and their feet looked more like pigs' trotters than anything human. Fortunately, the cultural fetish which inspired the binding of feet has finally died

EROTICA

Can reading sexy books in bed with your partner or watching – or making – a 'blue' video together enhance your sex life? Many couples may find erotica can help them learn more about each other's sexual preferences

Until recently, the popular image of the pornography consumer was a seedy man in a grubby raincoat who spent frenzied hours masturbating over a vast collection of salacious material. 'Dirty' postcards changed hands in foreign ports. Naturist magazines were sent through the post in brown paper wrappers. What were considered obscene works of literature were sold under the counter. And many classic works of medieval and oriental art were kept under lock and key in the great libraries of the world.

The 1960s changed all that. Sexually explicit 'girlie' magazines are now openly on display on the shelves of reputable newsagents. Long-banned books appear in paperback. Pornographic films and videos are freely available. There are sex shops in every major city. And even the newspapers – who often see themselves as guardians of the public morals – publish pictures of scantily clad, 'page-three' girls every day.

EROTICA OR PORNOGRAPHY?

But what exactly is pornography? The word means 'the writings of prostitutes'. But it is commonly used to describe films and books which depict 'lewd' acts with the sole intention of exciting the viewer or reader.

The word erotica, though, is derived from the name of the Greek god of love, Eros. It has come to describe any material – educational or artistic – that deals in any way with the act of love.

But one person's act of love is another person's lewd act. What some people find mildly titillating, others find deeply offensive. And where some find healthy stimulation, others find depravity.

The truth is there is no fixed line that divides pornography from erotica. The pornography of ancient Greece or medieval China – or even the Victorian era – may go on display at your local museum or art gallery as erotica because of its 'redeeming cultural value'. Books and magazines whose main function is to educate you about your own body and its sexual potential may, at the same time, make you more aware of your sexuality. And works of art – paintings, literature, sculpture, plays or films – may well show people and situations that arouse you.

Many people hate to admit that a visit to an art gallery or an 'intellectual' film can leave them feeling in the mood for lovemaking, but this is a common reaction. In some societies, such as Japan in the 17th, 18th and 19th centuries, no distinction was made between the artistic appreciation of a picture of a beautiful woman, say, and a sexual reaction. Both were equally complimentary.

MODERN PORNOGRAPHY

Today pornography is found in almost every media. Sexual feelings can be aroused at various levels and are often played on by advertisers who aim to link sexual stimulation with their product.

The commonest medium for pornography is daily newspapers. Most people see them at some time or other. Because of their wide circulation, the newspapers have to keep within firmly defined limits. Breasts and buttocks can be bared, but pubic hair is never shown. And when male pin-ups appear, only their chests and legs are exposed.

On the assumption that they are only seen by people who go out of their way to pay for them, magazines, books and films are less inhibited. Most can be divided into two categories – soft- and hard-core.

Soft-core pornography is available from newsagents, video and book shops and shows nude figures and often suggests various sexual acts, but it does not depict them explicitly.

Hard-core pornography, available only through specialist outlets, leaves nothing to the imagination. It also covers the more extreme areas of sexual practice such as flagellation, rape, bondage and sado-masochism.

WORDS AND PICTURES

It is often said that men fall in love with their eyes while women fall in love with their ears. According to researchers, this difference between the sexes extends into their attitudes to pornography too.

Men are turned on by sexually explicit pictures, while women prefer the power of the written word. The huge sales of romantic novels, therefore, can easily be seen as the female equivalent of the market for men's girlie magazines.

USING EROTICA

If you would like to bring pornographic literature into your life, where should you start? And what ground rules will you need?

The greatest fear any person has is of rejection and disapproval. And we all feel extremely vulnerable when it comes to our sexual prowess and tastes. Our natural impulse is to protect ourselves – and often the means of defence is attack. So it is important that both of you promise to respect each other. If confidences are to be given both of you must be equally frank. And you must agree that neither of you shares your secrets with anyone else, or uses them outside the bedroom in an argument.

You may like to start gently. If your daily newspaper has nude photographs, look at them and discuss your reactions. Does your partner find them stimulating? Which models does he like and why? How does she compare? If not, does it matter? Would she like to see an equivalent male pin-up? If so,

If you have a video camera you can make your own 'blue' movie. One person will have to act as cameraman and director as well. Think up a story line to give your picture – perhaps one of your shared sexual fantasies

what type of body would she like to see? What parts of the body does she look at?

You might like to set aside a particular time – an evening, morning or afternoon – when you know you will be left alone to pursue this. Each week, take it in turns to produce a fresh item to look at. From newspaper photographs, you can work your way up the ladder of explicitness. En route, you should gradually discover what it is that excites both of you.

USING MAGAZINES

Magazines for women sold in newsagents usually show men in relaxed positions. They are not allowed to show an erect penis and, consequently avoid simulating sexual positions.

But men's magazines always tend to show women in much more provocative and inviting positions that suggest availability and experience.

It can be dangerous to start out using such explicit material straight away though. For example, if a woman is deeply shy and finds sex and nudity deeply embarrassing she may well be even more intimidated if her partner ogles girlie magazines – especially if she feels that the bodies in the photographs are better than hers.

Men may well react badly to their partner taking an interest in pictures of other naked men, especially if he feels that his penis is small by comparison. But again, if the matter is brought out into the open he may gain confidence and discover that he is not as underdeveloped as he believes himself to be.

USING BOOKS

Books and magazines are often used to stimulate sexual fantasies during masturbation. But they can also play an important role in a loving relationship. Read separately they can be used to stimulate sexual fantasies during intercourse. They can also be used to extend the imagination into erotic areas and reinforce your identity as a sexual human being.

Reading sexual passages from books aloud to each other can be a powerful turn on. When shared like this, pornography can be used to broaden your mutual sexual horizons and help each of you discover what you really want. Some couples find it difficult to say outright what they want their partners to do. Material describing oral sex or alternative positions can be used as a cue. It is much easier to just say: 'Why don't we do that?'

LOVING ON VIDEO

The increase in ownership of home video machines has led to a revolution in the use of pornography. Few couples want to see sexy films in seedy – often male-only – cinemas. But now that explicit videos are hired out by most high street video stores, couples are able to enhance their love lives with pornography in the privacy of their own home.

The advantages of watching sexy videos at home are obvious. The couple using them can even watch in bed. But conditions at home are not always

The invention of the Polaroid meant that pictures no longer had to be sent out to chemists and processing houses. You must give each other strict assurances that your uninhibited shots will not be shown to the boys down the pub or the girls in the office

perfect for viewing explicit material and some attention needs to be paid to the surroundings before the 'play' button is pressed.

When you are watching a pornographic video you will not want to be interrupted. If you have a TV in your bedroom, so much the better. But if you only have one in the living room – and cannot move it – make sure you are not disturbed.

Close the curtains and turn the lights down low. Do not switch them off at first. Initially you might find the explicit acts portrayed unpleasant and offensive, and you will feel frightened and trapped in the dark.

Most video shops have a discount rate if you hire several tapes. And it is best to have a selection.

Again you can work your way up the ladder of explicitness, perhaps including in your selection a sexy film that has been on general release – like *10, Emmanuel* or *Last Tango in Paris*.

As you begin to watch more and more explicit videos, discuss what you like with your partner. This will not only improve your understanding of each other's sexuality, it will also help you know what to choose next time you go to the video hire shop. When a video excites you both, play it over again – or the specific parts you find exciting – and try pretending you are the actors.

There should be a word of warning here. Some modern pornographic videos contain a high level of violence – often with scenes of rape and sadism which can be frightening and most unloving. These can do more to turn you off than turn you on.

LOVING AND LAUGHING
Most people who visit a sex shop do go there for a bit of a laugh. They drop in to buy a nude toy for their boss, a Willie Warmer for their husband or a sexy novelty for their wife's wedding anniversary. But there is a lot more to a sex shop than that.

Most also carry a range of pornographic magazines and videos, sex aids and exotic underwear. All these are packaged and presented in a way that is not in any way seedy. In fact the inside of sex shop is much like any other shop on the high street.

The novelties are usually in bins or on shelves near the door. They include male and female toothbrushes, phallic soaps, breast-shaped mugs, sexy playing cards, suggestive greeting cards, explicit posters, sexy games, rude toys and risqué ornaments.

shaped. Some have forefinger and thumb attachments and anal stimulators.

If you use a standard vibrator in the vagina there is no danger that you might lose it. The neck of the womb is too narrow to let anything as broad as a vibrator pass. But if you use a standard vibrator or a special rectal vibrator to stimulate the anus, be careful. The digestive tract is very long and it is possible to lose things up the rectum.

OTHER SEXUAL AIDS

A range of exotic sheaths is usually on offer. Some give a three centimetre extension to the penis. Others have rubber lumps and bumps and feelers. As these only stimulate the inside of the vagina, they are unlikely to add any particular pleasure to the woman. Padded, ready-erect sheaths are also available for men who have trouble maintaining an erection. Most of these devices are re-usable but they do not give full contraceptive protection.

Ultra-thin contraceptive sheaths are available though, along with a whole range of condoms in various textures and colours.

As the clitoris is the centre of most women's erotic sensations, a clitoral stimulator worn on a ring around the man's penis can add a great deal to the woman's enjoyment. The stimulator itself is a small pad of rubber fingers which brush against the clitoris during intercourse. Other versions set angled fingers, along a broad band around the penis. But some women find them distracting and even uncomfortable.

The ring that the clitoral stimulator is fixed to often performs a double function. It helps maintain the man's erection and if the ring is tight, it prevents the blood flowing back out of the engorged penis.

Tight penis rings are also available without clitoral stimulators and come in other configurations. As well as the plain ring, there is one ring which has a slim rubber loop that draws tightly around the base of the penis, an 'energizing' ring generates a small stimulating electric current, and yet another encircles the root of the penis and the base of the scrotum with two linked loops.

'Penisators' also fit around the base of the penis,

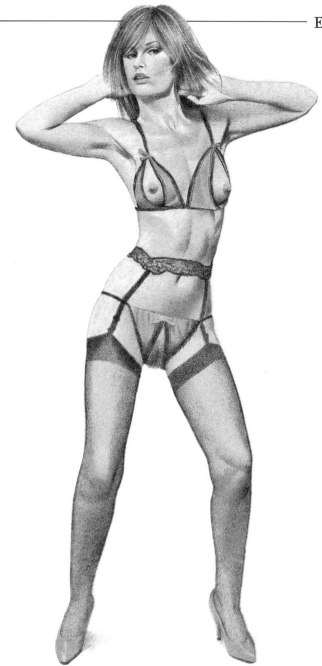

Crutchless knickers and peep-hole bras are only two items out of a whole range of underwear that can be purchased from the many sex shops now selling their wares behind blacked-out windows. Items such as these not only look sexy, they also make lovemaking easier as they are not a barrier to penetration or nipple stimulation

VIBRATORS

Deeper into the shop you will find a range of vibrators in all shapes and sizes. These are usually battery powered and their action varies from a fast tingling buzz to snake-like gyrations and deep thrusting motions. They come in a range of widths and lengths, with smooth and textured surfaces, hard and soft, rigid and bendy, straight and egg-

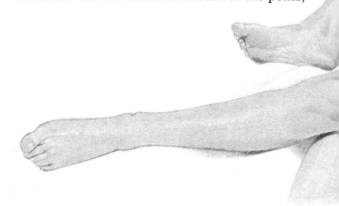

but they are electrically powered and produce a variable-speed vibration. The motor unit sometimes doubles as a clitoral stimulator.

Thai beads are inserted up the rectum on a string. When climax is reached, the string is pulled, stimulating the anus.

Geisha or duo balls, sometimes known as Chinese bells, are marble-sized pairs of balls that fit into the vagina. One is empty, the other contains mercury. Any pelvic movement, including walking, produces a stimulating sensation for the woman.

PILLS AND POTIONS
Sex shops tend to sell a lot of tablets. Some claim to increase a man's virility or turn a woman on. There are also creams which claim to increase the size of a man's penis. But they are usually overpriced and ineffective – and in some cases may even be irritating and dangerous. They are best avoided.

Some sprays and creams that claim to 'increase a man's staying power' do work to some extent. They tend to be a mild anaesthetic and prevent the man from becoming over-stimulated.

They must be applied with some care though. If they have not been fully absorbed by the skin of the penis, some of the anaesthetic will rub off on the woman's genitals, deadening her sensations as well.

Most sex shops also supply ranges of flavoured lubricants which aid intercourse and oral sex. Other 'boob drops' flavour the nipples.

EXOTIC LINGERIE
Most regular department stores carry ranges of frilly panties, scanty bras and suspender belts.

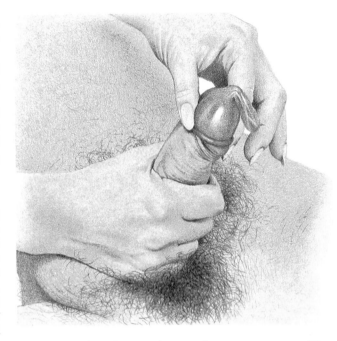

Coloured sheaths are fun, and your partner will gain extra pleasure if you slip it on for him

Selecting these as a couple can be a stimulating experience in itself. But in the sex shop you will find a much wider range of titillating underclothes – miniscule G-strings, panties with no crotch, bras that support the breasts from underneath without covering them, nipple pads and tassles, see-through nighties, French maids' outfits and nurses' uniforms.

It is usually only in the deeper recesses of the shop that you will find the more exotic gear – the leather and rubber wear, chains, double-ended dildos and inflatable dolls – it is entertaining to have a look.

Caressing your partner's genitals with a vibrator, while caressing her breasts with your lips, will spread a feeling of pleasure over her entire body

QUICKIES

Right: *Requiring no props, this is a position for the more adventurous couple as the man takes the full weight of his partner. Speed is the name of the game for all but the most athletic of men*

For much of their sex-lives together, lovers concentrate on how best to please each other. Yet periodically, a raw sense of urgency takes over and a couple want sex quickly

Many couples think of intercourse only as something that has to be worked up to gradually, and although this is enjoyable and an essential part of an intimate relationship, so too are those unplanned moments when you just feel like having sex with no preparation at all.

Some couples see sex as a ritual. They make love in a predictable way, even on a predictable night of the week. This can be fine for many couples, but others often complain of boredom or look elsewhere for sex in fact or fantasy. Yet why bother, when reality at home can be so much better?

The joys of quickie sex are often overlooked, even by quite experienced lovers. We have all tended to become obsessed with technique and we often forget the joy there is to be had in spontaneity.

There are many advantages to quickie sex:
■ It shows how much you fancy one another on a purely physical basis. Romancing and subtle foreplay are all very well, but there are times when one or both partners need to be shown that they are wanted urgently. Some women say that quickie sex is the best of all for them. As it is unplanned they have no part to play in making it happen – they are simply taken and overwhelmed by their man's ardour. In fact, some women only have orgasms during intercourse if it is a quickie.
■ Similarly, some men, if too much attention is focused on their penis, fail to perform well, or may even be impotent. The sight of their partner wanting sex urgently and uninhibitedly can be a real turn-on for such men, especially if the man believes (as

many unconsciously do), that women only have sex to please them, or as a sort of duty.
■ Quickie sex is often linked with taking chances of being found out. This can be highly exciting, as a degree of 'naughtiness' is essential for some people to enjoy sex at its best. Quickies in semi-public places build up this delicious feeling of naughtiness.
■ The kind of positions used during quickies are often very different from those a couple normally use in their bedroom. Unfamiliar movements and body positions produce new sensations – often unre-

For the man lying back on the bed, there can be few positions for quickie sex that are more erotic than when his partner, semi-clothed, straddles him, offering an undisturbed view of her buttocks

A bed is not just for lying on. It can become a delightful prop for lovers in a hurry – perhaps just before going out. All that is required is a minimum of clothing and for the woman to lean forward and support herself

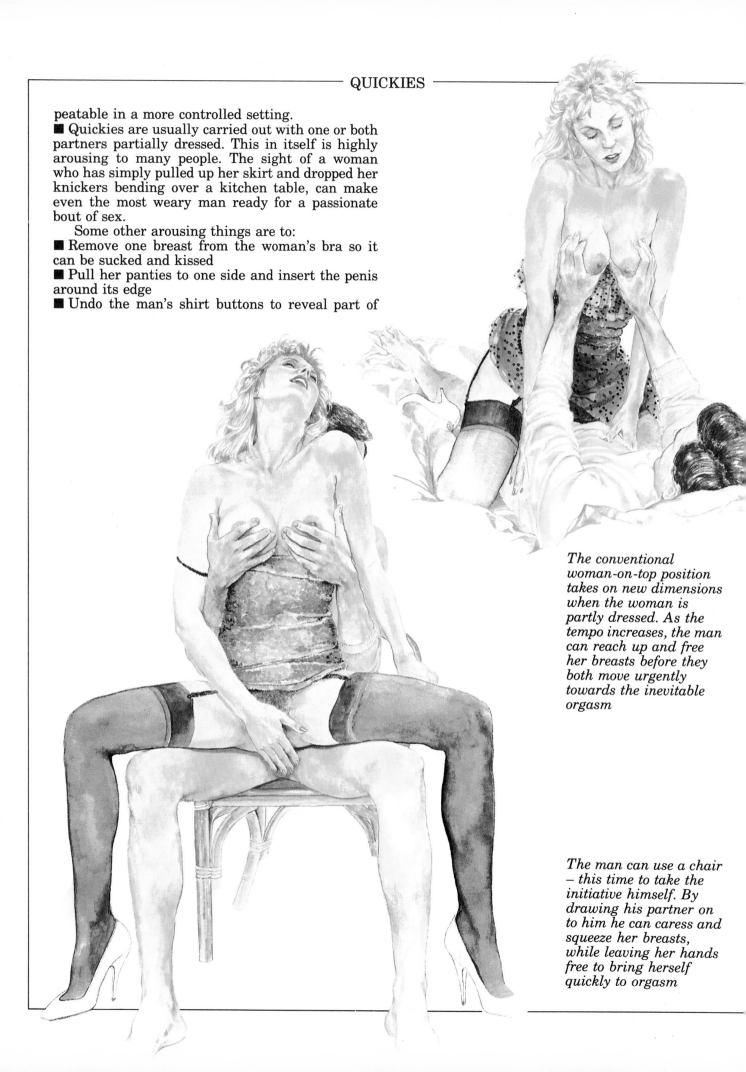

peatable in a more controlled setting.

■ Quickies are usually carried out with one or both partners partially dressed. This in itself is highly arousing to many people. The sight of a woman who has simply pulled up her skirt and dropped her knickers bending over a kitchen table, can make even the most weary man ready for a passionate bout of sex.

Some other arousing things are to:

■ Remove one breast from the woman's bra so it can be sucked and kissed

■ Pull her panties to one side and insert the penis around its edge

■ Undo the man's shirt buttons to reveal part of

The conventional woman-on-top position takes on new dimensions when the woman is partly dressed. As the tempo increases, the man can reach up and free her breasts before they both move urgently towards the inevitable orgasm

The man can use a chair – this time to take the initiative himself. By drawing his partner on to him he can caress and squeeze her breasts, while leaving her hands free to bring herself quickly to orgasm

his chest and just enough to insert one hand to caress him.

Quickies have other things going for them as well:

■ By not preparing for sex both partners are unwashed and therefore smell of their sweat and other body fluids. This earthiness greatly turns many people on, women especially who tend to make meticulous preparation ordinarily.

■ For many people, a quickie is an acting out of a sexual fantasy. Most people have fantasies of taking or being taken by a partner in various unconventional locations. Quickie sex can achieve this in practice. Given a choice and time to think it over, many people would not readily agree to sex in such a place or in that particular way – they would always find some kind of excuse. When it is 'forced' upon them they often greatly enjoy it, and may even then build the event into their fantasy lives to add to their enjoyment in future.

■ Some people are turned on by the touch or look of certain clothes. The silkiness of a dress, the sight of high heels or the feel of a man's jumper against bare skin can be an exciting bonus of being half dressed for quickie sex.

■ It is said that good sex depends on meticulous foreplay to arouse the woman so that her vagina is lubricated. But a woman's vagina can lubricate almost immediately when she is in the mood for quick sex. And some women are most turned on by quickie sex, because of the passionate feelings involved.

Sex between true lovers takes many forms and serves many purposes. One of them is that it reinforces their secret bond and by doing so builds up their unique relationship. If in this context, quickies can be especially delicious in the middle of an event at which others are present. Why not take your partner outside the room at a dinner party or other social gathering and make love. This is your private secret.

The time and place for quickies is only limited to your imagination. The inventive couple will always be able to find places and situations conducive to a bout of urgent lovemaking.

For sex without frills, almost any piece of household furniture comes into its own. When the woman wants to take the initiative, all her partner has to do is sit back in a chair

CHAPTER SIX

BECOMING AN EXPERT

ADVANCED LOVEMAKING

*For the loving couple who want to experiment
occasionally, there is always the opportunity
to try something new*

It is often assumed that all advanced sexual practices come from the East and the Indians and Chinese have a monopoly on the most adventurous and sophisticated sexual positions. But western cultures have some tricks of their own. In some of these, the male takes the more active role – in others, the female takes control.

Making love does not differ much between East and West. It is just that the East has all the good books. The Indian *Kama Sutra*, the Arabian *Perfumed Garden* and the Chinese and Japanese pillow books contain no real secrets – after all the human body and human sexual needs are much the same the world over. But these books have helped to systematize sexual behaviour and to allow people to try what others have tried before – and found successful – without just relying on their intuition.

THE FRENCH WAY

The French have put a lot of thought into lovemaking too. And they have come up with all sorts of interesting names for the more advanced sexual positions.

STANDING UP

The classic 'knee-trembler' can be an unpleasant strain unless the woman is a little taller than the man. Generally, woman are shorter than their partners. This can be equalized if she stands on something.

It is really safest to do it against a wall or some other solid object to give support. If you are having 'free-standing' sex, both of you should bend your knees and support each other by cupping your hands under each other's buttocks.

If her partner is strong enough, a woman can first curl one leg up around his buttocks, then lock both her legs around his waist, supporting the rest of her weight by locking her arms around his neck. After that, she can release her grip on his neck and fall back until she is completely upside down.

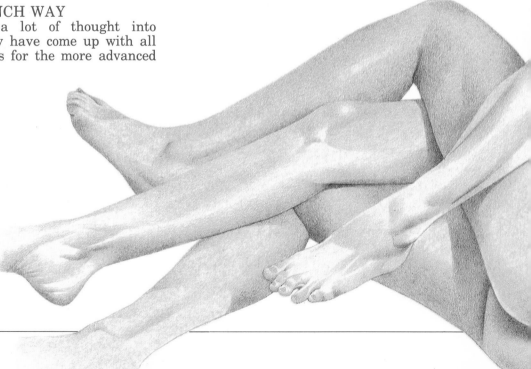

THE WHEELBARROW

If the standing sex starts the other way round, with the man entering the woman from the rear, you can end up in a wheelbarrow position. The woman simply bends forward far enough to rest her hands or elbows on the floor, then lifts her legs which he holds. But if you are not quite that athletic, it is much less tiring for both partners if the woman supports the upper part of her body on the bed.

VAGINAL CONTROL

Oriental sex manuals relate that once a woman has achieved ultimate control she can undulate her vaginal muscles like the fingers of a milkmaid forcing the milk down the teats of a cow.

Ancient training techniques are no longer available, but women can do much to tone up their vaginal muscles by regular pelvic floor pull-up exercises – squeezing and releasing their vaginal muscles. Start with three at a time, building up to ten contractions and releases, five times daily.

POSTILLIONAGE

The basic technique of postillionage is to insert a finger into your partner's anus as he or she is approaching orgasm. Both men and women enjoy it – but it does have its dangers.

First, you will need to have your nails cut short. Long fingernails can cause unpleasant cuts and abrasions. Second, it must be very well lubricated if it is not to be too uncomfortable.

Remember too that a finger that has been inserted into a woman's anus should never then be put into her vagina before it has been washed. It is especially important to remember this in the masturbation technique called 'a horse in both stables' where the man puts one – or more – fingers in the vagina and others in the anus.

THE 'FLANQUETTE' POSITIONS

In the *flanquette* positions, the man lies face-to-face with his partner but has only one of his legs between hers. He can either be directly on top of her, or they can lie side-by-side.

All the *flanquette* positions allow deep penetration and the position of the man's thigh also helps to ensure good clitoral stimulation. Many men also find the woman's thigh rubbing against their testicles stimulating. Others may find it threatening though. Any sudden movement could be painful.

THE 'CUISSADE' POSITIONS

The *cuissade* positions are similar, except that the man takes the woman half from the rear. Usually the woman lies on her back and the man lies beside her, then threads his leg under one of hers and over the other, effectively turning her pelvis. From here he can enter her from the rear, while propping himself up on his elbow so that they can still look at each other.

The *cuissade* positions allow the man's penis to enter the vagina at some very stimulating angles. If the man lies right back, it will enter her to a

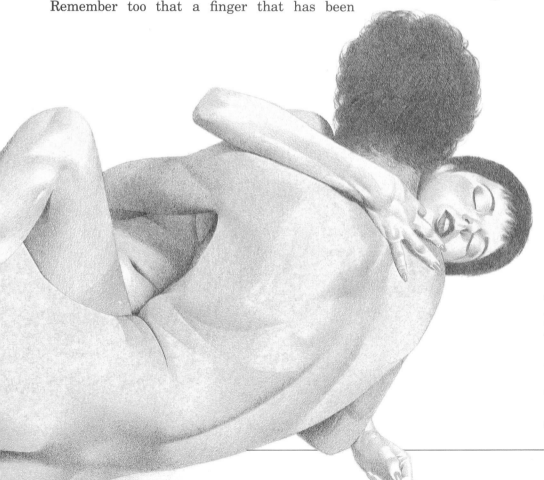

The cuissade positions
Here, the man takes the woman half from the rear. With both partners' legs entwined, the man can use his penis to vary the angle and degree of penetration

The Viennese oyster
*The woman lies back
and crosses her feet on
her chest or – for the
supple – behind her neck.
The man squeezes her
feet as he enters her*

The frog
*A woman-on top
position that allows full
contact along both
partner's bodies. The
woman rests the soles of
her feet on top of the
man's*

remarkable depth. Or, if he remains lying on his side, this is a very leisurely position for both partners – although none the less stimulating for that. It is one of those positions that a couple can finish an exhausting day with as it allows them to fall asleep while their genitals are still locked together. And if approached gently, it can be an interesting way for a man to wake up his partner in the morning.

THE BLACK APPROACH
The French often call rear entry position coitus à la négresse. There are two possible historical reasons for this label. Rear-entry positions were considered bestial, and much too base for 'civilized' Europeans to use. They were thought to be only suitable for the 'inferior' heathen races. They also tend to be submissive as far as the woman is concerned, and it may be that à la négresse has something to do with the advantage white plantation owners took of their female slaves in the 17th, 18th and early 19th centuries.

But in terms of the specific position that is usually referred to in sex manuals as à la négresse, the female is rather more active.

She starts by lying face down with her hands clasped behind the back of her neck and with her buttocks in the air. When the man enters her, she hooks her legs around his and uses them to pull him on to her. Using her legs in this way means that the apparently submissive woman can actually control the pace and depth of lovemaking.

THE VIENNESE OYSTER
The Austrians are also adventurous if the Viennese Oyster position is to be believed.

This can only be performed by an extremely supple woman. She must be able to cross her feet behind the back of her head. She assumes this position lying on her back. The man then lies full length on top of her and squeezes her feet. Apart from the stimulation of the soles of the feet, this position allows a unique rocking pelvic movement.

Those not so supple should try bringing their knees up to their shoulders and crossing their ankles on their stomach. Either way, the woman must be able to get into this position voluntarily. Do not try forcing it, it could be very painful.

SEX IN YUGOSLAVIA
The Slavs, it seems, find the smells of sex extremely stimulating and sexual odours play a very important part in their lovemaking.

According to folklore, they also like sex naked, simple and direct. So-called Serbian intercourse is essentially a mock rape. The woman is thrown down – preferably on a soft carpet – then the man grabs her ankles, raises them over her head and falls on her, entering her fully.

In many ways, this contradicts everything the enlightened westerner has learned about sex. Here, there is no foreplay, no tenderness, no gentle caressing of the clitoris. It is straight – almost brutal – penetration. But some women find this robust approach from their partners exhilarating once in a while.

THE WANTON WOMAN
Few men can resist the woman who takes the initiative in sex. And a new dimension can be added to the simplest woman-on-top position if the woman rests the soles of her feet on the top of the man's feet. This will usually make the woman splay her legs, and gives the name to the position *the frog*.

Here, the man and the woman have direct contact all the way down the front of their legs.

CROATIAN STYLE
The female equivalent of male-dominant Yugoslavian sex is called Croatian intercourse. First, the woman gives the man an intimate tongue bath, then climbs on top of him, and makes love to him until he is exhausted.

The woman can restrain him by locking her legs over his thighs and holding his arms down with her hands. Or, if she faces away from him, she can lean back, restraining his arms with her feet and hold his thighs down with her hands.

SEX FLORENTINE
Coitus à la Florentine allows a woman to enjoy a man even though he is not fully erect. She simply holds back his penile skin – and his foreskin if he is uncircumcised – with her forefinger and thumb so that it is stretched tight – both when it is going in and when it is coming out.

This sometimes makes the penis firm enough for intercourse, even if the man is not aroused at all.

She can also use the same technique to control – usually speed up – the time he takes to ejaculate. For the averagely awake, sober and potent man, Florentine sex is extremely stimulating.

SUPERIOR VARIATIONS
From the straight kneeling-on-top position, the woman can manœuvre one leg so that it is under the man's thigh, then bring her other leg over that same side of his body and rest it on his shoulder.

Now, still sitting on him, she can lean back so that his penis applies the maximum pressure on the front of her vagina and, hopefully, her G spot. This is known as the X position and helps to prolong intercourse.

It is often difficult for the woman to balance in this position and she may need to hold her lover around the neck or grasp his hand to steady herself.

FURNITURE FUN
The simplest woman-on-top position – out of bed – is on a chair. If the man sits down, the woman

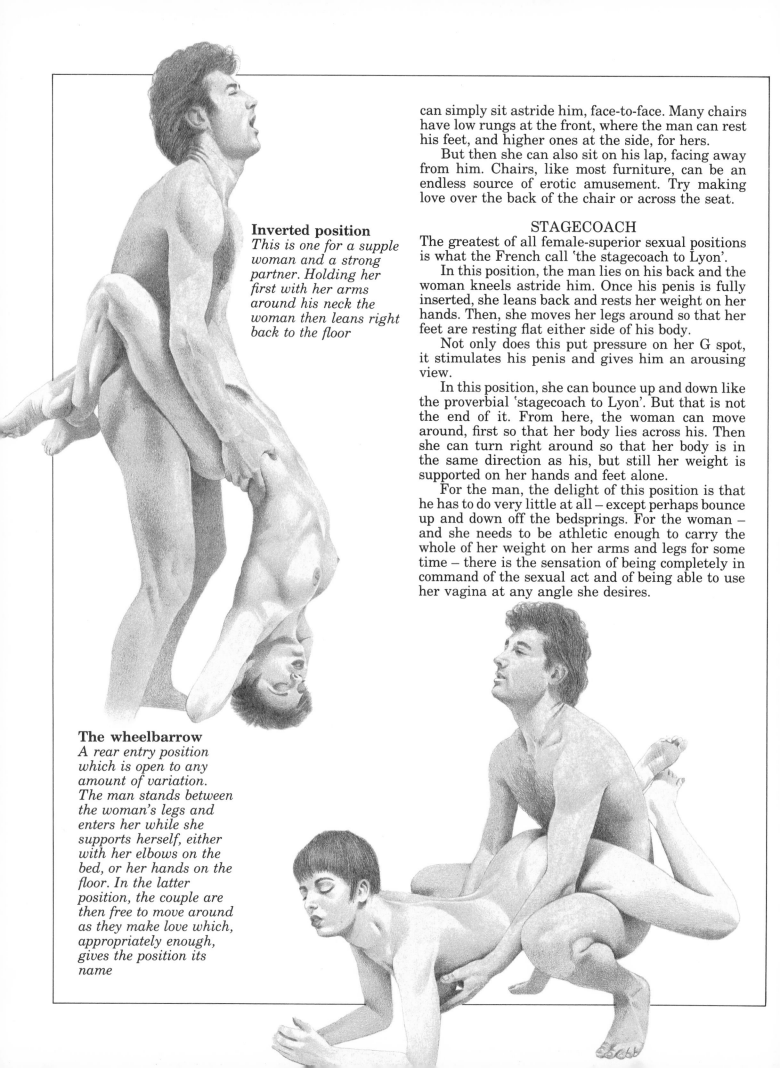

Inverted position
This is one for a supple woman and a strong partner. Holding her first with her arms around his neck the woman then leans right back to the floor

can simply sit astride him, face-to-face. Many chairs have low rungs at the front, where the man can rest his feet, and higher ones at the side, for hers.

But then she can also sit on his lap, facing away from him. Chairs, like most furniture, can be an endless source of erotic amusement. Try making love over the back of the chair or across the seat.

STAGECOACH

The greatest of all female-superior sexual positions is what the French call 'the stagecoach to Lyon'.

In this position, the man lies on his back and the woman kneels astride him. Once his penis is fully inserted, she leans back and rests her weight on her hands. Then, she moves her legs around so that her feet are resting flat either side of his body.

Not only does this put pressure on her G spot, it stimulates his penis and gives him an arousing view.

In this position, she can bounce up and down like the proverbial 'stagecoach to Lyon'. But that is not the end of it. From here, the woman can move around, first so that her body lies across his. Then she can turn right around so that her body is in the same direction as his, but still her weight is supported on her hands and feet alone.

For the man, the delight of this position is that he has to do very little at all – except perhaps bounce up and down off the bedsprings. For the woman – and she needs to be athletic enough to carry the whole of her weight on her arms and legs for some time – there is the sensation of being completely in command of the sexual act and of being able to use her vagina at any angle she desires.

The wheelbarrow
A rear entry position which is open to any amount of variation. The man stands between the woman's legs and enters her while she supports herself, either with her elbows on the bed, or her hands on the floor. In the latter position, the couple are then free to move around as they make love which, appropriately enough, gives the position its name

ORAL SEX

*Sharing the pleasures of oral sex is one of the
most intimate ways of making love*

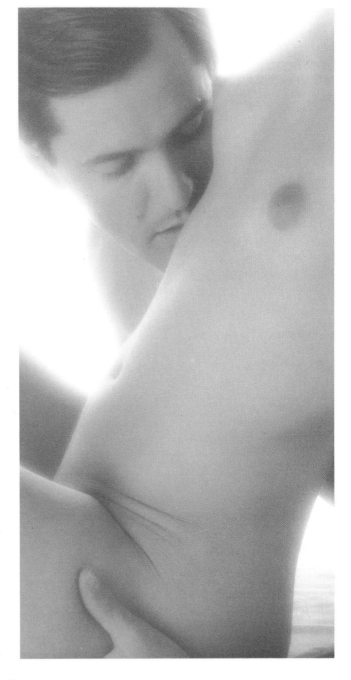

There was a time, not so long ago, when oral sex was widely regarded in western societies as a perversion. At best it was thought of as a naughty refinement, which should be left to whores and other 'professionals' – at worst it was shunned as disgusting and immoral.

Now it is generally recognized that oral sex offers a blend of intimacy, trust, generosity and tenderness which is often very different from intercourse. And it can produce a high level of excitement and satisfaction.

WHAT IS ORAL SEX?

Oral sex has two different 'names'. Kissing, licking and sucking the female sex organs, is called cunnilingus. Similar mouth contact with the penis is called fellatio.

The simultaneous performing of fellatio and cunnilingus by two people to each other is known as *soixante neuf*, the French for '69'. The numerals represent two people lying together head to toe.

Oral sex can be used as a complete sexual experience in itself with either or both partners being brought to orgasm. More often it is used as a part of foreplay before genital intercourse takes place.

For many women cunnilingus is more exciting than intercourse. Lubrication is more readily provided by the mouth than the vagina and a man has more control over his mouth than his genitals.

For a man fellatio is particularly exciting because it is so different from 'conventional' intercourse. The lips, lined as they are with tissues similar to the vagina itself, feel like a new vagina. It also shows a high degree of intimacy and it gives the man a chance to feel worshipped and play a passive role, which he may welcome from time to time. It is also an extremely effective way of restarting a man for a second round of lovemaking.

IS ORAL SEX NORMAL?

Many people still find the mere thought of oral sex distasteful. They may think it is 'dirty' to use your lips and tongue on the organs used for urination. Or they may simply be shy.

Women, especially, tend to have reservations

about being so closely 'inspected', often because their childhood left them with the feeling that their pubic areas are in some way unattractive.

Some men can also feel uncomfortable about oral sex, thinking it is unhygienic or even abnormal. They may also feel too vulnerable to trust their 'manhood' to a partner's teeth, or they may idealize women and feel that anything outside strict limits degrades them.

Another reason, perhaps, is that some men feel that any desire they have for oral sex is an expression of homosexual tendencies about which they may feel afraid and ashamed.

For healthy couples there is nothing abnormal, perverted or unhygienic about oral sex. It is merely an extension of other forms of sexual activity.

Most people kiss their partner's body when they have sex – the shoulders, chest, back, stomach and so on. Oral sex is a natural progression of this – a kiss that caresses the most intimate part of your lover's body.

Unfortunately, oral sex is often portrayed in a bad light in films and books and is a constant source of dirty jokes, which tends to foster existing misconceptions.

NOTHING IS COMPULSORY

A problem can arise in a relationship when one partner wants oral sex and the other refuses. Whether it is through embarrassment, fear or ignorance this can put real pressure on a relationship, even though in every other way it may be very good.

While being open and honest with each other about particular desires is positive in a relationship, no-one should be forced to do something they do not like. If you want oral sex and your partner does not, you should try to understand their reservations about it, and explain them away with understanding and patience. But nobody should be made to feel obliged by the demands of emotional blackmail or the pleas of an inconsiderate lover. Oral sex performed out of a sense of duty or simply because it is expected, would be an offensive chore rather than the loving, sensual experience it can be for many couples.

What a couple decide to do in bed is a matter of personal preference, and what feels right for both – not just one of them – at the time.

HOW ORAL SEX CAN HELP

Apart from providing pleasure, oral sex can, on certain occasions, be the most practical way to make love. This can be either when vaginal penetration is inadvisable – when contraception is unavailable, or after childbirth, for example. Or it can also be helpful if the man has 'come' too soon and wants to bring his partner to orgasm.

Oral sex can help solve certain sexual problems. Women who thought they were 'frigid' have enjoyed multiple orgasms from it. Impotent men are able to satisfy their partner with cunnilingus, and some have been helped – by fellatio – to overcome their sexual problems.

In any relationship, oral sex can add variety, and inject new drive and interest to a sex life that might be going a little stale.

The '69' position represents the supreme sexual sensation for some men, since they can give and receive pleasure simultaneously

HER FOR HIM

Although it is often thought that a woman kisses and sucks a man's penis because it is so pleasant for him, many women do it because it gives them such intense sensations. Indeed, a few women find it so arousing that it gives them – as well as their partner – an orgasm.

The idea behind fellating a man is to see it as a form of intercourse and treat it accordingly. No-one would dash into sex without foreplay and it is the same when fellating a man.

The only preparation necessary for fellatio is for the man to make sure that his genitals are clean.

HOW TO FELLATE A MAN

Once the ground rules are set and foreplay is well under way, find a position in which you can comfortably and easily enjoy your lover's penis. Positions can vary. Some men prefer to lie back in bed, others may prefer to sit down. A good position is for the man to stand with his hands on his hips and his erect penis at your face level. You can then kneel before him, leaving your hands free to caress him, and play with his balls and anus.

Next, take his penis into the palm of your hand and, keeping your teeth out of the way, moisten the head with saliva. Then put the head of the penis into your mouth as far as it is comfortable and move your head so that the penis goes in and out. The secret is to keep the teeth well out of the way at all times.

Once the man is highly aroused and excited, you can remove the penis from your mouth and run the tongue up and down the length of the organ and

TIPS FOR BOTH SEXES

Here are some do's and don'ts when you and your partner are having oral sex

■ *Never bite the genitals, however playfully. In the heat of the moment it is easy to get carried away and hurt your partner*

■ *Always be scrupulously clean. Wash your genitals every day*

■ *Agree on the 'rules' beforehand – especially as to whether the woman is going to swallow the semen*

■ *Be careful. A sudden thrust of the penis deep into a woman's mouth is not only inconsiderate, it can be dangerous as well*

■ *Never blow down the genitals. It can actually kill a woman by forcing air up her uterus and into her blood stream. It can also be dangerous for a man.*

One of the most comfortable ways for a woman to enjoy oral sex is to lie back with her legs apart, leaving her partner free to use his tongue to explore her most sensitive areas

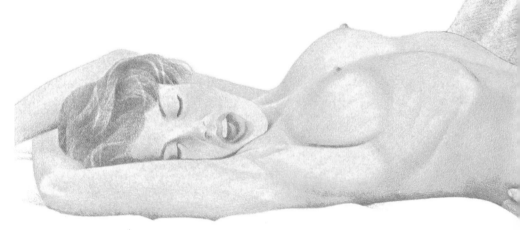

tease his balls too. This gives pleasure to most men, as does running and flicking the tongue over the frenulum, the little ridge of skin on the underside of the penis. After a few minutes' stimulation, stop and tease him by turning your attention elsewhere on his body – nibbling him, and kissing him all over.

Return to the penis and put it firmly into your mouth, squeezing his balls gently at the same time if he likes it. Be guided by the man as to how much in and out movement he likes.

Swirl your tongue around the head of the penis so that you never lose contact with it. Do this clockwise then anticlockwise. Dart your tongue into and out of the slit in the end of his penis, and then continue the swirling combined with the in and out movements. During all of this, make use of your hands, too – ensure that you are giving your partner ecstatic sensations.

If you have decided not to take the semen into your mouth, as he hardens finally – you will soon learn how to tell when this is about to occur – take

the penis out of your mouth and masturbate him so that he comes over your breasts. Do not try for vaginal penetration at this stage – it rarely works satisfactorily if a man is just about to come.

If you have agreed to take the semen into your mouth, shut off the back of your throat as he comes and let the semen pool in your mouth. Then either spit it out discreetly or swallow it, as you prefer.

Many couples do not take fellatio to the extent of ejaculation, but use it to one stage short of this as a form of foreplay soon to be followed by intercourse.

The secret here is to get to know your man's unique signs of arrival at the pre-ejaculatory stage by watching for muscle tension, breathing changes, noises and any movements he makes as he is getting close to orgasm.

If necessary, squeeze the head of his penis between your finger and thumb to cool him off for a while, until you are ready to be penetrated.

DEEP THROATING

A very few oral sex devotees claim to have trained themselves to be able to take a man's penis right down the back of their throat, but most women choke and panic if the man pushes his penis too far into the mouth. This should never be done unless the woman says in advance that she is willing and able to cope with it.

FELLATIO FOR RE-AROUSAL

As a re-arousal technique, fellatio takes a lot of beating. Even the most reluctant or exhausted penis can be brought back to life within minutes of tender and skilful oral caressing.

It can also work wonders for the older man whose powers of erection are declining or for when a man has already ejaculated but his partner wants him to penetrate her again.

A woman who genuinely wants to fellate her lover – either because she wants to give him exquisite pleasure or herself powerful sensations – will be able to produce an erection in all but the most stubborn penis. Few men fail to be intensely aroused by such intimate ministrations.

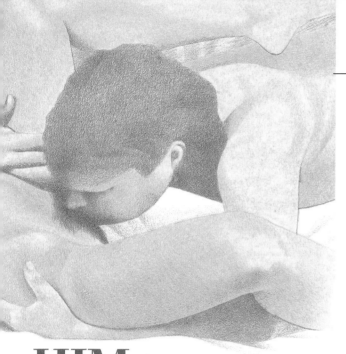

HIM FOR HER

Performing cunnilingus successfully is much more difficult than performing fellatio. Almost all men will become erect and come quickly with adequate oral sexual attention from a woman. For women things can be very different, mainly because individual women are so variable in their sexual needs and genital pleasures.

As with fellatio, the only prerequisite is cleanliness of the sex organs. Washing immediately beforehand, however, is unnecessary. Daily bathing is enough.

HOW TO DO IT

Put a pillow under the woman's bottom to raise her pubic area to make it more comfortable for both of you, and then nuzzle her all over and kiss her breasts and nipples. Tease her by running your lips over sensitive parts of her body but do not tickle.

Nuzzle into her vulva and kiss all round the area. Kiss her large lips and run your tongue along the length of them. Take one in between your lips and suck it. Suck the inner lips gently in this way as well.

Lick around the vaginal opening and the area between the vagina and the anus. Poke your tongue into her vagina and pop it in and out. As she becomes highly aroused and her vaginal juices start to flow, transfer your attention to the clitoris.

What you do to this sensitive organ will have to be dictated by what your partner most enjoys. Lick all around the area, but go gently on the tip itself as this can be exquisitely sensitive.

Some do not like the actual clitoris licked at all, while others enjoy very firm sucking and tonguing as they near their climax. As she becomes even more aroused, put a couple of fingers inside her vagina

and do what she most likes done with them. All the time keep on caressing the clitoris with the tongue.

From time to time stop the clitoral caressing, and concentrate on her vagina and other parts of her body. This will tease her and produce different sexual sensations. At this stage you could – if she likes – place a vibrator or a dildo inside her.

When she can stand no more, go back to caressing her clitoris and all around it with your tongue and mouth and bring her to orgasm. Be guided by what she wants. Some women who are normally multi-orgasmic find one orgasm produced in this way quite enough and do not want or need to go on any more. Others need several orgasms either by more oral caresses or from penis-in-vagina sex, which can be exceptionally erotic after all this attention to her genitals.

Many women greatly enjoy fondling their man's genitals as they are are being kissed and sucked, so ensure that you are in a position in which all this can happen too. The only aim is to give the woman the most sensual pleasure from the experience, so anything that she wants to do should be encouraged.

Some women feel that all this must be a bit of a chore for their partner and that they only do it because they feel they should or because the man loves her. Nothing could be further from the truth. Most men greatly enjoy performing cunnilingus on their woman and some are so excited by it that they actually come without any genital stimulation.

With some couples, where the woman has difficulty having orgasms in every other way, oral sex gives the man the pleasure of seeing his partner aroused and orgasmic when all else has 'failed'. This can be a great joy to both.

SOME MYTHS EXPLODED

There are probably more myths about oral sex than about any other aspects of male-female relationships. Here are a few of them. The only thing they have in common is that they are all false.

■ *Too much oral sex causes venereal disease*
■ *Men who enjoy being fellated are homosexuals*
■ *Women who enjoy fellating a man are submissive or they are whores*
■ *A man who enjoys cunnilingus cannot satisfy his partner properly*
■ *Swallowing semen can make a woman pregnant*
■ *Oral sex can lead to disease because of all the germs in the penis or vagina*
Many of the myths and misconceptions about the medical and hygienic aspects of oral sex have been dispelled. And though clear statements concerning oral sex are notably absent from the heads of the major religions, they have relaxed their old prohibitions about it being unnatural and sinful.

THE G SPOT

Making the most of the G spot can add a whole new dimension to a couple's lovemaking. It can also provide powerfully different types of orgasm – for both partners

It was generally thought, until the 1970s, that women were almost entirely aroused to climax by clitoral stimulation (even if it was indirect, during intercourse) and that men could only have an orgasm if their penis was stimulated.

But there is a hidden area in both men and women that – when stimulated correctly – produces intense excitement and orgasm. For men, this area is the prostate gland – in women, the area is called the G spot.

Many individuals had realized that there were such areas, because of their personal experience. But this did not prevent some 'experts' from denying the existence of 'alternative' pleasure zones.

ERNEST GRÄFENBERG

It was in the 1940s that the German obstetrician and gynaecologist Ernest Gräfenberg described a 'zone of erogenous feeling . . . located in the anterior [front] wall of the vagina'. It is this area that has become known as the G – for Gräfenberg – spot. Researchers have now investigated the G spot in more detail, and there is at least some measure of agreement about it.

FOR HER

In the 1980s, American researchers Beverly Whipple and John Perry followed up Gräfenberg's findings. Their work confirmed his, and they discovered that there is a small area inside the vagina that responds to stimulation.

They also discovered that if this area – which they called the G spot – is properly stimulated, the result can be intensely satisfying orgasms, and that if these orgasms do occur, the woman will very often ejaculate a small amount of clear fluid. Analysis revealed that this fluid was similar in composition to the seminal fluid from the prostrate gland that in the male protects the sperm.

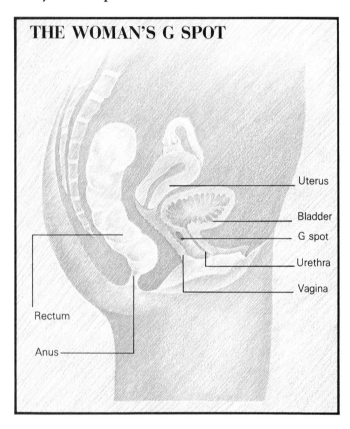

THE WOMAN'S G SPOT

Uterus
Bladder
G spot
Urethra
Vagina
Rectum
Anus

WHO HAS ONE?

Such findings were initially thought to be unbelievable by those who insisted that the clitoris, and only the clitoris, was the source of female pleasure.

But Whipple and Perry arranged for 400 woman volunteers to be examined – and every one was found to have a G spot. This seems to indicate that this hidden pleasure centre is not the exception, but the rule, among women.

WHAT IS IT?

The G spot appears to be a small cluster of nerve endings, glands, ducts and blood vessels around the urethra – the urinary passage running in front of the vaginal wall.

It cannot normally be felt when it is unaroused, only becoming distinguishable as a specific area during deep vaginal stimulation.

When this happens, it begins to swell, sometimes very rapidly indeed and a small mass with distinct edges stands out from the vaginal wall.

Because the fluid ejaculated during a G spot orgasm is very similar to the prostatic fluid (only without sperm), many scientists believe that the G spot is a rudimentary version of the male prostate gland which produces similar effects when stimulated.

Scientists cannot agree, however, whether the G spot has any organic function – other than helping a woman achieve an often unsuspected degree of sexual satisfaction.

A ROLE IN CHILDBIRTH?
It is thought that the G spot may well come into its own during childbirth.

To stimulate the G spot herself, a good position for a woman is to kneel with her knees slightly apart and sit back on her heels

The deep orgasms associated with G spot stimulation are often accompanied by a 'pushing down' sensation. Since this stimulation can be provided by the descending fetus during birth, it seems possible that the G spot's function could be to help the baby to be born as easily and quickly as possible.

WHERE IS IT?

Lying approximately halfway between the pubic bone and the cervix, within an inch of either side of an imaginary line drawn vertically down from the navel, the G spot is not the easiest part of the female anatomy to find. The problem is that it has to be stimulated to be found, and found to be stimulated.

FINDING THE G SPOT

It is a good idea for a woman to learn where her G spot is, if only to show herself that she does have one.

She cannot do this lying down, since gravity tends to pull the internal organ away from the vaginal entrance. A sitting or squatting position is preferred.

It is probably better for her to begin her search for the G spot while sitting on the lavatory. This is because deliberate stimulation of the G spot often causes an initial sensation that feels like a desire to urinate. If the woman makes sure that she has passed water first, but still remains on the lavatory, she will gain an added sense of security.

USE BOTH HANDS

Using her fingers, she should then apply a firm upward pressure to the front of the internal vaginal wall. Sometimes it helps if she uses the other hand to press firmly down on the outside of her tummy.

The G spot should now begin to swell, and will feel like a small lump between the fingers inside and outside the vagina.

Although, on average, the G spot appears to be slightly smaller than a penny piece, there is no real norm – and nor does size seem to have anything to do with the sensation produced.

THE G SPOT ORGASM

As the G spot continues to be stroked, pleasurable contractions begin to sweep through the uterus. Ultimately, a deep orgasm will be experienced that will feel totally different from one caused by clitoral stimulation. At this point, the woman may ejaculate a small amount of clear fluid from the urethra. Contrary to what she may feel – and the appearance of the fluid – this is not urine.

Once a woman has become used to these

Here, the woman can use her partner's penis to stimulate her G spot. Leaning forward allows exactly the right angle of penetration

sensations, she can continue to experiment while kneeling on her feet with her knees apart on the floor or bed.

JOINT DISCOVERY
Of course, a sympathetic partner can make the discovery far more intimate and enjoyable.

In this case, the woman should lie face down on the bed with her hips raised by one or two pillows. Her partner can then gently place two fingers inside her and begin to stroke the front vaginal wall.

By moving her pelvis, the woman can help locate the spot and also discover the most enjoyable kind of stimulation. The main point to remember is that the initial sensations felt are not those of a desire to urinate. In time, the woman will learn that these feelings are simply part of the run-up to vaginal orgasm.

THE IMPORTANCE OF POSITION
Alone among world cultures, Europeans appear to regard the missionary position as being the proven, natural way to make love. A number of other cultures see it as just another, possibly quaint, method – and not one calculated to totally satisfy the female partner.

In the missionary position the penis is usually

aimed at the rear vaginal wall. This can provide clitoral stimulation, but does not excite the G spot.

Probably the two easiest positions with which to achieve G spot stimulation are the 'rear entry' and 'woman-on-top' methods.

Rear-entry lovemaking allows the man's erect penis to stimulate the G spot on the front wall of the vagina – particularly if the woman swings and rotates her hips, so that she can direct her lover's penis to the most pleasurable spot.

WOMAN ON TOP
Woman-on-top positions also afford direct stimulation of the G spot, and allow the woman to control the direction and depth of the penis. If the man lies on his back, with the woman straddling his erect penis, she can also move forward or from side-to-side and guide his penis to the place that feels best.

The man can help by moving his own body and by pressing on the base of his own penis to make sure the head does make full contact. The result can be, and often is, a series of intense orgasms for both partners.

Both the rear-entry and woman-on-top positions were in widespread use in European countries, centuries before the missionary position took over as being the standard – possibly as a result of St Paul's teaching that the female should be subject to the male in all things. Certainly, the rear-entry position is most used in the animal kingdom.

MEDICAL IMPLICATIONS
Whipple and Perry, who are responsible for most of the research carried out on the G spot, have noted two important medical implications of their findings.

First, many women who use the diaphragm for contraception have complained that somehow it prevents them from experiencing the same degree of sexual satisfaction achieved when they were on the Pill, or when their partner used a condom.

The problem is that the diaphragm covers both the cervix and the front vaginal wall, and so can prevent direct stimulation of the G spot if it is located in the area covered by the diaphragm.

There are two ways of solving this problem. Either stimulate the G spot before the diaphragm is inserted, so that a G spot orgasm can be experienced, or change to the cap (which is smaller than the diaphragm and fits over the cervix itself) or to another method of contraception.

CAREFUL SURGEONS
Whipple and Perry stressed that in light of their findings, it is important that surgeons are very careful whenever they perform a hysterectomy to make sure that the front wall of the vagina is not damaged. Equally, the same kind of care should be applied to all other procedures that involve surgery of a woman's vagina.

FOR HIM

Men also have a sort of G spot. As with women, this area is located around the urethra at the neck of the bladder. It is called the prostate gland, and unlike the female G spot has a well defined function.

The prostate gland helps produce the fluid that carries the sperm into the vagina when a couple are having intercourse.

Many men have discovered that stimulation of the prostate gland prior to, or during, intercourse results in an orgasm of intensity never before realized. And not only do the feelings differ from the more usual form of orgasm, the way in which the man ejaculates is different too. After prostate stimulation, he ejaculates in a gentle flow, rather than in spurts.

FINDING THE PROSTATE

It is difficult for a man to reach his prostate gland himself, since to do so, he has to insert a finger – or thumb – into his rectum. But it is possible to reach it. The best position is if he lies on his back with his knees bent and feet flat on the floor, or with the knees drawn up towards his chest.

If he then inserts a thumb into his anus, and presses against the front rectal wall, he should be able to feel his prostate – it is a firm mass about the size of walnut.

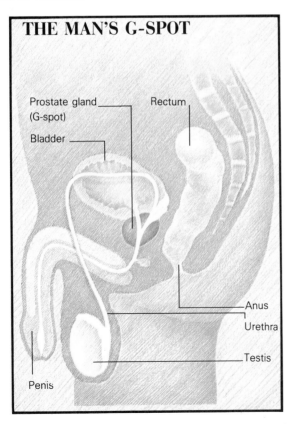

THE MAN'S G-SPOT

Prostate gland (G-spot)

Bladder

Rectum

Anus

Urethra

Testis

Penis

As with the female G spot, the discovery of this hidden pleasure centre is usually more enjoyable if it is shared with a loving partner.

If a woman wants to stimulate her partner in this way, here are a few tips.

■ Make sure your fingernails are not long as you could damage him inside.

■ Ensure that your finger is well lubricated. Unlike your vagina, the anus is not a naturally lubricating organ. Saliva is usually not good enough – you will need KY jelly or something similar.

■ Lie him down on the bed on his back and slowly and gently insert a finger into his anus. Wait for a few seconds as he becomes accustomed to your finger being there. Do not forget that his bottom may not be used to having things put into it – unlike your vagina.

■ Feel up the frontal rectal wall until you find his prostate – then massage it firmly. This can be fairly tiring, and can be made easier if he pulls his knees back towards his chest.

■ Even if you do not touch his penis at all he will probably become erect and have an orgasm

■ When you remove your finger wash it at once – do not touch inside your vagina or you could transfer bacteria.

If you are put off by the 'messiness' of all this, do not be. Unless a man is constipated there are no stools in his lower rectum – it is empty. Some women feel better using a disposal plastic glove.

To the man who enjoys prostatic stimulation, a skilful woman is highly cherished and valued. For the really adventurous, the woman can fellate the man as she massages his prostate.

NEW SEXUAL RESPONSE?

When Masters and Johnson wrote Human Sexual Response *in the 1960s, they proved – it seemed conclusively – that all women's orgasms were produced by clitoral stimulation.*

But many millions of women say they have orgasms without any clitoral stimulation at all, and some say that penis-in-vagina sex alone makes them climax. One US study of 131 women in 1977 found that 56 thought there were sensory nerve endings in the vagina (the medical world has repeatedly said that this is not so). 78 said that they had a particularly sensitive place in their vagina – when asked, 71 of their partners had found a particularly sensitive spot there too. 24 said that they had personally ejaculated. 42 had 'been afraid of urinating' when sexually aroused. 31 had thought they had urinated during intercourse. 30 experienced orgasm from vaginal penetration alone, and one third of diaphragm users said that pleasure was less with the diaphragm.

SIMULTANEOUS ORGASMS

For the loving couple, being attuned to each other so that they come at exactly the same time can be the ultimate goal of their lovemaking

To many couples the 'ideal' form of lovemaking is one in which they both have an orgasm at the same time – anything else is considered to be poor by comparison. Certainly, when orgasms do come together in this way they can be very pleasant, but to run lovemaking with this goal in mind is to store up a measure of disappointment and even resentment for the future.

TRYING TOO HARD

Try to imagine lovemaking as a dinner party where the purpose is to enjoy the food and the company of the guests. If you were to commit yourself to swallowing the last morsel of food at exactly the same time as your partner you would be preoccupied with timing, would not concentrate on the meal and, as a result, would not enjoy it. And then suppose you did finish the last piece of food at exactly the same time, would the occasion be any the better for that?

Unfortunately, for many couples the whole business of simultaneous orgasms is much the same – the very act of trying to come together prevents it from happening. The stress involved in trying to hold off his own orgasm, while the woman releases hers, can be very tiring for a man. It can interfere with his ejaculatory timing and so reduce the pleasure he gets from his orgasm. For the woman things can be equally stressful as she hurries her own orgasm to coincide with his.

SIMULTANEOUS ORGASMS IN INTERCOURSE

For men, an orgasm is an essential part of the procreative act. Without it, he cannot impregnate a woman. Male orgasm is thus a biological necessity.

Female orgasm, however, is much more elusive and less clear cut. All that is necessary, biologically,

is that the woman is sufficiently receptive so that the man can place his semen near her cervix. Orgasm during intercourse is not necessary.

Of those women who do have orgasms, twice as many get them from manual or oral clitoral stimulation as from intercourse. A United States survey of 106,000 women in 1980 found that 34 per cent usually had orgasms from intercourse, and the Hite Report of 1974 found 30 per cent to be the figure. So if simultaneous orgasms are to occur during intercourse – which is what most people mean when they use the phrase – few people, it seems, are likely to experience them.

SOME MYTHS DISPELLED

Some men blame their women for being 'frigid' if they do not have an orgasm during intercourse and especially at the same time. This is grossly unfair as frigidity is an entirely different thing from an inability to have orgasms.

Frigidity means an inability to respond sexually, in any way, of which having an orgasm is but one. To many a man, a woman who cannot, or does not, have an orgasm (and preferably during intercourse) is in some way lacking. This is an unfortunate, and even a harmful, concept because it judges women's sexuality by the same standards as men's.

Men are goal-centred in our culture and see the having of an orgasm on their part as crucial to any sexual transaction. As a result, most expect their woman to have one too. A large United States survey in 1977 of more than 4,000 men found that the majority defined the end of intercourse as occurring when 'both had had an orgasm'. Many, if not most, women would disagree.

There are currently two incompatible explanations as to why women, overall, have fewer orgasms than men.

The first is based on psychoanalysis and claims that all women are basically sexual and orgasmic, but that most of them are conditioned out of their capabilities by their culture telling them that sex is dirty, wrong or harmful. As a result, the theory has it, many girls never really discover their orgasmic capacity as boys do and so enter womanhood in a somewhat sexually crippled state. This state can be reversed, it is claimed, by undoing the old myths and harms that were previously done.

Clinical experience proves that there is a lot to this theory, but it seems incompatible with the other theory which derives from anthropology and states that human females are the only female animals to have orgasms. It goes on to suggest that orgasms are not biologically essential but are a rather specially-learned refinement of social behaviour, somewhat like learning to play the piano.

Whichever theory is right, simultaneous orgasm is not something that can happen as if by magic. But there are a number of things you can do to try and achieve it.

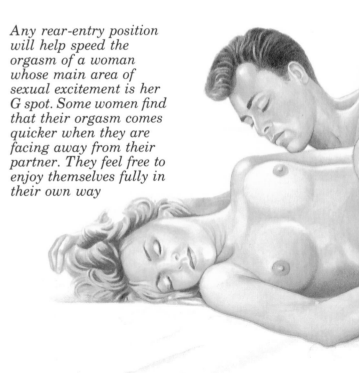

Any rear-entry position will help speed the orgasm of a woman whose main area of sexual excitement is her G spot. Some women find that their orgasm comes quicker when they are facing away from their partner. They feel free to enjoy themselves fully in their own way

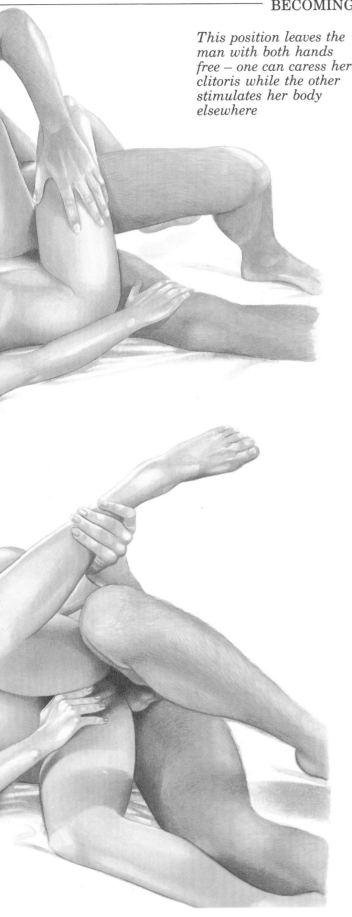

This position leaves the man with both hands free – one can caress her clitoris while the other stimulates her body elsewhere

TOWARDS PERFECT TIMING

Obviously, with something as uniquely individual as a person's sexuality, there can be no hard-and-fast rules about how to produce simultaneous orgasms, but clinical experience does enable us to learn from others. For the vast majority of couples, the woman will have to speed up her orgasm, and the man hold back his own, if simultaneous orgasm is to be anything other than a chance rarity. Here are some tips as to how to achieve this.

SPEEDING UP A WOMAN

■ Oral sex beforehand is a great favourite. If a man brings a woman to near-climax orally, and then penetrates her, she might well come almost at once. The final stimulation of penile thrusting is just enough to push such a woman over the edge to an orgasm she otherwise would not have had.

■ To the woman whose main area of sexual excitement is her G spot, rear-entry sex, and especially the doggy position, can help to ensure that she is stimulated where it matters most. Some women also have orgasms during intercourse in rear-entry positions because they are facing away from their partner, and so do not have him intruding visually on their lovemaking. Such women often fantasize about another man and their real man face-to-face 'gets in the way'. Another reason why such women have orgasms in this position is that they feel so vulnerable – they can be penetrated and feel completely at their lover's mercy to do with them what he will. Any couple who have found from vaginal play that that the woman has a sensitive G spot could well experiment with such rear-entry positions.

■ Use a favourite fantasy. Some women can take themselves from being 'pleasantly warm' to 'boiling point' simply by using a particularly arousing fantasy.

■ Foreplay is the answer to orgasms during intercourse for most women. This needs to be highly personalized to suit the individual woman. This may be why more older and married women have orgasms during intercourse than do the young and single – they have had more time to find out the best formula and to perfect it.

■ The couple should find a position in which the woman's clitoris can be stimulated easily and comfortably. One of the best positions in which to do this is for the man to lie at right angles to his partner's body and under her raised and parted

LEARNING THE SQUEEZE TECHNIQUE

The man should become aroused by reading something erotic and produce an erection by masturbating. When he has a really hard erection he should stop the stimulation and squeeze the head of his penis between fingers and thumb around the rim. This will make the erection subside very quickly. Once his penis is flaccid, he should re-stimulate it in his favourite way and go on with the cycle of arousal and stopping for as long as he can bear it.

He should build up the time he can hold off having an orgasm until he can go comfortably for half an hour.

Some men then go on to do all of this with their partner. This is good training because the erotic status is more realistic and closer to the true intercourse conditions. The woman who is training her man can stimulate him however she thinks best and then squeeze him to make him go slower.

After a few days of this training the man should be able to be given an erection and left for some time without ejaculating. He could, perhaps, do a job around the house or carry out a personal task for his partner. The couple then bring him to erection again.

As long as the training sessions always end with intercourse or masturbation for the man, no problems will result.

After a few weeks almost any man will be able to hold off his orgasm at will for almost any length of time. The secret is for him to become aware of when he is about to reach the point of 'no return'. He then tells or signals to his partner that his orgasm is imminent and she stops stimulating him. Later in intercourse he can recognize these sensations and can stop penile thrusting, actually come out of her vagina to be squeezed or do something else to control his progress to orgasm. After the early stages of training it is sensible to proceed very cautiously to vaginal penetration – this is best done with the woman on top.

Apart from the benefits of deeper penetration, many women find that they can control both their own orgasm and that of their partner if they are on top. And some positions, like this one, also makes it easier for the man to stimulate her clitoris as well

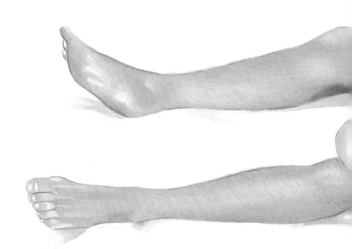

being penetrated and a number of men like this sensation too.

■ Have one orgasm before intercourse. This can make a penetration-induced orgasm much more likely.

Some women, even if they are highly (and multiply) orgasmic during masturbation and foreplay still never have orgasms during intercourse. Most sex clinics no longer consider such women as having anything wrong.

SLOWING DOWN A MAN

This is rather more difficult than speeding up a woman and the couple who try these manœuvres run the risk that the man may gain so much control that he can eventually end up unable to have an orgasm even when he wants to.

This is a real danger when meddling with male arousal. However, assuming that the man simply comes sooner than he would like to on various occasions and so cannot wait for his partner to come, here are some things that may work.

■ Talk it over with your partner – she may well be able to help you. Perhaps she stimulates you too intensely, kisses too passionately or, during foreplay, brings you to the point of no return and then wonders why you come so quickly and she is not ready. The secret here must be to balance your

thighs. This leaves both hands free so that one can caress her clitoris while the other pleasures her elsewhere on her body. There are many other positions in which the woman can caress her own clitoris while her man penetrates her. These include rear entry positions – the spoons (if she raises her upper leg), the woman-on-the-top – the inventive couple will soon find what produces the best results for them. Some women have orgasms only if they use a vibrator on their vulva or clitoris while they are

sexual paces. Spend much more time initially warming her up and only allow her to fondle and arouse you once she is getting close to her own orgasm.

■ Use a sheath for a few weeks. This can so reduce sensitivity that it can break the cycle of too-quick arousal.

■ Use a weak anæsthetic cream or ointment on the tip of the penis. This reduces its sensitivity and helps you last longer.

■ Try contracting your anus tightly at the end of each thrust.

■ Deep penetration helps some men because it reduces the amount of stimulation to their penis tip. This is because the woman's vagina is greatly expanded at its top when she is highly aroused and does not grip the penis so tightly.

■ Focus your attention on something non-sexual. Think about a problem at work, or almost anything that distracts you temporarily from the too-fast arousal you are trying to avoid.

■ Have a small alcoholic drink before intercourse. Some men are anxious, especially if their woman is putting pressure on them for simultaneous orgasms, and this relaxes them.

■ Learning the squeeze technique is a way a man can teach himself to have greater ejaculatory control.

Ejaculation training for men also has another positive benefit – it enables a woman to learn in intimate detail the warning signs of her man's imminent orgasm. This can be useful for her if she is trying to time an orgasm to coincide with his, or wants to slow him down to wait for her.

Similarly, a loving and caring man will learn by careful observation of his partner, both when she masturbates and during sex, what her final arousal signs are so that he can let go at the same time. Many couples have never invested enough time and care in learning these warning signs and then wonder why they do not ever have simultaneous orgasms.

Naturally, combining techniques which slow the man's orgasm and speed up the woman's tend to produce the best results. That way, provided that both partners can control their own orgasms and read the other's signs, they should be able to come together.

A NOTE OF CAUTION

If ever producing simultaneous orgasms becomes a chore or detracts from your enjoyment of sex, you should stop trying. It probably makes sense not to try for them too often and save simultaneous orgasms for special occasions or when you feel excep-tionally loving or rested.

CHAPTER SEVEN

PROLONGING THE PLEASURE

MAKING LOVE LAST LONGER

Do you hurry in love? Is your sex life active but short? It is time to find the time to make your love last longer

There are times in a sexual relationship when a swift bout of lovemaking can be exciting. The 'wham, bam and thank you Ma'am' style of love has its place, perhaps just before going out to meet friends for the evening, in a lunch hour or at the end of the day.

There are times, however, when partners will find sexual intercourse is only fully satisfying if it can be extended. Sensuous, prolonged intercourse can not only express an emotional commitment more thoroughly than a 'quickie', it can also be far more physically satisfying as both partners use all their love and skill to bring each other slowly to a peak of arousal and then satisfaction.

Prolonged lovemaking should not be seen as an end in itself. Some people make the mistake of believing that the ability to 'last' makes them good lovers. If you and your partner are not actually enjoying the experience, but merely enduring it to prove your stamina, it is an empty exercise.

The key, as in any sexual experience, is to share your thoughts and reactions and to be sensitive to your partner's needs and feelings.

IN THE MOOD

Sexual arousal can start long before sexual intercourse itself begins. It can be triggered by sensual kisses and caresses – and also by a wide range of other stimuli. Day-dreaming about your lover or a fantasy figure, hearing a certain song or tune, smelling an evocative scent, tasting a particular food or drink – all can put you in the mood for love. You can build up to lovemaking for many hours before actually touching each other.

If you want to prolong lovemaking, the best way is to extend not only the experience of making love, but both the lead up to it and the follow-on after both of you are satisfied.

STRIPPING FOR ACTION

There is nothing quite so potentially exciting, but also potentially ludicrous, as the taking off of clothes in preparation for making love. Men are often particularly clumsy, discarding shirts and trousers first and then wondering why their partner finds the sight of a man in underpants and socks funny rather than sexy.

Women can make the mistake of stripping too

quickly – a pity, since most men find the sight of a partially clad woman extremely arousing. 'Posing' in just jeans, or a T shirt and briefs can be very exciting. If both partners take their time and help each other with every item, you can get over any difficulties with stubborn zips or awkward clasps.

THE LANGUAGE OF LOVE

Your voice is as important a part of your body as your hands or lips. You can give as much pleasure to your partner by telling them how much you love them, how much their body gives you pleasure, how skilful they are as a lover, how you love the sight of their breasts or penis.

The most loving thing you can do is to praise a part of the body you know your lover feels is unattractive, and assure them that you find their tummy cuddly or small breasts gorgeous. By this time, you should both be fully aroused and can extend your caresses to every other part.

EXPLORING EACH OTHER

Before intercourse, you will want to explore your partner's body, and have yours caressed and soothed.

One of the best ways to start is to take a shower or bath together. Not only will you prepare your bodies for love and be confident that you can offer yourself smelling and feeling as good as possible, but you will find that under water and with soap and shampoo, your hand will glide easily over your partner's body.

Skin, with its different textures, scent and sensitivity to changes of temperature, is the largest non-genital sexual organ. Yet it is often greatly ignored in lovemaking, especially by men who are less sensitive to touch than women.

Experimenting with hands, fingers and tongue as you explore each other's bodies can prolong the sensual pleasures before intercourse.

You can use both massage or baby oil or cream to help you stroke your partner and make both of you relaxed and happy.

Spread a large towel over the bed or on the floor so you do not have to worry about stains, and take it in turns to oil or cream and caress each other. At this stage, stay away from the erogenous zones – they are of special sensitivity and excitement.

Leave the genitals, the insides of thighs and the breasts for a little later on and for now, concentrate on every other part of the body.

Let your fingers, palms, lips and tongue explore each other from the ends of your toes to the top of your heads. You will find gradually that every part of your body responds to your partner's touch and that some areas are more sensitive, and make you react more pleasurably than others.

Encourage your partner to make clear which areas of his or her body are most responsive to your touch and what sort of caresses he or she prefers –

DECIDING WHEN TO DO IT

Before embarking on a plan for a long session of sex you need to agree with your partner, if only tacitly, that this is something pleasant for both of you at that particular time.

From the moment you decide on a long lovemaking session concentrate on each other's needs. If you both feel valued and cherished you are far more likely to want to spend a great deal of time making love.

It is obviously easier during holidays and weekends to give your partner full attention and build up gradually and pleasantly towards sex. But even a working day can be made special through a few extra gestures – bringing your partner a cup of coffee in bed, a very loving kiss when you say goodbye and perhaps a phone call just to say 'How are you?'

Nearer the time when you plan to make love you need to make absolutely sure that the following conditions are satisfied – time is an obvious one. You can hardly set out to make slow, sensuous love if you are expecting an important phone message, or you know your children might be arriving home any minute or a visitor might call. Warmth and comfort are also essential. Goose pimples and shivers from the cold or a crick in the neck from an uncomfortable sofa are unhelpful distractions.

Finally, privacy is paramount. If you need to fit a lock on your bedroom door and take the phone off the hook, then do it. Sometimes we are conditioned to hurry sex because of early experiences when we were afraid of being interrupted by parents or flat mates.

and make sure you do the same yourself.

THE TONGUE BATH
Try using your tongue as well as your hands. Use long, broad, slow strokes of the tongue and apply as much saliva as possible. Cover every part of your partner's body, beginning on the back and then turning them over to cover their front.

As you reach the erogenous zones try blowing as well as licking – the sensation of air drying wettened skin can be enough to send a member of either sex into ecstasy. Do not, however, blow into your partner's ears or you will deafen them and never blow into a woman's vagina as this can cause serious damage – even death.

SLOW POSITIONS
There are several lovemaking positions which will help you maintain intercourse for long periods. All rely on giving the woman control of coital movement. Generally, the aim is to slow down the male partner for as long as both partners find desirable.

While a woman can experience several orgasms and continue to enjoy intercourse, once the man has come that stage of lovemaking for him is over for some time.

If he enters the plateau phase, it can often be difficult for him to stop his movements. But if his partner has control she can slow everything down. She can also withdraw his penis and use the squeeze technique to stop ejaculation. To do this she places her thumb on his frenulum, her index and middle finger on the other side of his penis, and gently squeezes.

THE WOMAN ON TOP
One position is 'female superior', where the man lies on his back and the woman sits astride. She can sit upright or lie full length on him, with her legs outside or inside his. By pressing a hand on the small of her back, this position gives stimulation to her clitoris by compressing his penis between her

body and his and allowing her as much freedom to move as gives her pleasure. Her partner can caress her breasts, and buttocks while she moves.

THE LAP OF LUXURY
A supple back is needed for this position – so if you have back troubles, be very careful. In this, the man sits on a bed with his legs outstretched. His partner lowers herself into his lap, stretches her legs over his and, providing both partners are ready, takes his penis into her vagina.

She can wrap her legs around his back, or relax with her legs stretched out on either side of him.

Both can sit back, supporting themselves on their hands, or she can cling around his neck, further clasped by him. He can also sit on her lap, with his legs over hers or wrapped around her back.

In a further variation, he can double his legs in a kneeling position, and she can lie back.

By raising one knee and resting her foot against his chest, she can control his thrusts by rocking her foot against him. He, in turn, can kiss and caress her foot – a very erotic action to many women.

SIDE-BY-SIDE
A particularly relaxing position is 'side-by-side'. The woman can rest on her partner's thigh, or he on

Side-by-side is a perfect intermediate position between the man on top and the woman on top. It allows you to keep the rhythm of lovemaking constant and saves wrenched muscles when you change

hers. Movement is restricted and so this position is ideal for slow, leisurely love.

In this position, both are able to use a hand to caress the other and can exchange long looks and kisses. Side-by-side is an ideal 'resting' position, which you can roll over into and use as a means of slowing down excitement for a while.

HOW TO MOVE

Movements are usually an 'in and out' thrusting, and it is these that primarily stimulate the man by rubbing the glans and the shaft of his penis. However, the clitoris can be equally stimulated by a side-to-side and swirling motion, similar to the 'bump and grind' movement made by strippers. Such movements can be highly exciting to the woman, while keeping her partner on 'hold'.

Most eastern societies practised the art of reserving ejaculation. A great lover was considered to be a man who could give his woman 'a thousand loving thrusts' and bring her to orgasm many times without himself ejaculating. The ideal seemed to be one emission every 100 bouts of love.

Most western men will feel that having both enjoyed the sensations and shared the closeness of prolonged intercourse, and having made sure his partner is satisfied, the best end to lovemaking is

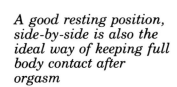

A good resting position, side-by-side is also the ideal way of keeping full body contact after orgasm

the gradual build up to and explosion of, orgasm.

GOING FOR AN ENCORE

In prolonged lovemaking, you will probably find that the woman is able to enjoy more than one orgasm. Depending on the age and fitness of the man, he too may want to 'go for an encore'.

A man over the age of 30 is likely to find the period his body takes to recover from orgasm is longer than when he was a youth. Even the youngest and fittest will need at least 20–30 minutes before his body can respond.

A shower or bath, a time of lying together, talking and enjoying each other's bodies, can some-times lead to a surprise – especially if the female partner uses her lips and tongue on his penis. However, if this part of his body is unable to oblige, remember that you do not need an erect penis to 'make love'.

THE MOMENTS AFTER

Using the rest of your body, you can continue to make love by caressing each other for as long as you choose. Many women say that the moments after sex are the most pleasurable. This is because their partners hold them and display affection.

After intercourse we can feel at our most relaxed, confident and trusting.

MULTIPLE ORGASM

Many women are capable of having multiple orgasms, but do not realize it. With care and tenderness from a loving partner they may reach heights they never thought possible

There are four stages of arousal and orgasm in a woman. In the first – the excitement phase – the woman's nipples become erect, her heart rate quickens, her breasts swell. Her vagina expands and lubricates and her clitoris enlarges.

In the next – plateau – phase the clitoris withdraws, and the top end of the vagina balloons out, and she progresses towards the third phase – orgasm.

Here, her breathing may become heavy, she may twitch or writhe with pleasure and cry or shout out. The muscles of her vagina contract rhythmically. After several contractions at the climax of her orgasm, her body goes into the final – resolution – stage. Things settle down and slowly, over perhaps ten minutes to half an hour, and if unstimulated, her body returns to its sexually unexcited state.

It is during this last – resolution – phase that many woman can have another orgasm.

HOW MANY WOMEN CAN HAVE THEM?

In the 1940s, the American sex researcher Kinsey found that one in seven women sometimes experienced multiple orgasms. Terman, another researcher, found the figures to be much the same. However, in the 1960s Masters and Johnson discovered that, given enough stimulation, most women were capable of having more than one orgasm. And they found that, in most cases, a woman was 'capable of having a second, third, fourth or even fifth and sixth orgasm before she is finally satisfied'. Many of the woman in their study were able to have five or six full orgasms within as many minutes.

More recent experience gathered in the *Cosmopolitan* report – a survey of 106,000 American women of all ages – showed that 67 per cent of the sample had multiple orgasms most of the time, with one in seven of all those over 35 saying that they

had them every time they made love. Of those who had multiple orgasms, 66 per cent had up to five in a single sexual episode, 13 per cent had between six and ten and 6 per cent had eleven or more.

MULTIPLE ORGASM AND MASTURBATION

Clearly, many more women have multiple orgasms than is generally realized, but the vast majority do not have them from intercourse alone. It is this that makes many men think that their partner is not multi-orgasmic when she is.

Most women have multiple orgasms only when masturbating – probably because they can control the situation and maintain stimulation for far longer than is possible during intercourse.

Masters and Johnson found that the largest numbers of orgasms occurred when women used vibrators.

The woman should show her partner what she most likes, letting him know exactly where to put his hands and how to use his fingers, then lying back to enjoy his attentions. When she is totally relaxed he can begin oral sex again, skilfully using his tongue on her outer and inner lips and her clitoris to bring her to orgasm – this time the first of many

IS ONE ENOUGH?

Some women – probably about one in three – are totally satisfied with a single climax, in the same way that a man is. Indeed many women say that stimulation after orgasm is painful and unpleasant and that it kills any further pleasure for them.

But just because direct clitoral stimulation produces their best orgasm first time, it does not mean it should be used for subsequent orgasms. Indeed, because the clitoris in the resolution phase is still erect and has now re-emerged from under its protective hood, it is still highly sensitive and direct stimulation may feel painful.

The secret is to use other methods of stimulating the clitoris indirectly. These include caressing the whole vulva area (keeping away from the clitoris), intercourse itself and stimulating some other part of the woman's body altogether.

This is why it is so common for a woman who has climaxed before intercourse (by direct clitoral stimulation) to come again when the couple are having intercourse (when clitoral stimulation is usually indirect).

ARE MULTIPLE ORGASMS NECESSARY?

Although, when it comes to human sexuality, there is no absolute truth in the 'more is better' theory, many women claim that their second or third orgasm is much stronger and more enjoyable than the first one.

For a woman on her own, the pleasure of multiple orgasms is purely selfish – and why should it not be? Women, unlike men, have been endowed with the capability to climax time and again until they are exhausted physically.

But many single-orgasm women put an unconscious brake on their ability to enjoy themselves. They may unconsciously ration themselves both in and out of bed, and as a result may never get the best out of all kinds of activities in life – not only sex.

FROM TIME TO TIME

Naturally, not all women have repeated climaxes every time they have sex or masturbate. The best times according to most women are just before, during or just after a period, during the middle three months of pregnancy and under extreme stimulation. While a few women have multiple orgasms every time they masturbate or make love, most need the mood to be just right and to have plenty of stimulation and foreplay and prolonged stimulation of the right areas of their body.

For the woman who feels she might be multiply orgasmic and has contented herself with a single orgasm, there are a number of things she can do. Even if it does not work out, the tips are pleasurable in themselves.

■ Start experimenting on your own during masturbation. Next time you feel especially sexy, perhaps around period time, get very aroused and then when you have had one orgasm, experiment with other ways of stimulating yourself until you have another. If you usually climax with your fingers stimulating your clitoris try a vibrator around the area until you come again.

If the clitoris is tender after the first orgasm, do not continue to stimulate it – find other ways of

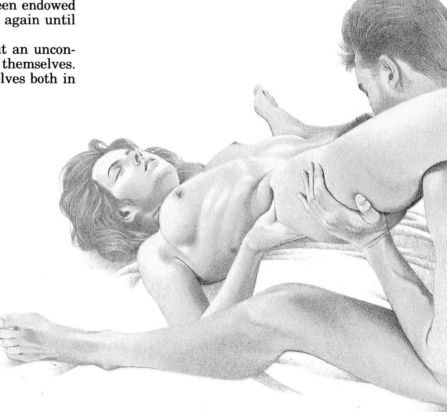

From kissing his partner's breasts, the man can move down her body and use his tongue to tease her clitoris, bringing her to the brink of orgasm

doing so indirectly. Try a vibrator or dildo inside your vagina. The rhythmical in and out movement will pull on the lips and stimulate your clitoris again.

Naturally, you may find, as many women do, that simply repeating what you did to get your first orgasm produces several more.

Do not forget to use all your favourite fantasies and erotica during this early stage. Once you have learned to have several orgasms you are ready to involve your partner.

■ When you are feeling very sexy, encourage your partner to stimulate your clitoris – possibly with his tongue – and give you a really enjoyable first orgasm.

Then, guided by what you have learned during masturbation, tell him what you would most like next. Do not expect him to be able to keep an erection for as long as you will need. Encourage him to use a vibrator or dildo on or inside you.

When you feel you have nearly had enough, let him make love to you. At first, he may be so excited at your new-found orgasms that he will come very quickly. As he becomes used to it, however, he will be better able to control his speed to orgasm.

If you want to have several orgasms, and he does not want to go in for that much stimulation, ask him to cuddle you or suck your breasts, while you masturbate and have several climaxes yourself before inviting him inside you for the final one.

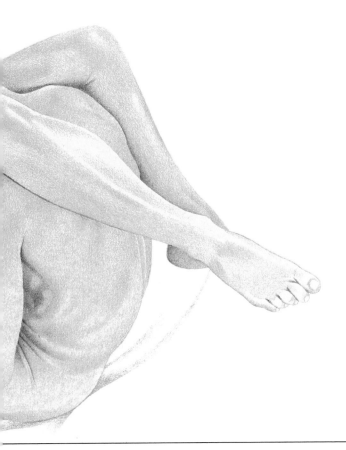

MEN AND MULTIPLE ORGASMS

Multiple orgasms in men are very rare. Young men in their teens and early 20s may be able to ejaculate several times one after the other, but few men over 20 can do so regularly.

In a man, the pleasurable sensations of orgasm come from the seminal fluid hitting the first part of the urinary passage deep in the prostate and expanding it.

When a man ejaculates after a day or two's abstinence, the volume of semen is the most it is likely to be and it explodes into the prostatic part of the urethra giving him intensely pleasurable sensations.

If he comes again within a couple of hours, the sensations are usually much less intense, because there has been insufficient time for fluid to build up again. This is all the more true if he is stimulated again within minutes of an orgasm.

The link between orgasm and ejaculation in men is a very vexed one. It is certainly true that men can have an orgasm – a feeling of intense excitement and release – without having an erection. This can be achieved by massaging the man's prostate gland. This almost always produces some sort of ejaculation – although it may appear feeble compared with one produced by direct stimulation of the penis.

A few men claim to have 'dry orgasms' – that is orgasms without ejaculation. They can have repeated orgasms – with all the physical and emotional signs, yet not ejaculate. This occurs most frequently in men who have already come several times in one lovemaking session, but it can also occur in some who have not.

The control of ejaculation is dealt with at great length in most eastern love texts, where methods that involve both psychological and physiological training are explained. Pressure on an acupuncture point above the male right breast creates a 'short circuit' and aids the retention of semen. This can be helped, according to tantric texts, by 'pressing the heel into the space between the scrotum and anus'.

■ Practice makes perfect and you may be surprised how quickly you become multiply orgasmic with less and less stimulation. If you then only have one orgasm on a particular day, do not worry. Your old pattern will soon come back.

■ Do not forget the G spot. Women who enjoy the front wall of their vagina being stimulated to orgasm say that the sensation is totally different from that produced during a clitorally induced orgasm. It is much 'deeper' and envelopes the body in a more voluptuous way.

DEEP PENETRATION

Few couples use positions for deep penetration every time they make love. Occasionally, however, a couple wish to experiment with positions that offer deep penetration and enjoy new sensations

Most men enjoy penetrating a woman's body as deeply as possible. Some see this as a total acceptance of them as men and lovers – others see it as demonstrating the control they have over the woman.

Deep penetration is also greatly enjoyed by some women, but most find it less attractive than do men. This is because the most erotic parts of a woman's vagina are at the entrance and the areas immediately inside. Generally the deeper a man goes in, the less sensitive are a woman's tissues.

THE MALE URGE
Men have an almost primitive urge to thrust deeply as they ejaculate and for many, if not most, men this deep thrusting is regarded as the best part of intercourse. Most women, however, prefer less deep penetration – at least on most occasions.

This is another area of give and take in a sexual relationship. The loving woman who may not particularly enjoy deep thrusting can, from time to time

when she is exceptionally aroused, allow her man to penetrate her deeply, even if it hurts for a few seconds. This can be a tremendous turn-on for the man who perceives that filling his woman so completely is a sign that he is in charge of lovemaking. At both the conscious and unconscious levels this is a game that some couples enjoy.

Many women like to be told that they are about to be penetrated very deeply indeed and some ask for more and deeper penetration, especially when highly aroused. Few men are unaffected by such behaviour, especially in a woman who is otherwise rather shy.

WHY BOTHER?

When a woman becomes sexually aroused the lower third of her vagina becomes greatly engorged with blood to form a 'barrel' of spongy tissue that grips the penis and makes the vagina feel 'tight'. Because of this swelling, deep penetration is not essential for a man to enjoy intercourse and many women claim that quite shallow penetration is especially exciting for them. However, occasionally, a couple will want to experiment with techniques which involve deep intercourse. There are several reasons for wanting to try it.

Deep penetration can be very passionate and exciting, especially as the woman has to press her thighs back against her stomach to let her partner penetrate her deeply. This 'opening up' of the whole of her pelvis to her man makes him feel especially wanted. And women similarly claim that they want their man to 'fill them up' and other such phrases.

For the couple who like very deep penetration it can provide entirely new sensations. The aroused vagina widens very greatly at the top end and this

The woman who wants to open herself up completely to her lover can take him into her while her legs are over his shoulders. This is a good position in cases where the man comes too fast since the woman's pelvis is stretched and direct stimulation to the penis diminished

means that deep penetration, rather than offering more stimulation to the head of the penis, actually stimulates it less. This gives a new dimension to the feel of the vagina for both the man and the woman.

Some women like deep penetration even when they are not fully aroused. The intense stretching caused by the penis deep inside her produces novel sensations and sometimes even some pain. For those who enjoy a little pain during sex this feeling can actually intensify the excitement.

THE BENEFITS

Deep penetration can also be useful for the man who has trouble with coming too soon. If his partner is aroused, her vagina will have expanded at the top end and so will offer less stimulation to a 'trigger-happy' penis. So, ironically, deep penetration can help him make love longer, whereas for the average man deep penetration makes him come.

The woman's thighs are pressed back against her stomach to allow deep penetration

ARE THERE ANY PROBLEMS?

Usually, deep penetration is highly arousing and the majority of couples greatly enjoy it. However, some do not.

A man with a tight foreskin which gives him little trouble in shallow intercourse can be in considerable pain when penetrating a woman deeply. If this is the case, he should see a doctor to have the problem sorted out. Apart from this, and the difficulties of the man who needs lots of penile stimulation if he is to climax, there are only rarely any problems with men when it comes to deep penetration. Some men may find that their penis tip receives little stimulation in deep penetration and that they have difficulty coming. The solution is simple – the couple should use positions that enable the penis to be grasped by the lower third of the vagina.

In women, there are several potential problems with deep penetration. A few perfectly normal, healthy women, find that really deep penetration hurts, especially if their man has an exceptionally long – as opposed to thick – penis. The answer is to find positions that do not put pressure on the sensitive areas.

Any woman who experiences true pain, rather than discomfort, in deep sex should see her doctor to sort out what the cause might be.

Another group of couples that benefit from deep penetration are those who are having difficulties conceiving. Even a relatively infertile couple – especially if the man has too few sperms – can conceive if they make love every other day around ovulation time (the fourteenth day of the average cycle) and the man penetrates his partner very deeply. If a couple is trying to conceive, the idea is to place the man's semen as close to the cervix as possible – and to keep it there.

Many women get up immediately after sex to wash or to go to the toilet. This should be avoided. She should remain lying down, preferably with her hips up on a pillow, for about half an hour after intercourse to make conception more likely.

If her uterus is retroverted (pointing the opposite way from normal) her doctor will tell her. Then if she wants to conceive it is best to use a rear-entry position – preferably an all-fours position with the woman's forehead on the bed. Again she should keep in this position for some time after sex to allow the sperm to enter the uterus.

THE NEED TO EXPERIMENT

For some women, very deep penetration brings their partner's pubic bone into contact with their clitoris, causing intense excitement from the repeated friction. For many women, though, this has no effect

and the pressure of their man's pelvis comes in entirely the wrong place and can be unpleasant. There is only one way to find out – experiment.

The cervix is the lowest part of the uterus and projects down into the top of the vagina. It can usually be felt by a woman herself if she squats and inserts her middle finger into her vagina. Almost all men can play with the cervix during foreplay.

Women vary in how much they are aroused by cervical stimulation, but some are very excited by being touched either by their man's fingers or his penis. Deep penetration positions enable such a woman to enjoy her man's penis stimulating her cervix, and this can be exceptionally nice for the man too. Some men say that hitting the cervix with their penis is one of the best parts about intercourse.

OTHER POSITIONS

Deep penetration in rear entry positions is very pleasant and highly arousing for those women who have a sensitive G spot. In front-entry positions the G spot does not become stimulated. Deep rear-entry positions are excellent for such women.

Some women greatly enjoy being on top of their man and then positioning their body so that they can direct the penis tip to stimulate the front wall of the vagina. Many men find this exciting because the woman is totally and wholeheartedly using his penis to bring her to her own climax.

During the middle three months of pregnancy, when the vagina is widening and lengthening, some couples find that normal intercourse positions feel 'sloppy' or 'loose' for the penis. This is the time when deep penetration can be very exciting.

In the last month of pregnancy it is probably not

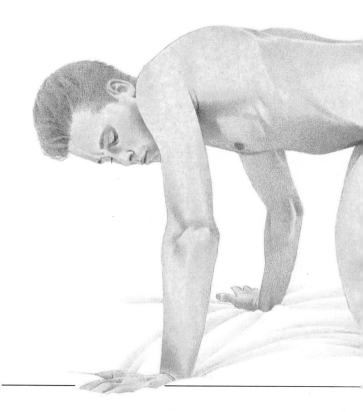

sensible to use deep penetration positions just in case it starts off labour. This is especially likely to occur in a woman who has a history of premature labour. However, deep penetration can be a very pleasant way of starting off labour if you are overdue. The direct penile stimulation, the high level of excitement and the absorption of muscle-contracting prostaglandins from the semen all help to begin to contract the uterus.

Positions for deep penetration can be simplified to a single rule. Any position in which a woman's thighs are close to her tummy will provide the right opportunity for deep penetration. There are, however, a few that are exceptionally successful.
■ The missionary position, but with the woman's thighs drawn back with her hands behind her knees and her bottom on a pillow.
■ The missionary position, but with her legs over his shoulders as he bears down on her. If she is very supple she can place her knees on her breasts. For the athletic, her toes can touch the bed at either side of her head. Another variation of this is for the woman to get into this last position and for the man to penetrate her facing away from her head.
■ Spoons position. The man cuddles into the woman's back as she lies facing away from him. She draws her knees up to her chest and he penetrates her deeply. This is very relaxing – probably the most relaxing of the deep penetration positions.
■ Woman on all-fours facing away from the man. Any of the all-fours positions give deep penetration, but the best ones involve the woman placing her forehead and the top of her chest flat on the bed. Her bottom then sticks right up in the air and he can penetrate her deeply.

Standing with his woman in his arms, her body pressing gently against his, allows for very deep penetration, and special kind of intimacy

■ The woman sits on the man. Most of these are not very deep penetration positions, but if the woman is sufficiently supple and can squat on the man's penis with her feet flat on the bed or floor she can angle the penis to stimulate her cervix or her G spot. However, this may take a lot of practice.
■ Standing. For the athletic and strong man, sex in a standing position can offer very deep penetration. The woman holds on around his neck and grasps him with her legs by winding them around his back. Little movement is possible but penetration can be good. It is, however, very tiring for the man.

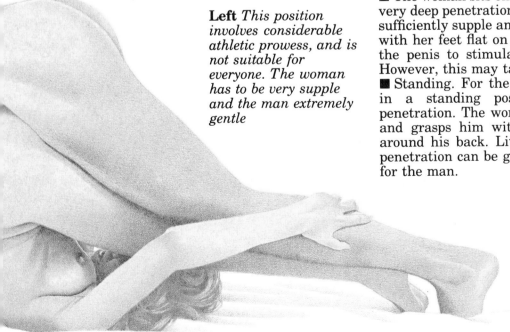

Left *This position involves considerable athletic prowess, and is not suitable for everyone. The woman has to be very supple and the man extremely gentle*

IMPROVING YOUR ORGASMS

*You can achieve better
quality orgasms and gain maximum
pleasure from your lovemaking*

Orgasms vary from day to day, from year to year and from partner to partner. In a woman, the time of the month, the man she is with, her previous sexual experience and her current emotional state can all affect the quality of the orgasms she experiences. And in a man, outside factors can also work to enhance or inhibit his ability to achieve pleasurable orgasms.

For those people who feel that the quality of their orgasms could be improved, there are a few self-help techniques that can go some way to achieving this. For the woman, these include becoming more aware of her sexuality, and more familiar with her genitals.

All women have sexier and less sexy times of the months. Most women feel at their most arousable just before, or just after a period, but some feel sexiest during a period or in the middle of the cycle at around the time of ovulation.

By charting your cycle for several months, and seeing how pleasurable or frequent your orgasms are, you will soon get to know how sexy you are likely to feel at certain times and how good an orgasm you are likely to achieve.

If, for example, you feel very un-sexy and take ages to become aroused just before menstruation, it will explain why orgasms are difficult to come by or are of fairly poor quality at this time. Once you know this, it takes pressure off you (and your partner) and you can settle for fewer orgasms, or less pleasurable ones, knowing what the reason is.

SELF-PLEASURING

Next, embark on a programme of self-pleasuring. The idea is to learn how best to pamper yourself. Learn how to enjoy a long bath. Massage yourself with soap and find which areas of your body feel most sensitive.

When you are dry, lie on the bed and repeat the procedure with some body oil or talcum powder.

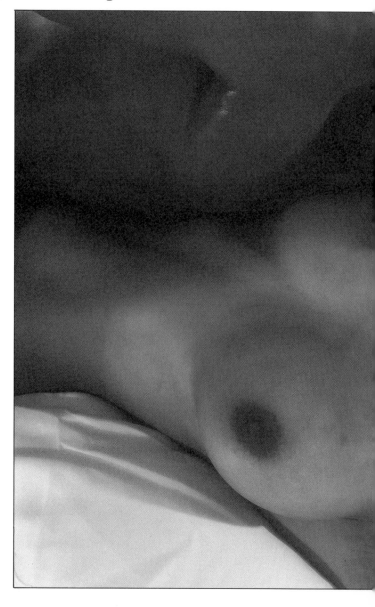

Slowly discover what best excites you. This knowledge can then be incorporated into your foreplay or masturbation, as the mood takes you. All this enhances arousal and can greatly improve the quality of your subsequent orgasms.

KNOW YOUR GENITALS

Self-examination can be very instructive. Most women know little about their own genitals and a large minority have never really looked at them. As a result, they harbour all kinds of unconscious fears and worries which in turn can harm their potential for orgasms. Lie down one day when you are relaxed and have just had a bath, take a hand mirror and, in a good light, look in detail at your vulval area.

Next, put a finger inside and feel the vaginal walls. By inserting the finger deeply, you will come to the cervix – a part of the womb that feels like a nose-tip with a hole in the end. Explore this and see

how it feels when you touch and stimulate it.

Now squat down and try to feel up the front wall of your vagina and see if there is an area that is especially arousing to stimulate. There often is one about two thirds of the way up the front wall. Massage this area (the G spot) deeply and see how it feels. Some women experience far better orgasms from this kind of stimulation than they do from stimulating the clitoris.

If you wish, you can buy a vaginal speculum (disposable plastic ones are available in surgical stores and larger chemists) and actually look inside your own vagina. This helps many women to realize just what 'normal' is for them and demystifies their genitals.

A man can easily become familiar with his genitals, but it is easy to forget that so much of importance in a woman lies inside her and thus cannot be seen without making a special effort.

AROUSAL

A very useful part of this self-examination programme is to repeat it all when you are aroused. Some women who believe that they do not ever become aroused find it instructive to see their vaginal lubrication increasing and their outer and inner lips swelling. This can help the shy woman acknowledge that her body does in fact react normally to sexual excitement.

SENSUAL MASSAGE

Now learn sensual massage with your partner. The idea is for the receiver to say exactly what she wants and most likes when being massaged and for the giver to adhere exactly to what is requested.

This unconditional, no questions asked, type of giving and receiving can be a wonderful prelude to sex or simply a good way of sharing without sex in mind. Certainly, the massage itself should be non-genital and avoid the breasts and nipples.

Many women who have reasonable orgasms will usually feel so relaxed and 'safe' with their partner after a massage that they will have more or better orgasms, or both.

STRENGTHENING YOUR PELVIC MUSCLES

Exercising your pelvic muscles greatly enhances the quality of your orgasms and can even make a non-orgasmic woman more likely to have one.

Sit on the toilet and, as you pass water, stop the flow using the muscles deep in your pelvis. Keep on stopping and starting until you can do this easily.

Now pretend that your vagina is a lift and slowly, and in a very controlled way, raise the lift from floor to floor right up to the top and then lower it slowly again. Repeat this many times a day at first – in the car, in the supermarket queue, or wherever you like.

The most severe test of pelvic muscle control and a way of knowing that you have done all you can, is to insert a pencil (blunt end inwards) a few inches into the vagina. Now, try gently to pull it out against the grip of your pelvic muscles. If you can grip it firmly, your muscles are about as strong as you will ever make them.

Not only will this greatly enhance the enjoyment of your orgasms but it will, if you use the muscles during intercourse, also make sex more exciting for your partner.

SEX ENHANCERS

Sex aids, and especially a vibrator, can make all the difference between having a good orgasm and having a really great one. Use the vibrator around the vulval and clitoral areas until you find the best way to excite yourself. The place you will need to stimulate may change within any one arousal experience.

You may like to put something inside your vagina, too, to enhance your orgasm. The best by far is a finger or two, but some women like to have a vibrator or dildo inside them. It is purely a matter of individual taste and style.

Teach your partner to stimulate you better during loveplay. This is probably the single most valuable thing to do when going out for better orgasms during lovemaking.

BETTER STIMULATION

Almost all women learn how to have orgasms first during masturbation, and thus become experts in their own arousal. Many men ignore this and do things they want or things they believe their partner may want, rather than what actually best pleases their woman. In most relationships, it is up to the man to experiment. This is especially so if the woman is shy and cannot or will not say what she best likes.

One way around this is for the man to watch his partner masturbating and then to mimic what she does. Any enhancements, such as different types of clitoral stimulation or a particular sort of vaginal activity can be added as a result of trial-and-error experimentation.

EMOTION AND ORGASM

The quality of a woman's relationship with her man greatly affects the quality of her orgasm. Few women who are hostile, unhappy, unloved or badly treated will relax enough to get the best out of their orgasms. This could mean doing something about your relationship, perhaps with the help of a

Most women best know how to arouse themselves, so try to overcome any shyness you may have and let your partner watch you masturbate. This will allow him to see what you like best and in future lovemaking sessions he can incorporate what he learns into foreplay and increase the enjoyment for you both

Once you have mastered the self-help technique your lovemaking can reach new heights of pleasure for both partners

professional counsellor or therapist. Many women who have poor quality orgasms greatly improve when their love and romantic lives are sorted out.

Sex usually suffers in both quality and quantity, if a couple's relationship is bad, so any improvement you can make in this area will almost certainly pay off handsomely.

USING FANTASY

Fantasy plays an enormous part in the quality of most women's orgasms. At one end of the spectrum are those women who cannot fantasize at all.

At the other are those who can turn an average orgasm into a stunning one simply by changing their fantasy.

Most women, and indeed men, have a small bank of fantasies that work for them, but it makes sense to add to them over the years so as to keep your fantasy life rich and growing.

EXERCISES FOR BETTER ORGASMS

It is usually easy for a man to explore his genitals – at least when compared with a woman – so that there is not the same mystique surrounding them.

Most men can learn at least something, however, from a study of their arousal cycle – something which can then be incorporated into their foreplay, or even intercourse, to improve their orgasms.

Penis exercises, like pelvic muscle exercises in women, have a valuable part to play. The best

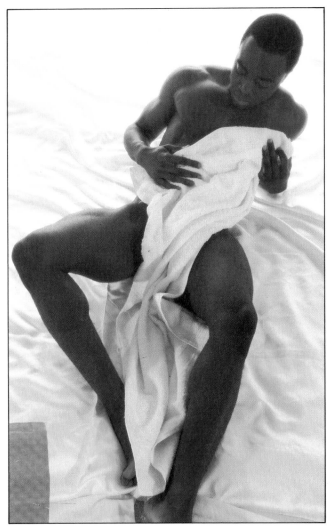

Explore your body to discover the areas that are most sensitive to touch – you may find some surprises

starter exercise is the 'stop-start' game. In this the man obtains an erection, and then stops stimulating the penis, perhaps also squeezing the top between thumb and two fingers, until it goes down.

He then re-excites it and repeats this procedure several times until he feels that he has good control and can restrain himself from having an orgasm until he really wants one.

The next penis exercise involves hanging a small towel or similar object on the erect penis. By using his pelvic muscles, he can keep the erection hard and the towel in place. As he becomes more ambitious, he can add more weight to the penis in the form of more, or wet, towels.

This type of training improves penile stamina and often the quality of erection and orgasm. If the man's partner is delighted by these attributes, which she almost certainly will be, and things go well for them both, as a result of her pleasure alone, he will have a better-quality orgasm.

CHAPTER EIGHT

LOVE POSITIONS

MAN ON TOP

*Lovemaking positions where the
man is on top are not always
passive for the woman. With many
of them, a woman can control the degree of
penetration and dictate
the pace of intercourse*

For most couples, the most popular position in which to make love is the so-called 'missionary position' in which the woman lies on her back with her legs open as she is penetrated by the man who lies on top of her. This is the basic model of all man-on-top positions – all the others tend to be variations on the same theme.

The missionary position is the most popular of all lovemaking positions for many reasons:

■ It is considered by many women to be the most romantic of positions. This is almost certainly because the couple are always face to face. Every expression can be noticed, they are free to kiss if they wish, and each partner can see that they are being loved – something that is not possible in some other positions, such as the rear-entry ones.

■ Also, the missionary position, being such a passive one for the woman, absolves her of the responsibility to make anything much happen. Some women can relax and enjoy lovemaking more if they do not take the dominant active role.

■ Many women experience great pleasure from being dominated during intercourse. Such women enjoy sex particularly if the man is in control and makes everything happen. The missionary position is ideal for this. The man, being on top, controls the thrusting and can pin the woman down to the bed and take her roughly and at his pace.

■ Being 'taken' like this can be highly exciting to some women. For the woman who is at all guilty about her sexual needs and appetites this position leaves her free of guilt, because she can think of herself as being overpowered by a much stronger man.

■ For the woman who is aroused by nipple stimulation, the man-on-top position allows the man to kiss her nipples.

■ By altering the angle of her thighs to her tummy the woman can change the degree of penetration even if the man stays in exactly the same position.

One of the great benefits of the missionary position is that it allows a couple to kiss and caress each other. And perhaps more importantly, it allows them to talk to each other easily. This is particularly useful for a couple who are making love for the first time and have little knowledge of each other's preferences

As she brings her knees nearer to her chest, the penis goes in deeper. The woman can find just the right angle to give her the best sensations – perhaps as her lover stimulates her cervix with the tip of his penis. A more sophisticated variation of this is for the woman to rock her pelvis backwards and forwards. If, at the same time, she 'milks' her partner's penis by contracting and relaxing her pelvic muscles, this can be extremely exciting for him.

■ The man-on-top positions are very good for couples who are trying for a baby, because penetration can be very deep.

If the woman holds on to her legs behind her knees and draws her thighs right back, sperm can be deposited deep in the vagina – at the neck of the womb. This provides the best chance of conception occuring.

■ Because it is a romantic, yet fairly unadventurous position, it is a particularly good one when having sex with a new partner. While you are still learning about one another, it makes sense to go for a position that is non-threatening and loving. It allows a couple to kiss and caress. The woman's hands are free to caress the man. This could be especially valuable – showing him that he is loved and wanted in the new relationship. The missionary position lays neither partner open to strangeness, anxiety and unfamiliarity.

■ Because the man has control of the thrusting he can control his speed to orgasm. This is good news for the individual who fears losing control of ejaculation. A 'trigger-happy' man can thus stop when he feels ejaculation approach, and a man who needs a great deal of thrusting to maintain his erection will also benefit.

■ For the man who loses his erection in woman-on-top positions – erections are harder to maintain when the man is on his back – the man-on-top position is ideal. Indeed, it might be the only way he can maintain an erection, especially in middle age.

THE EASTERN WAY

The *Kama Sutra* and Chinese pillow books list numerous variations on the missionary position. Often the difference is in slight detail only, but there are many other simple, man-on-top positions that can be tried for a change.

■ Missionary position with one of the woman's legs pulled back to her chest. This is a pleasant variation that skews her pelvis and can enable the man to stimulate her ovary on one side. This may be tender for some women, so the man should be careful.

■ The man kneels and raises the woman's buttocks on to the lower part of his thighs as he penetrates her. She crosses her ankles behind his back. This reduces the depth of penetration considerably, but can be a very exciting position for the woman who enjoys having her vaginal opening teased and stimulated.

■ The man kneels between her open thighs, penetrates her, and the lifts her bottom from the

Here, the man kneels on the bed and raises his partner's buttocks on to the lower part of his thighs as he penetrates her. She can then cross her ankles behind his back. This considerably reduces the degree of penetration possible, but gives increased opportunity for the man to stimulate his partner's vaginal opening

A relaxing position for the woman but a potentially tiring one for the man. The woman relaxes on a bed, her legs hanging over the side. The man enters her and leans forward on her body, taking most of his weight on his forearms or hands. This position offers little scope for movement and limits the degree of penetration

bed so as to bring her as close as possible to his pelvis. This can produce superb sensations for both partners, but it is tiring for the woman to keep her back arched in this way for very long. One answer is to put a couple of pillows under her bottom – although these can get in the way.

■ The woman lies over the edge of the bed or a low stool with her legs open. The man enters her and leans forwards on her body, taking most of his weight on his forearms or hands. This can be very tiring for the man, because movement is restricted. It is, therefore, not a very suitable position for the couple who enjoy, or need, deep thrusting during lovemaking.

■ The woman lies on her side and raises her upper leg. The man cuddles into the front of her body and penetrates her. She curls her upper leg over his body. Here again the angle of entry of the penis can be to one side, stimulating unfamiliar parts of the woman's pelvic organs. Most couples find this a very loving and restful position – the man does not have to support his weight. However, movement is restricted and the woman may have to contract her pelvic muscle to give her man the best pleasure.

■ A variation is for the woman to raise her upper leg so as to open up her pelvis further and 'release' him from the clamping effect around his waist. This now allows him considerable movement, even though they are both on their sides, and she can obtain new and different sensations as she angles her upper leg differently.

Positions in which the man lifts his partner's bottom and thighs off the bed allow her little movement but enable him to thrust deeply, giving her unforgettable sensations

ADVANCED POSITIONS

Some of the positions described here require both partners to be in tip-top condition physically, so you will need to train yourself to fitness before attempting the more athletic ones.

■ The woman lies face up on the bed and draws her knees up to her chest. The man then enters her and she puts her ankles over both of his shoulders. The woman will find this position more comfortable if she places a pillow under the small of her back.

If the man pushes his partner's knees right on to her breasts and kisses her while her ankles are still over his shoulders, he will achieve exceptionally deep penetration.

This position calls for suppleness on the part of the woman. A good exercise for this is for the woman to lie on her back, and slowly – over several sessions – try to get her feet further and further back over the body until she can touch the ground behind her head with her toes.

If the couple stay in this position for some time after sex, with the man on top taking the weight of his body on his hands, it gives the woman the best chance of conceiving as semen bathes the cervix and none spills out of the vagina.

■ The man kneels down in front of the woman who has her hips raised very high. He supports her hips with both hands and penetrates her. This angles the penis horizontally, while the woman's vagina is nearly vertical. This allows the penis to stimulate the front wall of the vagina and stretch the vaginal opening. This can be highly exciting for the woman who enjoys having her G spot stimulated. The man can, by adjusting his partner's position, get his penis tip into just the right place to do this.

■ Making love with the woman lying back in a large armchair can be very relaxing for her and stimulating for the man. She lies with her hips very near the front of the chair. He kneels between her open legs and can hold her legs wide apart while he penetrates her. She can easily reach down and caress her clitoris with one hand and her breasts or nipples with the other.

This is a very good position for learning about sex with a new partner, because it enables the woman to stimulate herself to produce the best sensations while she is being penetrated. It is quite awkward for the man to caress her clitoris, but it can be done.

Movement is easy in this position, and the man can thrust as deeply as the angle of the woman's vagina will permit.

Penetration is quite deep – but not so deep that the position cannot be used during pregnancy. If the man angles his penis correctly he can stimulate the G spot, and his hands are free to caress all the front of her body.

■ The woman lies with her bottom close to the edge of a bed. The man lies on top of her – facing away from her with his knees either side of her chest. His weight is taken by his hands on the floor as he lies over the edge of the bed. His penis penetrates her in the reverse way to normal as she puts her feet on his shoulders.

This is a position for occasional fun and variation and is ideal for the man who likes his anus being played with or his G spot stimulated during intercourse. There are only a few positions where this can be achieved.

■ For the really adventurous and athletic, the woman can lie as a bridge, her legs on the bed and her head and shoulders on a chair at the front of the bed. She opens her legs and the man straddles her hips and penetrates her facing away from her face.

This position is fairly uncomfortable for all concerned, but if the woman arches her back and both partners move their pelvises they can achieve a stimulating sensation.

■ A more realistic version of this is for the woman to lie flat on her back on the bed with her legs apart. The man faces away from her and kneels with his legs either side of her chest. She draws up her legs, he penetrates her and rests face down on the bed, possibly supporting himself on his elbows. She puts her feet on his back.

Like all reverse-entry positions in which the man faces the opposite way to normal, this position brings the penis into contact with unfamiliar parts of the woman's anatomy, particularly the back wall of the woman's vagina.

The bottom of the penis shaft stimulates the clitoral area and this suits the woman who likes clitoral stimulation during intercourse. If the man leans forward a little, his penis goes more vertically into her vagina and leaves her room to caress her clitoris.

The position is very restful for the woman and would be suitable for early pregnancy and for the woman whose back vaginal wall is exceptionally sensitive. (Most women find that the front wall is most arousable, especially in the area of the G spot.)

■ The woman lies flat on her back with her head on a pillow. She raises her legs in the air and parts them slightly. The man kneels with his knees on either side of her waist and penetrates her facing away from her with his legs either side of her hips. Again, he may well have to support himself on his forearms or hands. The woman can easily stimulate her clitoris and caress his anus or G spot.

■ The woman lies on a low table with her feet flat on the floor and wide apart. The man enters her. Penetration is shallow, but can be greatly enhanced if she raises her legs to put her ankles over his shoulders. He can hold her legs apart with her soles facing the ceiling as he penetrates her deeply and with good, long thrusts.

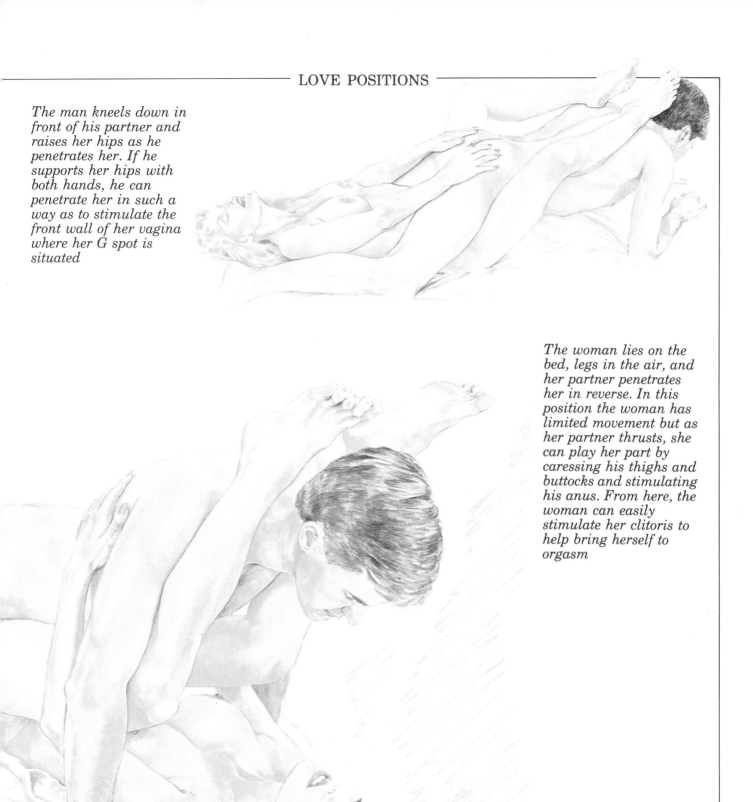

The man kneels down in front of his partner and raises her hips as he penetrates her. If he supports her hips with both hands, he can penetrate her in such a way as to stimulate the front wall of her vagina where her G spot is situated

The woman lies on the bed, legs in the air, and her partner penetrates her in reverse. In this position the woman has limited movement but as her partner thrusts, she can play her part by caressing his thighs and buttocks and stimulating his anus. From here, the woman can easily stimulate her clitoris to help bring herself to orgasm

If the woman lies close to the edge of the bed and pulls her knees towards her chest, the man can lean over her, supporting his weight on his hands and penetrate her very deeply. This is another ideal position for the couple who want a baby

WOMAN ON TOP

*For the woman who likes to take the sexual
initiative and the man who enjoys watching
his partner as they make love, woman-on-top
positions cannot be beaten*

With today's vogue for women having a greater say in their sexuality, woman-on-top lovemaking positions are becoming more popular than ever. Until fairly recently, it was considered that only a very 'abandoned' woman or a whore would take the lead in this way. Today, rather like oral sex, it has become a fashionable alternative to man-on-top positions that is widely practised. Certainly, the woman-on-top positions have several advantages:

■ Perhaps the biggest single advantage of woman-on-top positions is that the woman is, and feels, in control. This can be of benefit to both partners. Almost all men say that on some occasions, at least, they like to have the initiative taken away from them, and just as some women feel flattered to be pinned to the bed and taken with great ardour, so it is also true that many men like to be 'taken' by their female partner in this way.

For some men, this will have to be a frequent occurrence because they do not have sufficient self-esteem or sexual drive to be able to make things happen themselves. The woman taking the lead can be a life-saver in this type of relationship. Real trouble arises if both partners are so inhibited that nothing much happens at all.

■ Making love with the woman on top gives her the opportunity to angle her partner's penis to exactly where she most enjoys it. She is also in control of it in a way she cannot be when being penetrated in a conventional man-on-top position.

■ For the woman who needs very specific stimu-

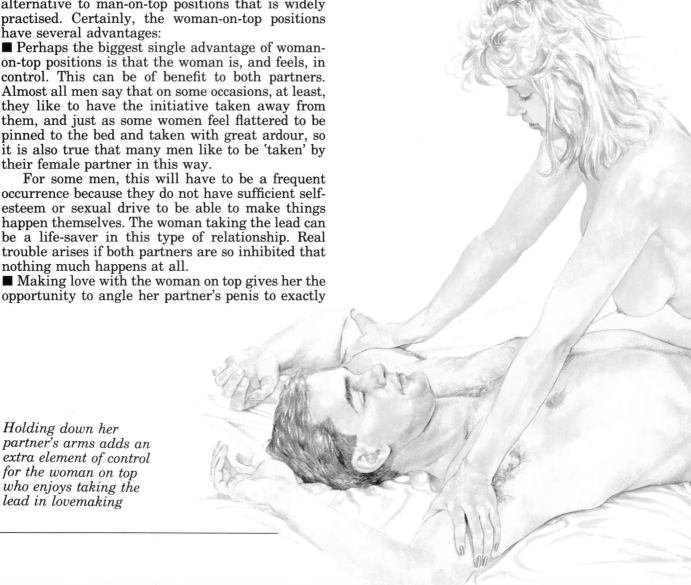

*Holding down her
partner's arms adds an
extra element of control
for the woman on top
who enjoys taking the
lead in lovemaking*

lation which her partner may be too lazy, or unable to provide, the position can make all the difference between her really enjoying intercourse (with or without an orgasm) or not.

■ The woman's G spot is more easily stimulated in this position. The woman can angle her body in such a way as to allow the penis to stimulate the most sensitive part of her vaginal wall.

■ The woman can control the depth of penetration. As she kneels over the man and takes his penis she can control not only the amount of penetration but also the speed of thrusting. At the same time she can caress her clitoris very easily. This provides yet more excitement and can all help to produce more or better orgasms than in other positions.

■ They are ideal positions for a woman when she is pregnant. There is no pressure on her stomach and she can control penetration depth, angle and speed in a way which causes her no discomfort. The man can see her stomach, caress it and her enlarged breasts, and the whole episode can be highly arousing for both partners. Using a woman-on-top position, a pregnant woman can go on having intercourse until very late pregnancy.

■ Some men climax too quickly, and premature ejaculators need to gain more control. A man's erection and ejaculation reflexes are slowed down when he is on his back – so these woman-on-top positions are a real help. If the man feels he is coming too soon he can signal to his partner who can then get off the penis and squeeze it until he loses the urge to come. She can then re-erect it by stroking, kissing or caressing it and intercourse can resume until he learns to gain ejaculatory control.

■ Woman-on-top positions are also good for when the man is very tired or ill and cannot take the lead sexually. This can be especially useful after the man

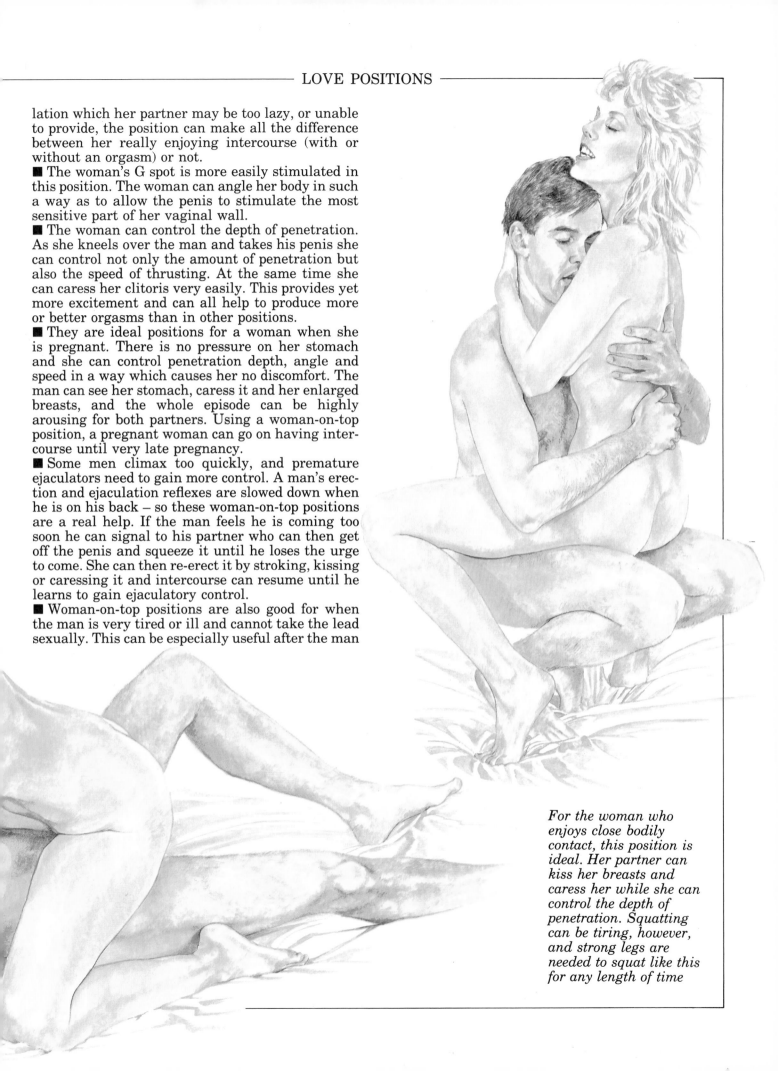

For the woman who enjoys close bodily contact, this position is ideal. Her partner can kiss her breasts and caress her while she can control the depth of penetration. Squatting can be tiring, however, and strong legs are needed to squat like this for any length of time

has recently had a serious illness or surgery. By using a woman-on-top position the couple can get back to sex much sooner than they otherwise would if the man were having to be more active.

■ If the woman squats or kneels over the man's hips, penetration can be really deep. By angling her body forwards or backwards she can greatly improve the sensations for both of them.

■ The positions are also exceptionally good for the cautious or anxious woman who is being treated for vaginismus (painful spasm of the vaginal muscles), after a vaginal operation, or even after a baby.

In many lovemaking positions, the woman's movements are restricted. This is fine for the passive, inhibited woman who sees sex as something that is 'done to' her. Most woman-on-top positions, though, offer a wide range of movement. Apart from

moving up and down on the penis, she can move around on it, rock backwards and forwards on it, and even keep it inside her and turn completely around.

A sequel to this is that many of these positions can also be adopted with the woman facing away from the man's head.

Now, more than ever, she can fantasize and can more easily reach down and caress her clitoris, because her body faces away from his and she does not feel so shy. Of course, when facing away from the man, she loses all possibilities for kissing him, his kissing and caressing her breasts, and both of

This position is fairly restful and comfortable for both partners. Penetration can be very deep and the woman can add to her pleasure by stimulating her clitoris. If the man uses one hand to support his weight, he can use the other to fondle his partner's breasts

them watching one another's reactions and pleasure. But this need not be a disadvantage. It is simply a matter of going for different sensations at different times.

If the woman kneels over her partner's hips, for example, and takes the penis inside her, she can lean forward and display her thighs and bottom to him in an enticing way. For the bottom-centred man this is highly pleasurable and he can, if she likes it, stimulate her anus and cuddle her buttocks.

Kneeling positions are fine, but any form of squatting position can be very tiring and call for strong legs.

Perhaps the most basic, simple position, is with the man lying flat on his back.

■ Here, the woman kneels over her man's body facing his head and inserts his penis. By moving her body up and down she can control both the speed and depth of penetration. She can arrange things so that penetration is very deep. He can caress her body, and breasts especially, which hang down tantalizingly close to him and bounce around as she moves. This can be very exciting for the man. Also, he can see his penis going into her vagina, which again is stimulating. Because her weight is being taken on her legs her hands are free to caress him.

■ A variation of this position is for the woman to lean forwards so that her breasts are on his chest. This reduces movement severely but she can still raise and lower her hips. The danger here is that, depending on the anatomical position of the woman's vagina, the penis can pop out easily.

■ It is important to remember when thinking about any sex positions that women's vulvas are very different. Some women's genitals are set very much more forward than those of others. This brings the penis into contact with the clitoris in a different way and means that deep penetration for one couple will be shallow for others. Experimentation is the name of the game. Discovering what is best for both partners can also be a lot of fun.

■ Finally, the woman can kneel over the man's penis, facing away from him. This gives deep penetration and allows him to stimulate her bottom and anus. He can watch the penis going in and out of her, especially if she leans forwards. If she is strong enough to support herself on one arm, she can stimulate her clitoris with the other hand.

ADVANCED POSITIONS

Probably the biggest advantage of woman-on-top positions is that the woman herself can control the proceedings. Yet in a number of the more 'advanced' positions, this is not the case. In fact, many of them allow very little room for movement or penetration at all. In spite of this they all have several points to recommend them.

■ They show the man that his partner is willing to be inventive in lovemaking.

■ For the woman, some of the positions give novel pelvic sensations that cannot be achieved in any other way. Just how worthwhile such relatively uncomfortable positions are for any one woman is clearly up to her. Perhaps even a few minutes in one of these positions would be enough to stimulate a part of her pelvis so as to arouse her as no other position can.

■ Most of the positions are restful for the man and so are good if he is ill, very tired or recovering from an operation or illness.

■ They are also very good for those women who want to use their pelvic muscles to stimulate their man while he is inside them. This can be combined with squirming movements of the pelvis and even perhaps some rotation of the pelvis. All of this is extremely attractive to the man who greatly enjoys his penis being 'used' by his partner for her personal and private pleasure.

■ Some women greatly enjoy having a finger, vibrator or dildo in their anus as they are penetrated vaginally in one of these positions. For the woman who can not actually make this happen in practice, even the fantasy of it in one of these positions can enhance her enjoyment of the act.

A CAUTIONARY NOTE

When adopting one of the positions in which the man stimulates the woman's anus, he must never put a finger that has been inside her anus into her vagina. This can cause a transfer of bacteria that can produce a urinary infection.

TRIAL AND ERROR

As with all lovemaking positions, experiment with what you think might work and if it produces pleasant sensations for either one of you, share your feelings and pleasure with your partner. Often, such athletic positions do not produce benefits on a par with the effort and discomfort that they involve. Do not persevere if any position hurts or annoys your partner. Go back to one of your tried-and-tested ones and perhaps try one of these more unusual ones

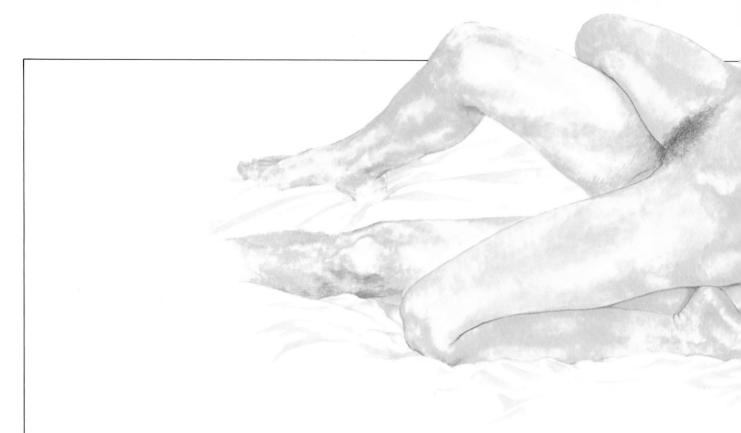

another day when the woman is at a different part of her menstrual cycle, is more aroused, or when you both want some fun before actually getting down to making love in one of your favourite positions.

Just because a particular position does not do much for either or both of you on any one day, it does not mean that you will never get anything out of it. Try it again and see what, if anything, becomes arousing or simply enjoyable.

The woman who is hesitant or shy about taking the lead in lovemaking should first experiment with woman-on-top positions which allow her partner to hold her. If she sits astride him, face forward, for example, she can lean forward and he can cuddle, kiss and caress her as they make love.

Once she has become more used to these positions she can try the more inventive and athletic woman-on-top positions. Many of these are difficult to maintain for any length of time, but they can produce new and different sensations.
■ The man lies flat on his back on the bed with his bottom on the edge and his legs supported on a chair. The woman stands astride his closed legs and inserts his penis into her vagina. She then leans forwards, facing away from him, to lie on his legs, supporting most of her weight on her feet and and forearms.

This is expectionally good for the man who finds his partner's bottom stimulating to look at while making love. If the couple enjoy it, it is very easy to stimulate her anus and buttocks and the man can, by simply looking down, watch as his penis penetrates her.

Movement is not all that good unless he pushes her bottom up and down with his hands. Anything else is very tiring for her unless she has strong legs.

She can kiss his feet and stroke her breasts across his lower legs to add pleasure to the whole position. The man is, of course, virtually pinned down and and can do almost nothing in the way of thrusting. This can be a pleasant position for the woman who wants a lot of bottom stimulation and possibly her anus played with or penetrated with a finger.
■ The man sits on a chair with his legs wide apart. The woman kneels on the seat of the chair with her legs either side of his pelvis, and her back to him and sits on his penis. She then leans forward to support herself on his knees with her hands. He holds her around the waist and can not only steady her in this rather unstable position but can also, to some extent, control penetration by putting her on to his penis or pushing her further off it.

Movement is not very good and penetration is poor, but short jabbing motions are possible and some women greatly enjoy this. Once again the woman's bottom is very much on show and the man can closely watch his penis penetrating her.

The position is, however, rather tiring on the woman's arms. A way around this is for her to lean right forward to rest her hands on the floor between his feet. She can even rest her forehead on the floor on a pillow. The man's penis now enters her at a very different angle and the change can be exciting for the woman who likes the back wall of her vagina stretched by her lover's penis.

Obviously the woman cannot caress her clitoris, and neither can her man, so the woman is unlikely to experience a clitorial orgasm in this position. It can nevertheless provide a change once in a while for the agile couple.
■ The man lies on his back and pulls his legs right back on to his chest. The woman pulls his penis out

The woman turns her back on the man, kneels astride him and lowers herself on to his penis. If she lies back he can caress her breasts

and downwards between his legs and sits on it with her back to his legs. He can rest his legs on her back to support both his legs and hers and she can support her weight by resting her hands on his thighs.

Very little movement is possible but she can, as in all these restricted movement positions, contract her pelvic muscles and wriggle her bottom about to stimulate them both.

Not many couples will be able to sustain this position for long because of the strain on the man and the fact that many men find it uncomfortable or even painful to have their erect penis at such a downward angle.

■ Another woman-on-top position is particularly suitable for the pregnant woman. The man lies flat on his back on the bed and the woman kneels over his pelvis, facing away from him. She inserts his penis and sits on it. Now she leans right back and lies on his chest. He can caress her whole body and especially her breasts and can reach down and stimulate her clitoris.

The only tiring part about this position is that many women find that their legs and knees becomes strained, but this can be overcome, at least to some extent, by lifting their knees off the bed a little.

■ Penetration is not deep but the penis is forced into the front wall of the vagina quite hard and this can be pleasant for the woman who likes her G spot stimulated during intercourse. The couple can kiss and her body is very open to caresses but she can do little herself to please her man. The penis slips out very easily with women whose vaginal opening is high up in the front of their pelvis.

For most couples, this will be a transitional

position that they adopt during the run-up to the final lovemaking position in which their orgasms will occur. It is, nevertheless, worth trying from time to time, especially for the breast-centred woman who likes her nipples and breasts caressed while she stimulates her clitoris.

■ This position is somewhat tiring but fun for a change, or for a while during any single lovemaking session. The man lies on his back on the edge of the bed with his feet and lower legs on a chair. The woman sits on his penis facing him and with her legs on either side of his chest. She leans back and supports herself with her hands on the arms of the chair.

Little movement is possible and penetration is not especially good. The man can watch his penis entering her and he can lift up a little to increase penetration, but the fact that she is supporting her weight so much on her arms is somewhat tiring. The man can reach in between her legs and caress her clitoris, but many woman will need to be highly aroused in advance if they are to have an orgasm from this position because they will be unable to maintain the weight on their arms for long.

The point to remember about advanced positions – whether they are for the woman-on-top, man-on-top, rear entry or whatever – is that they are only guidelines. Most are adaptable and a shift or slight change of position for either partner can mean all the difference between comfort and extreme discomfort.

For the couple who fancy a change, but feel that a particular position may present difficulties, it is worth seeing whether it can be adapted to their specific needs. The inventive couple will usually find a way around most problems.

REAR ENTRY

*Of all the rear entry positions, the 'doggy'
position is the best known. But the loving
couple can find others even more stimulating*

Intercourse face-to-face is by far the most popular form of lovemaking, for a variety of reasons. First, most women like to be held and have a good deal of close bodily contact during their lovemaking.

Second, a woman's breasts and lips – two major sources of erotic stimulation – are on the front of her body where they can be seen and made use of by her lover during sex.

And third, many women associate rear-entry sex with animal behaviour and therefore find it a turn-off.

For a couple who make love several times a week, however, making love in positions that involve the man penetrating the woman from the rear can be a refreshing change and can add a touch of variety to their sex lives.

And with such a spate of recent interest in the G spot, it has been suggested by researchers in this field that rear-entry lovemaking could actually be preferable from the woman's point of view.

In these positions, the man's penis stimulates the front vaginal wall and is therefore highly exciting to a woman who has a sensitive G spot.

PRACTICAL ADVANTAGES

Whatever the physical and emotional advantages and disadvantages of rear-entry positions, there are many practical benefits for the couple who enjoy making love in this way.

■ In a rear-entry position, the woman feels exceptionally vulnerable to her man. Some women find this highly stimulating. The thought of being penetrated and taken in an 'animal-like' way

The woman lies on her stomach, legs apart, and the man enters her from the rear, taking his weight on his hands. Deeper penetration can be achieved if the woman raises her bottom off the bed

greatly turns them on. However, other women find it a turn-off because they prefer positions which they consider to be 'romantic'. And rear-entry lovemaking, for all its pleasures and advantages, is not very romantic. However, for many couples this is no drawback, as the woman will want to be taken with ardour on some occasions, while on others she will want tender, loving and romantic intercourse. As humans, we have a vast range of emotions.

■ It is fashionable today for women to talk of caring men in bed who spend ages with detailed and prolonged foreplay, but this should not become a boring routine, however pleasant it might be. Many women, in therapy, say that they greatly enjoy being taken roughly. This proves to them that they are so desirable that their man cannot keep his hands off them, which is in itself sexually flattering. It also absolves them from having to put up with much foreplay which they may find contrived, boring or repetitive.

■ There is a time and a place for everything in sex and rear entry, forceful sex can be very exciting as a change. For the man who likes to see his woman's bottom and anus, rear entry positions (or at least some of them) can be excellent. If both partners like it the man can caress her bottom, stimulate her anus and so on. Because in many rear-entry positions, the woman's thighs are at an angle to her body (this is especially true of the classical 'doggy' position) penetration can be very deep.

■ For the woman who has a sensitive G spot, rear-entry positions can be especially good. The man's penis can be arranged to hit the right spot or to massage it gently, whichever the woman prefers. Even if the woman is not sensitive to G spot stimulation, she will experience very different sensations, many of which are highly arousing, if only because of their novelty to her.

■ A woman who is shy, who wants to fantasize about another man, or who wants to be sexually satisfied but would rather not be reminded too blatantly of her partner for some reason, may find rear-entry a good way around her problem. By facing

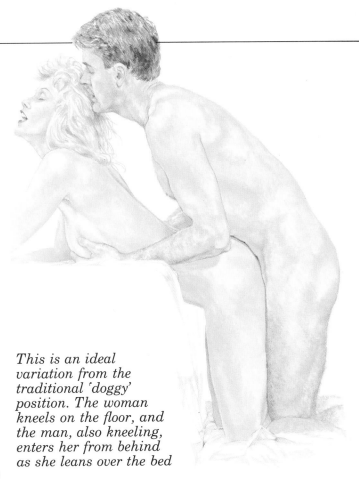

This is an ideal variation from the traditional 'doggy' position. The woman kneels on the floor, and the man, also kneeling, enters her from behind as she leans over the bed

away from the man she can enjoy her partner's penis and caresses in a somewhat anonymous way.

■ Rear-entry positions leave the man's hands free to caress and stimulate the woman's body, breasts and clitoris.

■ In some rear-entry positions, especially the 'doggy' position, the man has considerable freedom to thrust and can alter the amount and angle of movement his penis makes almost better than in any other position.

FOR THE ATHLETIC

Rear-entry positions range from the simple 'doggy' position to some highly adventurous positions that will please more athletic lovers.

Whatever variation you choose to try, make sure it suits both partners. For if one or other partner finds a particular position awkward, painful or tiring, this will detract a great deal from his or her enjoyment of lovemaking.

■ Probably the best-known and most widely used is the 'doggy' position. In this the woman kneels on the bed or the floor and her partner kneels behind her and enters her. She can angle her pelvis in several different way according to how far she leans forward and how she supports herself.

Each position gives new sensations to both. The woman can, for example, keep her body horizontal by resting on her hands and knees. She can rest on her elbows, or even lie with her arms back along

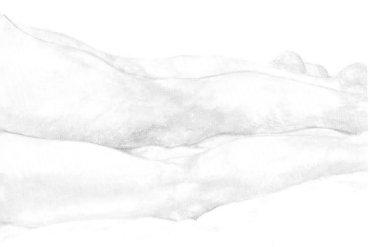

her body, or put them under her forehead or her breasts to support her upper body.

Penetration is extremely good, especially if the woman lies with her chest on the bed. The man has a large range of possible movements and the woman can be taken very forcefully, which many enjoy.

A few women find that air becomes pushed into the vagina in some of these positions. This need not necessarily be a problem, but if the penis traps air and pushes it up into the top end of the vagina, it can cause pain.

When the woman turns over, the air comes out with an embarrassing noise, but most couples either ignore this or make a joke out of it.

■ A modification of the 'doggy' position is for the woman to kneel on a low stool or table (covered with something that is not too hard on her knees). The man stands behind her between her open legs and enters her.

■ For the more athletic, another good rear-entry position is to ask the woman to bend over with her legs wide apart and rest her hands on the floor in front of her. Her bottom and vulva are now exposed and the man can, by bending his knees a little, enter her from behind.

Movement and penetration are good (at least for the man) but the woman is totally fixed, apart from being able to wiggle her hips from side-to-side to enhance their pleasure. She can, of course, as in all rear-entry positions, contract her pelvic muscles to make it more stimulating for them both.

■ A restful and very enjoyable rear-entry position

The man lies on his back with his knees pulled up to his chest. The woman then eases herself on to his penis as he uses his legs and hands to support her

The man lies flat on his back, legs together, and the woman sits astride him facing away. In this position, penetration is exceptionally deep and the woman controls any thrusting

is the 'spoons', which can be modified to become a side-by-side position (see following pages). The woman lies facing away from her man with her knees drawn up. The man cuddles into her body from behind and curls around and enters her. They can lie still with his penis inside her or he can move around. Penetration can be deep if she angles her body down towards the foot of the bed. He can reach round and caress the front of her body.

■ The man lies on the bed with his legs together and the woman kneels over his hips facing away from him. She takes her weight on her hands placed either side of his legs. She can control the amount of movement in the rear-entry, woman-on-top position and he can see and caress her bottom and anus.

■ Another position is only suitable for a woman

with strong arms. Here, the woman leans over the bed supporting her entire weight on her arms and the man lifts her open legs off the ground and stands between them as he enters her from behind. Movement is limited in this position, but penetration can be quite deep.

The woman squats on the seat of a chair, using the back of the chair as support. The man enters her from a standing position

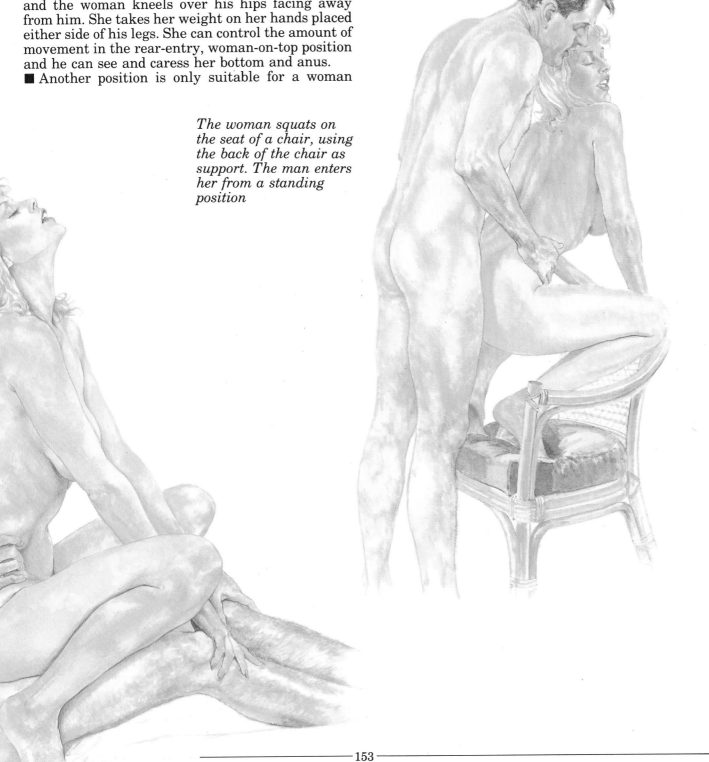

SIDE-BY-SIDE

*For couples who prize intimacy
and close contact when they
make love, side-by-side positions
give maximum opportunity for
cuddling, caressing and kissing*

Most couples like to bring variety into their sex lives by using positions that suit their mood at the time. And for couples who make love several times a week, lovemaking can range from the warm and intimate to the highly adventurous.

Athletic positions which require the couple to be fit and supple can be very enjoyable from time to time but they do have their drawbacks.

Many of the more adventurous positions, while providing stimulation in new and different ways, are often tiring and are rarely romantic.

POSITIONS FOR INTIMACY

Side-entry positions allow for maximum body contact, are restful and are ideal for occasions when intimacy is the order of the day.

They are particularly useful when one or both partners feel tired, or when the woman is pregnant.

In many of the side-entry position the man is able to cuddle his partner, his hands are free to caress her, and for the woman or man who likes their lovemaking to be accompanied by words of love, these are among the best positions for intimate conversation.

Without a doubt, the best known of these positions is the 'spoons'. This is an exceptionally good position for during pregnancy because the woman's stomach can lie flat on the bed and it is very restful for her in the last few months.

■ The couplé lie on their sides with the man cuddling into the woman's back as she draws her knees up towards her stomach. He tucks into her and penetrates her.

Penetration can be very good, especially if the woman angles her body down towards her feet and the man can, in a limited way, make thrusting movements. He can reach around and stimulate her clitoris or she can open her legs and do so herself. He can also reach around and caress her breasts and stomach and, at the same time, kiss her neck and back. The area of skin contact is extensive and

'Spoons' is one of the most comfortable and affectionate of all lovemaking positions because it allows for maximum skin contact and the man can easily kiss, caress and talk intimately to his partner

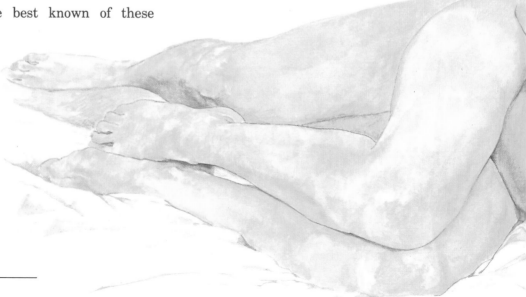

this can be very romantic and sensuous.

This is a very pleasant position for the couple who like to fall asleep after sex – it is quite possible to go to sleep with the penis still in the vagina.

■ A variation on this position is for the woman, once penetrated, to roll over on to her back a little and to place one leg over the upper leg of the man. This opens up her vulva considerably and leaves her clitoris available for her or her partner to caress. She now has both hands free to caress herself, or her lover.

Her stomach is totally free, again making this position good for late on in pregnancy. Penetration can be good but is not exceptionally deep, and any thrusting movement is somewhat restricted.

From the woman's point of view it is restful and she can stimulate herself and her partner's scrotum. In some women the man's penis stimulates the G spot in this position, giving extra sensations.

■ The couple lie on their sides facing one another. The woman draws up her legs to her chest and opens them widely. The man enters her and she holds her legs around his back. She also cuddles him around the shoulders with her arms.

Penetration can be very good but movement is somewhat restricted. The couple can kiss very easily and passionately. There is a lot of skin contact and the couple can feel very 'at one' with each other.

This position is not suitable for the very fat or for women who are pregnant.

■ One of the best lovemaking positions of all is a side-entry one. The woman lies on her back and the

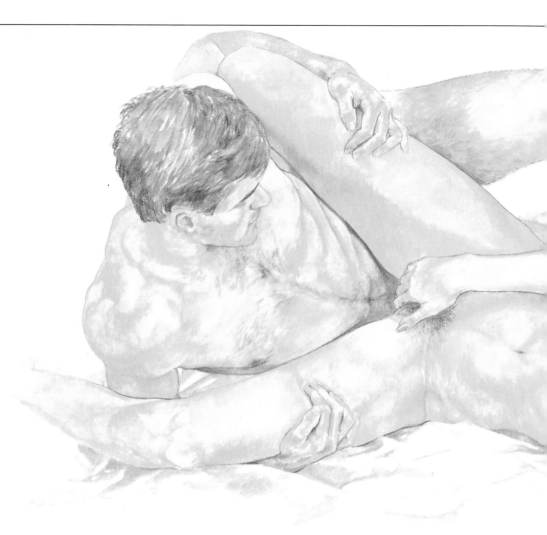

man on his side at right angles to her body. She draws her thighs back towards her stomach and he enters her as he lies underneath them.

Penetration is deep and movement can be good, but not excellent. It is another restful position during pregnancy or for the obese woman. Both partners can reach the woman's clitoris to stimulate it and the man can caress most parts of her body.

It is a good position for a 'quickie' because it involves very little undressing. It is also good for conceiving, especially if the woman remains with her legs in the drawn-back position for a few minutes after intercourse.

The anus of both partners is accessible for those who like anal stimulation and it is a good position for inexperienced women who have difficulty having orgasms during intercourse.

■ The woman lies on her side, turning slightly on to her front and supporting her top half with her forearms on the bed. The man cuddles into her back just as in the spoon position, then puts his upper legs over her hips as he penetrates her.

It is a pleasant position for the man to be able to caress the woman's back with one hand but she can do very little. Penetration is not especially good because her legs are fairly straight, but he can make quite good movements.

This can be a particularly exciting position for a man who likes to watch his partner's vulval area when making love. Both can reach the woman's clitoris to stimulate it

She lies on her front, her bottom raised slightly, and the man lies over her at right angles and penetrates her from behind. The woman's movements are restricted because she is pinned down by her partner, but he can thrust without restriction and caress her body

CHAPTER NINE

OVERCOMING PROBLEMS

WHEN A MAN CAN'T COME

Many men experience impotence at some stage but a loving couple should be able to sort out the problem

Many men, perhaps even most men, have, at some time or other, found themselves in the situation where they cannot sustain an erection long enough to have sex, or indeed even manage to achieve an erection. The reasons for this can be too much alcohol, tiredness or simply not being sufficiently attracted to the woman.

These 'one-off' occasions are part and parcel of the male sex life and, provided they occur only infrequently, there is obviously no need to worry. If they are the general rule, it is a more serious problem that can wreak havoc in a couple's lives.

PERFORMANCE PRESSURES

If a woman cannot come, sex is still possible if the man is able to function normally. But when a man cannot achieve, or maintain, an erection, intercourse is virtually impossible. Also, women can easily fake orgasms, and some frequently do – but a man cannot, and this puts considerable performance pressures and anxieties on to him.

Impotence is a term that can be applied to masturbation as well as intercourse. Some men who are impotent in intercourse and mutual masturbation can come perfectly well and enjoyably when masturbating alone. In therapy, some men who successfully masturbate lose their erection when asked to fantasize about intercourse with a woman, indicating that they are obviously, but unconsciously, avoiding sex.

Discovering, or rediscovering, the pleasures of being masturbated by his partner – with both knowing that she will bring him to orgasm – is a necessary step before the temporarily impotent man should attempt full intercourse. The watchwords are relaxation for the man and a sensuous, regular rhythm for the woman

WHAT CAUSES IT?

There is no single reason why impotence should strike. The causes are numerous and varied. Some stem from medical problems, others from psychological ones. And sometimes a man's general lifestyle or the state of his present relationship can bring about the condition.

By far the most common causes for a man not coming are connected to problems in the mind. Some can be treated by the couple, others may require professional help.

■ Penis size can be a real worry to a number of men. Almost all men have at least some sort of view about the adequacy of their penis and many are convinced that it is too small. Men who are ashamed

One of the most powerful resources a woman has to counteract her partner's impotence is her own body. With the man relaxed, and without using her hands, she can use her breasts or tongue to trace a lingering path along his body from head to toe

of the size of their penis may fail to erect in the presence of a woman because they fear she will find it wanting. This is a groundless fear because most women are not that bothered by penis size. Curiously, this fails to convince a high proportion of men.

■ Stresses such as moving, a bereavement, redundancy (or even the threat of it), business worries, financial concerns and problems with the children can all disrupt a man's ability to become aroused. These problems usually only produce a short-lived sexual problem but, given the complexity of modern life, a man can be off sex for long periods if the worries pile one on top of the other. Many men live at a level of stress that means they are rarely

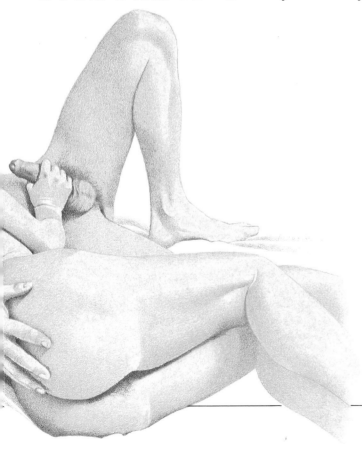

relaxed and so hardly ever come when they want to. This is one reason why some men look outside their one-to-one relationship – it is only when stimulus is very high (in a 'forbidden' relationship) that they can function properly.

■ A fear of assertive women is an increasingly common cause of impotence. Today's woman is more assertive in bed – and out of it – and many men with a poor self-esteem simply cannot cope. Almost all young men who are apprehensive about intercourse have the occasional bout of impotence. Sometimes, especially if the woman is sexually experienced and he is not, this can make him fear her criticism so much that he cannot get erect.

■ A fear of pregnancy or VD is a common cause of impotence. A number of extramarital affairs are, to some extent, blighted by such fears and, as a result, cause impotence in men who are normally good performers. As with almost all matters pertaining to sex the real damage is done unconsciously. At the conscious level the man thinks he is having a good time and, given that the level of excitement involved in illicit sex is so high, he cannot explain why it is that he fails time and again in such situations. Unconsciously, though, his guilt, his concerns about any long-term implications of the affair, and his fear of VD and getting the woman pregnant turn him off.

■ Previous failures loom large in the minds of many impotent men. They have odd failures (for perfectly rational and understandable reasons) but generalize from these isolated experiences to the point where they fear the next sexual encounter because their penis might let them down again. Having a failure in sex is rather like falling off a horse – you must get right back up and ride again. It is interesting that many men see even quite rare failures as a sign of impending age and its resultant sexual decline. This is especially true of middle-aged men. The trouble with erections is that if the man believes he is about to fail, he probably will, unless he has a really active and passionate partner to bolster his lack of confidence. Unfortunately, many women pull the man's leg about his occasional failures, or even frankly criticize him for them, both in and out of bed. This sows the seeds of future failures in the mind of the man.

■ Illness can affect a man's ability to have an orgasm and certainly a man with an acute infectious illness will be less likely than usual to come. What is often overlooked is that many men, especially after a heart attack, are so worried about the negative effects that an orgasm might have on their health that they simply do not have one.

■ A fear of injuring the woman is another cause of impotence. Many men say that if their partner has just had a baby, a gynaecological operation, an abortion or indeed almost any operation or illness, they would rather not run the risk of hurting her.

■ Latent homosexuality is undoubtedly a feature of some impotent men. Often, quite unconsciously, they wish they were not making love to a woman at all – not just to that particular women. Some men function perfectly well for years in a marriage if they can fantasize about intercourse with a man while they make love with their wife.

SORTING OUT THE PROBLEM

The first step is to sit down and talk about the problem and to try to get to the root of it. If the couple can talk frankly they are half way to sorting it out. It is important at this stage for the woman to accept that this is her problem as well. If she can recognize this, the prospects for a solution are good.

RELAX – DON'T DO IT

The next step is to stop attempting to have intercourse. It is amazing how alleviating the pressure to perform can help the man to achieve confidence again. While the couple are abstaining, it greatly helps if the woman continues to reassure her lover that she is happy to forego intercourse.

During this period, a return to courtship behaviour is beneficial. Both partners should take every opportunity to show their love for each other short of intercourse. Kiss more and try to increase your physical closeness by hugging each other. Taking an extra pride in your appearance and dressing in ways you know please your partner can help.

The emphasis should be on closeness, cuddling and massage. Maximize the power of touch. When you go to bed, stroke your partner's back, shoulders, limbs, face and buttocks – but stay clear of the genitals. Take it in turn to massage each other. Learn to relax together and put out of your mind any notion that these activities have a purpose beyond the simple pleasure of touching your partner's body.

EXTRA STIMULUS

Another ploy that helps is to raise the general level of eroticism in your relationship. Reading erotic literature to each other, browsing through 'girlie' magazines, or watching sexy films or videos will all help to this end.

At this stage the man will still be extremely vulnerable, so it is essential that the woman is careful to avoid any kind of dominating behaviour. Suddenly becoming a 'sex siren' to turn him on, wearing all kinds of sexy underwear and so on may prove to be intimidating rather than helpful, so take things gently and slowly.

Along with this, the man should establish self masturbation. Fantasies of enjoyable, successful, intercourse should also prove helpful.

ORAL SEX

When the man has achieved an erection, the couple may still not be ready to attempt intercourse. In this situation oral sex should be the next stage.

The woman should take her partner's penis in her mouth and use her tongue and lips to tease him. She should take as much of the penis into her mouth as feels comfortable and use regular, rhythmic movements up and down. She can use her own body to keep his excitement going. If her partner wants to come in her mouth she can let him, provided she is happy with this. Otherwise the couple may now be ready to attempt full intercourse again.

Once the man can achieve an erection and ejaculate through self masturbation and mutual masturbation, and possibly oral sex, his sexual confidence will usually return and with it the ability to enjoy successful sexual intercourse with his partner.

NON-COME INTERCOURSE

As well as men who cannot come there are also some who simply choose not to. The technique of 'non-come' intercourse has long been practised in the Orient, where one man had to keep many wives sexually satisfied. It enabled the man to have sex several times a day, perhaps with all his partners having several orgasms each, yet he would come only at the end of the day with his last intercourse.

'Non-come' intercourse is, to some extent a case of mind over matter, and involves the ability to control the degree of arousal felt during intercourse to such an extent that ejaculation can be delayed indefinitely. A simple first step is for the man to try and concentrate on something other than what he is doing – analysis of the pattern of the bedroom wallpaper or counting the curtain rings. By doing this, he can delay ejaculation a little more each time until, eventually, he will be able to concentrate on what he is doing yet still be able to control his state of arousal.

Once learned, this technique can be excellent if his partner takes a long time to come. It is useful also for men who fear a loss of vitality or get tired if they have sex in the morning. Indeed, men who use this technique say it greatly adds to their sense of well-being and vitality during the day.

WHEN A WOMAN CAN'T COME

Although there are a multitude of reasons why a woman may be unable to come, curing the problem is often surprisingly straightforward

Problems with orgasm are more common than is generally realized. According to a large survey carried out in 1984, one in three married women had orgasm difficulties at least half the time they made love, and only one in five never had any difficulty.

Although some sort of trouble with orgasm often occurs during intercourse, most of the eight out of ten women who claimed to masturbate had orgasms when doing so.

THE ELUSIVE ORGASM

Perhaps the most common form of orgasm failure is seen in the woman who feels sexy and becomes aroused but does not actually experience orgasms.

Some women can have an orgasm in a particular position, but not in others. Other women have difficulty experiencing orgasms early on in a relationship, but find that things improve as they become more relaxed and their lover becomes more expert at stimulating them.

Alternatively, there are women who have orgasms early on in a relationship when sex is 'naughty' or 'forbidden', but lose them after marriage when sex is 'allowed'. Most are inhibited and find that orgasms are possible only if they are extremely aroused, as they were when the relationship was fresh.

As soon as the excitement level falls, even a little, they are unable to have orgasms because their

Probably the most valuable time a woman can spend learning, or relearning, to have an orgasm is spent on her own – relaxing and exploring her own body

If the man plants lingering kisses over her body, making sure he does not miss any part, he will help to keep the mood going

fears and inhibitions now tip the balance out of their favour.

Some women masturbate and say that they feel relaxed and satisfied afterwards, but have little or no awareness of having an orgasm. Their problems can be recognizing that they are having one and being able to enjoy it. Their unconscious mind blocks out the realities of the orgasm and allows such women even to deny that they masturbate.

This is a common story in girls who are brought up to adhere to a strict religious code. This is why so many women claim, quite sincerely, not to masturbate. By denying the pleasure, they can deny the act.

For some women, orgasms during intercourse are often plentiful and enjoyable because they are 'allowed' in their eyes – at least if they are in love with, or married to, the man.

Here, at least the woman can enjoy her orgasm and recognize it for what it is.

PHYSICAL PROBLEMS

Almost any illness – especially an acute, physical or emotional one – can make a woman less likely to have an orgasm. Severe illnesses such as advanced diabetes and certain disorders of the nervous system, can also prevent orgasm in a woman who previously had them. And *anorexia nervosa* frequently produces a cessation of orgasms.

Many women feel mutilated after gynaecological operations, and it is not at all uncommon for a woman to go off sex entirely after a hysterectomy or a breast removal for cancer. Most regain their sex drive and are able to have orgasms again, but it can take months.

Certain drugs kill orgasms in women, especially anti-depressants and anti-blood pressure drugs.

Hormone deficiencies which occur in some women can be to blame too.

EMOTIONAL ORIGINS

Shyness is a common reason for women not to come, especially in new relationships.

A woman who is unsure of her partner simply may not be able to let go and might take weeks or months to become sufficiently at ease to have an orgasm in his presence.

Depression is a very common cause of orgasm failure. An inability to relax is another common cause. Some women, especially young, busy mothers – particularly those trying to do a job as well – are simply exhausted.

A fear of pain is a less common cause, but is not all that rare. If ever you have pain during intercourse, see your doctor.

A recent bereavement can turn a woman off sex or having orgasms. This includes miscarriage.

Pregnancy is a common cause of a lack of orgasms in many guises. Some women cannot come if they are contraceptively safe.

Other woman fail to have orgasms because they are not contraceptively safe, and are tense about the possibility of an unwanted pregnancy.

Many women see their man as a father figure in certain situations. A few, however, are still very much attached to their father and treat their partner, unconsciously, as if he were the father. Because sex between father and daughter is wrong, the woman can never have an orgasm.

This feeling may be confined to one individual partner who particularly reminds the woman of her father. In another relationship, she might be quite capable of having orgasms.

Women often strongly identify with their mother – whom they see as sexless. A woman who has become a mother herself may stop having orgasms because she is now a mother, not a lover.

Some women have been psychologically damaged during childhood and made to wish they were a boy. They will only really enjoy being on top during intercourse, when they can pretend that they own the penis they are sitting astride.

Adverse sexual experiences during childhood, including incest and rape, can have serious consequences. As child molestation is so common – and probably always has been – it can often be at the heart of orgasm failure. Again, this is an area that needs professional help to sort out.

A surprising minority of women have unconscious, and sometimes conscious, lesbian thoughts and fantasies and find that these inhibit them having orgasms when with a man.

AWKWARD SITUATIONS

Some women make a lot of noise when they come and some fear that the neighbours, the in-laws or the children might hear, so they may stifle their orgasms and eventually stop having them. Other noisy women cannot come with a man they love and respect, in case he thinks her to be some sort of slut for being so abandoned, but come perfectly well in extra-marital sex which is 'forbidden'.

Many women do not come because their partner does not do what they most enjoy.

LATE DEVELOPERS

A late developer has to realize is that she is simply under-developed psychosexually and that she can fairly easily develop herself, even if it seems rather late in life. Some things that can be done are:

■ Learn to strip in front of a mirror and then do a striptease to music.
■ Become used to looking at your vulva before and during sexual arousal. Some women who think they cannot be aroused are amazed to see their vulva react vigorously as they become excited.
■ If you do not normally stimulate your vulva by hand, you should start to do so and try – by clitoral stimulation – to bring yourself to orgasm.
■ Join a pre-orgasmic group. There are several in larger cities in the United Kingdom.
■ Learn to fantasize more. Many women who do not have orgasms find fantasizing difficult. Some do have fantasies but always as onlookers, never as participants. Erotic books and videos help, as does reading about other women's fantasies.

INVOLVING YOUR PARTNER

Once things are well under way, it is sensible to enlist your partner's help. Any caring man will be only too delighted to enter into the spirit of the exercise. Gradually, the woman can teach her man to masturbate her as well as she herself can – or even better – perhaps by using a vibrator on her while making love or using some other variation that pleases her.

The time a woman spends using a vibrator to bring herself to orgasm – or the brink of it – can be used to teach the man what she likes best

WHEN A MAN COMES TOO SOON

*Premature ejaculation is a distressing
problem in any partnership, but with
perseverance a couple can soon get back on
the road to a satisfying sex life*

There are few men who have not, at one time or another, wished that they could have carried on making love a little longer – either for their own pleasure or that of their partner. But, because a man climaxes earlier than he or his partner would like, it does not mean he is a premature ejaculator. Premature ejaculation is a relative concept, and 'coming too soon' can be a problem in one relationship but not in another, even for the same man.

The 'experts' have had difficulty trying to define premature ejaculation. There are literally scores of different definitions, including the concept that a man suffers from the condition if he ejaculates before his partner has had her orgasm. This definition would swell the ranks of premature ejaculators to include most men at certain times in their sexual life, and so is clearly nonsense.

No matter how else premature ejaculation is defined, however, it is generally seen in psychosexual terms as an unconscious way that a man can avoid sex.

It can happen in masturbation or fellatio, as well as during intercourse. The man, for one of many reasons, wants to get sex over with quickly, or even to avoid it altogether. Unfortunately, because this desire is often totally unconscious, he does not, and cannot, acknowledge it.

*With the rear-entry
position the man can
achieve deep penetration
and at the same time be
able to control the
rhythm of the
lovemaking – the minute
he feels an orgasm
coming he can stop
thrusting*

TREATING YOURSELF

Premature ejaculation is one of the easiest problems to treat yourself. A loving couple who really want

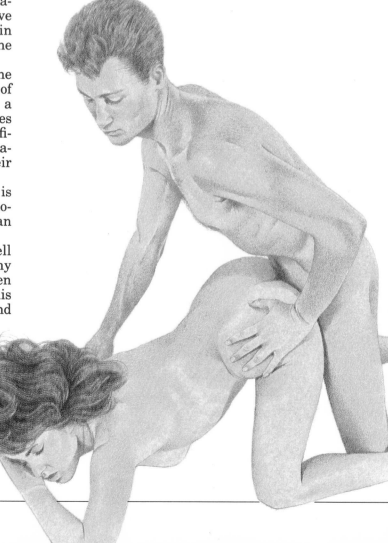

If the woman straddles her partner she can stop any thrusting movement if the man feels he is about to ejaculate

to make things work, and who do not want to 'prove' something to one another, or go in for one-upmanship games, can usually sort things out between them when it comes to premature ejaculation. The following self-help programme works for many couples.

Have orgasms more frequently This is especially useful in young men who are 'trigger happy'. They are greatly helped by masturbating a few hours before they are about to have sex. If you are going to be apart from one another for any length of time, it makes sense for the man to masturbate at some stage close to his return so that the first bout of lovemaking does not end prematurely.

Talk it over between yourselves This usually helps, as with most sex problems. Perhaps there are simple answers that could easily be arrived at. For example, some women become so excited after a lot of foreplay that they over-stimulate their man with kisses and caresses. He understandably cannot take too much of this and climaxes very quickly. She may simply have to indulge in less foreplay so that she is less aroused, or not stimulate him so powerfully if she wants him to last longer.

Alternatively she could enjoy an orgasm or two first to 'defuse' herself. Then her partner could take his time. A good way of achieving this is for the man to perform oral sex on her or to make love to her using a dildo or vibrator first.

Masturbation training The next stage is for the man to teach himself to masturbate in such a way as to be able to learn to recognize the sensations associated with impending ejaculation. He should start off by reading erotic material, watching sexy films or videos, or whatever turns him on in reality or fantasy. In this way, he obtains a really good erection. He then concentrates on all the sensations in his genitals and continues to masturbate, being very aware of both the physical changes and changes in sensation in his testes, penis, scrotum, breathing, heartbeat and internal sex organs. All this may sound very contrived, but it is the starting point to becoming more aware of what is going on.

The key sensations that have to be noted are those that occur in the immediate run-up to ejaculation. As the man feels he might be nearing these mini-orgasms deep inside his pelvis, he should stop stimulating his penis and let the erection go down.

He can repeat this stop-start exercise until he learns what it feels like to be getting very close to an orgasm. It also gives him confidence that, after recognizing these changes, he can do something to prevent them from going on to produce an orgasm. This sense of being in control of the previously uncontrollable is the first step on the road to success.

OTHER AIDS TO SUCCESS

By this stage, the man may feel ready to go back to intercourse, if he has stopped during his training period. This is not necessary, however. The masturbation training can go hand-in-hand with continuing to have intercourse.

Wearing a sheath can work wonders for some men. The latex reduces penile sensations just enough to make him last longer, and if the man has not known his partner long, the use of a sheath is to be recommended anyway.

Some men have success with weak anaesthetic creams. They are available from most sex shops.

Contracting the anus tightly at the end of each thrust can also help. Some men find that really deep penetration with very small penile movement is an answer. In a highly aroused woman, the top end of the vagina balloons out and, ironically, actually stimulates the penis tip less.

STOP-START INTERCOURSE

Stop-start intercourse can work very well, too. In this, the man inserts the penis tip and then keeps it still. Slowly, over several stages, he inserts it deeper and then cautiously thrusts and stops when he feels he is anywhere near climaxing. Such a 'teasing' approach can greatly excite the woman, but it is best in the early training days if she tries not to show it. This could so arouse her partner that he will yet again come too soon.

KEEPING YOUR MIND OFF SEX

All the classical sex books talk about psychological manoeuvres such as counting backwards from 100 in fives, counting the rings on the curtain pole or thinking about some difficult work problem.

Some men find that once they are advanced in their premature ejaculation training they can concentrate more on pleasing and pleasuring their partner. Concentrating on her takes his mind off himself and can work wonders. She enjoys the added stimulation, especially after the disappointment of

premature ejaculation, and he has something more interesting and valuable to think about than problems at work.

THE SQUEEZE GAME

Once a man has gone this far with his premature ejaculation training he should be very nearly cured of his problem – indeed many men will have been performing normally long since. But if not, there is still one more tried-and-tested method that is worth trying. It is called the squeeze game.

In the squeeze game, the couple settle down into a comfortable position, with the woman sitting on the bed between his open legs and her back supported. She now stimulates his penis, as he lies back and enjoys the sensations. She arouses him orally or manually and then continues to do so until he says that his pre-ejaculation sensations are coming on. After the first couple of times, no words are necessary, he can simple raise his hand or give some other signal they have previously agreed.

The woman now stops stimulating him and squeezes the tip of his penis firmly with her thumb over the little ridge on its underside and two other fingers on the opposite side of its rim. She applies a first squeeze for 15 seconds, or thereabouts, and the man loses his erection almost at once. In this, he can gain control with her very powerful and erotic stimulation. As days go by, she can make things more realistic by using KY jelly or baby oil on the penis.

TAKING TIME

Over a few weeks, the man should become totally confident that he is in charge of his ejaculation and is never taken by surprise or overtaken by his orgasms. Now the couple can decide on a time span and keep the man erect for almost all of it, before allowing him to ejaculate at will. If this is too boring or frustrating for the woman it makes sense to satisfy her first before the squeeze game begins.

Once this is going really well, the woman can straddle the penis one day without prior agreement and the man can become used to being contained in her vagina, yet not ejaculating. If he feels he is about to come he tells her, she gets off and squeezes him until he gains control.

When they both think he can cope, they go on to penile thrusting, again, perhaps with her on top controlling the pace. As soon as the thrusting produces sensations of being about to come, the man stops short. By this stage they probably will not have to resort to squeezing the penis. As the days go by thrusting can become more powerful and vigorous and, eventually, the man can ejaculate whenever he or his partner wants him to.

A premature ejaculation programme such as this could take up to two months for a couple to work through, but it is very effective and well worth the investment of time and love.

SEXUAL DISEASES

*Sexually transmitted diseases are on the
increase throughout the world, and young
people form a high proportion of those
affected. But if diagnosed early some of these
infections can be cured*

Any disease that can be passed on from one person to another by sexual contact is called a sexually transmitted disease, or STD. In the past the term VD (short for venereal disease) was much more commonly used, and usually referred to gonorrhoea and syphilis, the more serious of the diseases, apart from the killer disease AIDS, which is discussed fully in the following pages.

For many people, VD was not merely a term describing an infectious disease transmitted sexually – it was regarded as something that was only caught by people who indulged in immoral behaviour. This attitude has changed a great deal in recent years, so that today STDs, and departments of genitourinary medicine where they are treated, are usually thought of with less embarrassment than in the past.

WHO SUFFERS?

Anyone can catch an STD by oral and anal sex as well as vaginal intercourse, in most cases the treatment is not painful or difficult, but as with most diseases, the earlier it is diagnosed, the easier it is to cure.

Generally, the most severe consequences of neglected STD fall upon women and their babies. Women are far less likely to have the recognizable symptoms that make early diagnosis easy. That is why the follow-up of contacts by an STD clinic is so important.

Not surprisingly, some 60 per cent of those infected worldwide are under 24. The effect on young women can be particularly devastating if the untreated disease leads to infertility. So, if you think you could have caught an infection, even though you have no symptoms, go for a check up anyway – nobody is going to criticize you for being safe rather than sorry.

SYPHILIS

Syphilis, one of the most serious of all STDs, is becoming less common in Great Britain and the western world generally, while increasing in the developing world. There are about 20 to 50 million cases in the world every year. There were just over 3,000 cases reported in Great Britain in 1983, 6 per cent fewer than in the previous year – with ten times more men than women contracting the disease.

WHAT IS SYPHILIS?

Syphilis is caused by a corkscrew-shaped organism which is present in the blood and body fluids of an infected person. It can only live in the warm environment that the body provides, and it dies within a few hours outside it. The likelihood of you

*One of the most important elements in the treatment
of STDs is the tracing of contacts, particularly as
many women have no symptoms*

contracting syphilis if you have sex with an infected person is thought to be about one in two – particularly when it is in the early stages.

When the disease is passed on (by contact with a sore or ulcer), a hundred or more of the minute organisms called triponemes, pass through the skin. After only half an hour they have passed to the lymph nodes in the groin and next they pass into the blood stream and are distributed to the whole body. It takes about three weeks before the body's defence mechanism begins to work against them.

THE FIRST SYMPTOMS

The first visible symptom of syphilis is a raised pimple on the vagina or penis (although it can sometimes occur on the mouth or anus from oral or anal contact).

Next, hard tissue forms around the pimple. The pimple becomes a painless ulcer or sore from which fluid oozes, and finally heals leaving a scar, usually taking about three weeks to do so.

Most people seek treatment when the sore appears, and the doctor will take a sample of the fluid from the sore to examine under a microscope and will also look to see if the lymph nodes of the groin are swollen.

The doctor will also take blood tests to see if antibodies to the organisms have been manufactured by the blood.

EFFECTS ON THE FETUS

Transmission of syphilis to an unborn baby occurs by way of the placenta. A blood test done, for example, in the first ten weeks of pregnancy, can

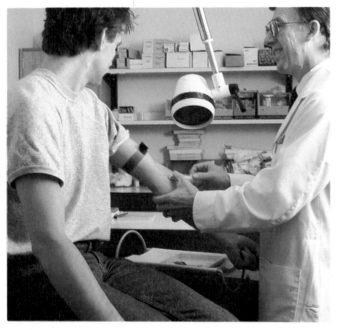

A blood sample is taken from a patient with a suspected STD then a laboratory technician examines it

diagnose the disease in the mother before it is passed on to the baby – which does not happen until after the twentieth week. She can be cured with penicillin and produce a perfectly healthy baby.

TREATMENT

The chances of curing early syphilis by penicillin or other antibiotics are excellent, and even the advanced disease can be arrested. Daily injections of penicillin (together with Probenecid which maintains high levels of the antibiotic in the bloodstream) are given for about ten days, or a single dose can be injected into a muscle. Alternative antibiotics are given to those allergic to penicillin.

GONORRHOEA

Gonorrhoea is much more common than syphilis – about 50,000 new cases are diagnosed in Great Britain each year. It is the third most common STD, after non-specific genital infections and thrush, but much more common than herpes.

More than half of gonorrhoea cases are among under 24-year-olds, with three to five times as many cases among young men as among young women. Today there are probably between 200 and 500 million new cases every year in the world.

WHAT IS GONORRHOEA?

The gonorrhoea organism is small and bean-shaped, and is passed on by sexual intercourse – oral and anal as well as vaginal. It can therefore be passed from the urethra of a man, to the cervix, urethra, throat or rectum of his partner. It can be passed to a male as well as female partner. A woman can pass it on to the urethra of her male partner during penetration.

Since the organism (gonococcus) dies very quickly outside the human body, it is virtually impossible to pass it on without sexual intercourse. So you need not worry about catching it from a lavatory seat or towel. But if you do have sexual intercourse with someone who has gonorrhoea, you have more than an even chance of catching it.

THE SYMPTOMS

The symptoms are different in men and women. While only one man in ten is symptomless, more than half the women who develop the disease have no symptoms at all.

The first signs for a man occur between three and five days after contact. They start with a tingling of the man's urethra, followed by a thick, creamy-yellow discharge, which drips from the penis. At the same time there is a burning pain on passing urine.

Although at first he feels well in himself, if the infection is not treated and spreads, he may well begin to suffer from fever and headaches within ten to fourteen days. Infection can then travel to the prostate gland, the bladder, the testes or the epididymis. Scarring of the epididymis – the two long

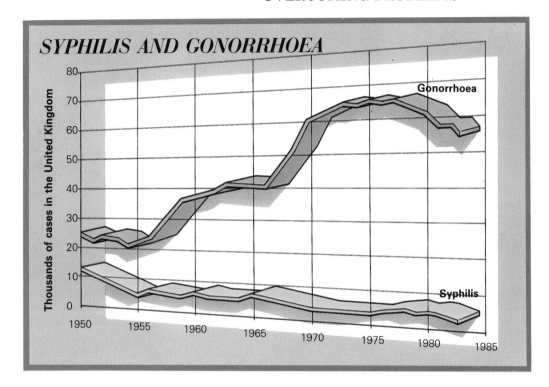

SYPHILIS AND GONORRHOEA

Thousands of cases in the United Kingdom

80
70
60
50
40
30
20
10
0

Gonorrhoea

Syphilis

1950 1955 1960 1965 1970 1975 1980 1985

narrow tubes where sperm normally mature before they are ejaculated – can cause permanent sterility if both are affected.

Symptoms of gonorrhoea in a woman may include vaginal discharge or a burning feeling when passing urine. One painful complication occurs when the glands which supply secretions to keep the vagina moist – known as Bartholin's glands – become swollen and tender.

If the infection is not treated, it may spread upwards, often during menstruation, and affect the Fallopian tubes. This may happen in as many as one in ten women who contract gonorrhoea, and is accompanied by fever, headaches, and severe pelvic pain. The inflammation of the tubes, known as salpingitis, can be serious enough to need emergency hospital admission, and the resultant scarring and blocking of the tubes can lead to permanent sterility.

TREATMENT

A positive diagnosis, found by microscopic examination of penile discharge, or of a smear taken from a woman's urethra, vagina or cervix, is followed by treatment with penicillin. If oral sex has taken place, a swab is taken from the throat, and if anal intercourse has occurred, one is taken from the rectum.

Treatment today usually consists of one large dose of penicillin in tablet form, together with Probenecid which maintains high levels of the antibiotic in the blood-stream. While treatment is taking place, alcohol and sexual contact must be avoided.

A week following treatment, more swabs are taken and checked for gonococcus. If none is present the man is considered cured, but a woman needs to be checked again, after her next period. Certain types of penicillin-resistant gonorrhoea, found most frequently in South East Asia, need to be treated by another antibiotic called Spectinomycin.

PREVENTION

For both syphilis and gonorrhoea, the condom may provide some protection, and the diaphragm or cap can protect the cervix from infection. Passing urine after sex may also help a woman to avoid gonorrhoea, although none of these measures guarantees protection.

CHANCROID

The STD chancroid is most common in tropical climates, but with the increase in travel between tropical countries and the rest of the world, the disease is likely to become more widespread.

Chancroid is caused by a small organism which is transmitted by sexual intercourse. Symptoms develop after three to seven days, with painful pimples on the man's penis or the woman's labia. When the pimples break to form ulcers, these too are painful (unlike syphilis ulcers) and they bleed easily. The lymph nodes of the groin become swollen and tender.

Diagnosis is made by taking a sample from the ulcer, and identifying the organism responsible under a microscope. It is cured by taking sulphonamides. This is not an antibiotic and therefore does not suppress syphilis if the two STDs occur together. When the chancroid is cured, further check-ups will be made for syphilis.

AIDS

Will AIDS kill more than one million people in the United Kingdom within the next ten years? This is the question that people have been asking with increasing concern, while scientists struggle to find a cure

Much of the hysteria about AIDS has been generated by society's attitudes towards some of those groups most likely to be affected – homosexuals, bisexuals and intravenous drug users.

This has resulted in an outbreak of hysteria as devastating in its way as the disease itself, which has earned the tags of AFRAIDS and AIPS (AIDS Induced Panic Syndrome). Children have been barred from classrooms, dentists have refused to treat gay patients and cameramen have boycotted interview sessions featuring victims.

The disease itself has confounded doctors and scientists alike since it was officially recognized in July 1981 in San Francisco.

WHY AIDS KILLS

The acronym AIDS stands for Acquired Immune Deficiency Syndrome which spells out about as much and as little as we know about the disease. It is *acquired* and not inherited, it strikes at the *immune* system, the body's natural defence against hostile invading organisms, it produces a deficiency in its ability to fight infection, and it is a *syndrome*, that is a collection of symptoms which seem to occur together and very probably have the same cause.

Victims die not from AIDS itself, but from one of a host of· diseases to which the human body deprived of its immune system can fall prey.

Chief among these are Kaposi's sarcoma, a rare and disfiguring skin cancer and a type of pneumonia (*Pneumocystis carinii pneumonia*) hardly ever seen except in cases of AIDS. Together or separately, these two diseases have caused about three quarters of the deaths of AIDS victims in both Britain and the United States.

UNKNOWN ORIGIN

Equally puzzling is the origin of AIDS. Many researchers believe the virus was perhaps passed from animals to humans in day-to-day contact.

Monkeys in Africa, pigs in Haiti, even sheep in Iceland have all been singled out as possible one-time hosts of the virus, but no-one really knows how and why it claimed humans as its victims.

There is mounting evidence that AIDS is in fact

As with most living organisms, the AIDS virus must kill in order to procreate and survive. Unfortunately, its natural prey – the T4 cell – is part of the immune system. And while the virus is as fragile as a soap bubble outside the human body, once it reaches the blood stream it becomes, to date, impossible to destroy

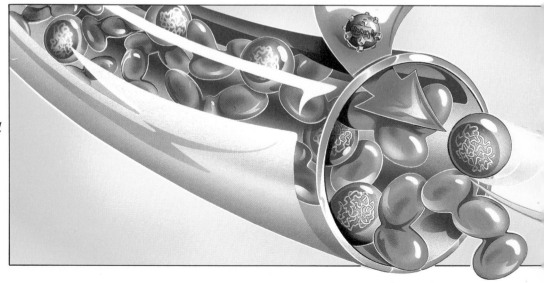

THE SAFER SEX CODE

1. *Only solo sex is guaranteed safe.*

2. *Avoid any contact with your partner's semen, bodily fluids or blood.*

3. *Have sex where you do not orgasm inside your partner's body, or if you feel you must do so, use a condom.*

Supplied by the Terence Higgins Trust.

an old disease from Africa, where the cancer Kaposi's sarcoma is thought to have been known long before the current outbreak.

AIDS IN THE USA

Wherever it came from, the disease has spread extremely rapidly over long distances in a very short space of time. The problem is that whereas most diseases increase arithmetically (2, 4, 6, 8 and so on) AIDS increases exponentially (2, 4, 8, 16, 32), and this is what has led to the cliff-face rise in the numbers affected. In America, five cases of *Pneumocystis carinii pneumonia* in Los Angeles and 26 cases of Kaposi's sarcoma in New York and California heralded the arrival of the disease in the summer of 1981.

Two years later in the autumn of 1983, some 2,300 cases had been reported, over 900 of them fatal. By the end of 1984 AIDS had taken its toll of 7,700 citizens, 3,700 of whom had died, and just nine months later the number of cases stood at 13,000 with 6,800 deaths. It is thought that this rate of increase was because some gays were considerably more promiscuous than heterosexual men or women. However, as the latest figures for gonorrhoea show that incidences within the gay community are declining – whereas heterosexual cases are still increasing – it can be assumed that homosexual promiscuity has declined. This, together with increasing awareness of safe sexual practices, has made doctors hopeful that the increase in gay AIDS cases will begin to decline.

AIDS IN THE UK

Hot on the heels of the American outbreak of the disease came its British appearance, and although the numbers involved are far smaller, the rate of increase in the numbers of AIDS sufferers in the United Kingdom has been equally dramatic.

The first case of AIDS in the United Kingdom was reported in December 1981, with the first death, that of a 37-year-old-man, on the 4th July 1982. By the end of 1984, 108 AIDS cases and 46 deaths had been reported, numbers which by December 1985 had risen to 257 and 140 respectively. Seventy per cent of those who contracted the disease in or before 1982 were dead by the end of 1984.

AIDS WORLDWIDE

By the end of 1985 AIDS had affected some 16,000 people worldwide and countless others have now been exposed to the virus. US victims still account for the vast majority of cases, but there are few countries which have escaped the disease.

Russia has finally acknowledged that it does have the beginnings of an AIDS problem, but the governments of other countries, particularly those dependent on their tourist trade, are keeping quiet about the actual incidence of the disease. Undoubtedly, AIDS is no respecter of borders – cases are

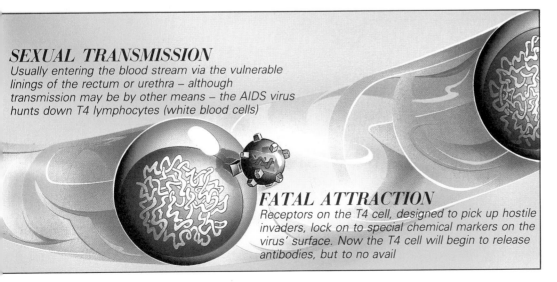

SEXUAL TRANSMISSION
Usually entering the blood stream via the vulnerable linings of the rectum or urethra – although transmission may be by other means – the AIDS virus hunts down T4 lymphocytes (white blood cells)

FATAL ATTRACTION
Receptors on the T4 cell, designed to pick up hostile invaders, lock on to special chemical markers on the virus' surface. Now the T4 cell will begin to release antibodies, but to no avail

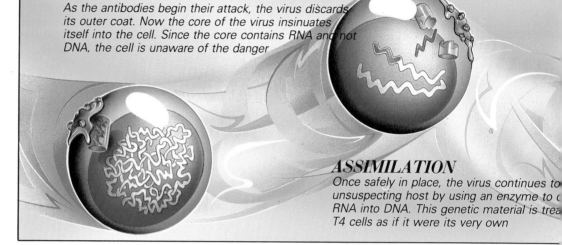

INSERTION
As the antibodies begin their attack, the virus discards its outer coat. Now the core of the virus insinuates itself into the cell. Since the core contains RNA and not DNA, the cell is unaware of the danger

ASSIMILATION
Once safely in place, the virus continues to [...] unsuspecting host by using an enzyme to [...] RNA into DNA. This genetic material is trea[...] T4 cells as if it were its very own

being identified in developing nations as in the West, in small towns and in the country, as well as in larger cities.

NOT A HOMOSEXUAL DISEASE

Although AIDS has been dubbed by some as the gay plague and has even been described as being the result of the wrath of God brought to bear on homosexuals, it is by no means exclusive to the gay population, nor even the male population.

In Europe and the US, male homosexuals have made up the majority of victims to date (71 per cent in the US and 86 per cent in the UK), but other high risk groups include intravenous drug users, haemophiliacs using blood products, bisexuals and prostitutes. In the US and UK a number of sufferers are heterosexual men and women, proof of the fact that anyone who has sex is now at risk.

Outside of the western world, the concentration of AIDS in the gay population has been far less of a feature of the disease. In Central Africa, for example, where as many as one in 20 people are affected in some areas, AIDS is spreading rapidly through heterosexual contact and women are just as likely as men to fall victim to the disease, particularly prostitutes. This may be because of poor standards of hygiene in hospitals and clinics. But it may also be the result of the widespread practice of anal intercourse as a form of contraception in some African countries.

VIRUS ISOLATED

When people were first stricken by AIDS, doctors were mystified and the actual cause of this deadly disease was only isolated in 1985. The culprit is thought to be a virus which attacks the very cells which protect us from infection. This rod-shaped bug has been labelled the HTLV III virus (or human T cell lymphotropic virus, Type 3) by American scientists, and LAV (lymphaedenopathy associated virus) by French scientists. They have now compromised

and the virus is known as LAV-HTLV III.

How this virus spreads from one person to another is still not completely understood. Scientists have isolated it in most body fluids of AIDS victims – in blood, semen and saliva. But because the virus can be isolated in a laboratory test tube does not mean that it can be passed on through contact with all these fluids. AIDS is predominantly a blood-borne disease, although semen is also a likely carrier.

What is clear is that those in normal daily contact with AIDS victims are not necessarily in danger.

The most common method of transmission is still through anal intercourse. The reason why anal intercourse allows the virus to cross over from one host to another is because the membranes of the rectum are more more delicate than those of the vagina, and hence far more likely to tear and bleed.

Unlike the vagina, the walls of the rectum allow fluids to pass through into the blood stream so that viruses from contaminated sperm could enter another person's body in this way.

There are two other ways in which the virus might be spread by blood to blood contact. The first is by exchanging and using infected needles, a common practice among intravenous drug users, and the second is by transfusing contaminated blood or blood products.

OTHERS AT RISK

Haemophiliacs have found themselves in a high risk group because of their treatment with the blood clotting agent, Factor VIII.

However, these two routes of transmission – blood transfusions and contaminated Factor VIII – should have been blocked by the introduction of tests for all blood donors and of heat treating all blood to kill off any AIDS viruses present. These measures have been mandatory in the United Kingdom since September 1985.

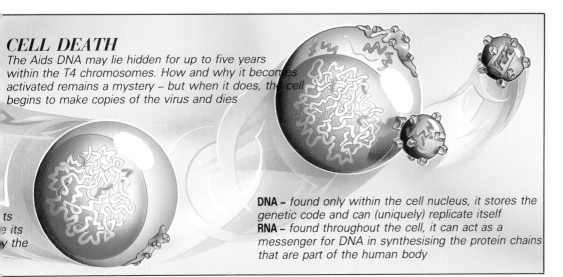

CELL DEATH
The Aids DNA may lie hidden for up to five years within the T4 chromosomes. How and why it becomes activated remains a mystery – but when it does, the cell begins to make copies of the virus and dies

DNA – found only within the cell nucleus, it stores the genetic code and can (uniquely) replicate itself
RNA – found throughout the cell, it can act as a messenger for DNA in synthesising the protein chains that are part of the human body

MANY SYMPTOMS

When they do develop, the symptoms of AIDS are those of an array of diseases which the immune deficient victim has fallen prey to, making it difficult to tell whether someone actually has the disease. These include swollen glands in the neck, armpit or groin, weight loss, high fever and night sweats, diarrhoea and persistent coughs or shortness of breath.

There may also be skin changes with pink to purple flattish blotches or bumps occurring on or under the skin, inside the mouth, nose, eyelids or rectum or blemishes in the mouth.

Where any of these symptoms occur alone, or even in twos and threes, it is extremely unlikely that AIDS will be found to be the cause, and because the fear of AIDS can be almost as debilitating as the disease itself, it is important to seek medical advice.

COMPLETE CURE NOT YET IN SIGHT

As yet, the prospects in terms of the prevention and cure of AIDS look none too hopeful.

No known cure has yet been found for the disease and the best that can be done, medically, for victims is to help alleviate the symptoms. Nor is there any effective vaccine at present, and according to scientists there is no chance of there being one before 1990.

The virus probably has several different forms, each capable of mutating (changing), which makes the development of a vaccine difficult. Many of the drugs currently being tested as possible cures for AIDS are aimed at stopping the virus reproducing after it has entered the body, but progress is slow. According to a report in the New England Journal of Medicine, doctors have isolated the virus in brain and spinal fluid from AIDS sufferers. The implications are that the virus 'hides' in the brain – and this could make eradication difficult, though probably not impossible.

Despite the anxiety among health care workers, and those involved in caring for AIDS victims, their chances of contracting the disease themselves seem remote.

Apart from one case in the UK of a nurse who contracted the disease by acidentally innoculating herself with a small amount of blood from an AIDS patient, there have been no known cases of disease among doctors and nurses.

It is, however, now known that an infected mother can pass on AIDS to her unborn child, possibly through the placenta or else during the actual birth when blood is lost by the mother.

VIRUS NOT NECESSARILY FATAL

As yet there is no test which shows categorically whether a person has AIDS. Anyone who has come into contact with the virus will make antibodies to it, and will show up as 'antibody positive'.

But although the presence of antibodies gives no protection against the disease, only 5–10 per cent of those who are found to have LAV-HTLV III antibodies in the blood will go on to develop a fatal case of AIDS.

Some will develop milder, less life-threatening infections, and a sizeable number may develop no obvious symptoms at all.

AIDS CARRIERS

Exactly what makes one person develop the disease while others remain unaffected is not known exactly, but carriers – those who have antibodies without symptoms – will still be capable of passing the virus to others, who in turn will stand much the same chance of developing AIDS.

The other worrying problem about AIDS is that symptoms may take anything from two, possibly as long as seven years to emerge, which means that sufferers may unwittingly be infecting a large number of other people before realizing that they have the disease.

CHAPTER TEN

ALTERNATIVE LIFESTYLES

HOMOSEXUALITY

*Although prejudice against homosexuals has
lessened since the 1960s, the decision to
'come out' can still be a difficult one to make*

Society's attitude towards homosexuality has changed greatly in the past 20 years. But since the AIDS virus, the heterosexual community has focused its fear on homosexuals once more. Like many such fears, this attitude is often based on a misunderstanding of what being homosexual – gay – really means. The gay population is large and varied, and its members do not always conform to society's stereotypes.

Most researchers agree that about one in twenty men, and a slightly smaller number of women, are gay throughout their adult lives. But the number of people who experience erotic involvements with members of the same sex at some point in their lives is far greater.

A SEXUAL CONTINUUM

The sex researcher Alfred Kinsey interviewed thousands of American men and women in the 1940s, and researchers agree that his findings on the frequency of homosexual activity are still the most reliable. Kinsey came to the conclusion that sexuality should not be seen in black and white terms of either being exclusively heterosexual or exclusively homosexual, but that it was more a question of degree. He stressed that for many people sexual interest can change considerably over the years. Humans explore and experiment, settle down for a while, and then often explore again a little later in their life.

According to his findings, 37 per cent of men and 13 per cent of women had sex to the point of orgasm with members of the same sex at some stage in their life between adolescence and old age.

Given the increasing openness about homosexuality since the 1940s, the numbers may well be higher than this now. For Kinsey's figures were gathered at a time when homosexuality was very taboo and hence very secretive. As it becomes more freely talked about, more people perhaps are willing to experiment.

Certain societies accept homosexuality very easily – it was accepted and widely practised in

Ancient Greece, and it is still widely prescribed among the Sambia in New Guinea. All young men there are expected to perform fellatio with the other young men.

But in western culture, homosexuality was outlawed from the Middle Ages until relatively recently. Religious prohibition, followed by legal and medical condemnation, turned homosexuality into a sin, a sickness and a crime.

Since the 1960s, however, there has been a remarkable modification of society's attitudes towards homosexuality.

The law has been changed in many countries, so that homosexuality is no longer illegal for consenting adults. And in 1973, psychiatrists agreed that homosexuality was not a 'sickness' but a 'normal sexual expression'. Opinion polls show that the general public are more and more accepting of homosexuality – about a fifth of the population now say they have gay friends, and the younger generations seem much more at ease with the issue.

BEING GAY

So why are some people gay? There are many theories, and experts still fail to agree on the reason.

One group of German researchers, for example, has suggested that too much or too little of certain sex hormones while a baby is in the womb can lead to later homosexual orientation. The idea is that too much testosterone before birth could predispose to adult lesbianism. Too little testosterone could lead to male homosexuality.

This prenatal explanation is very controversial, but there are many theories that link homosexuality to early child-rearing experiences. Boys might over-identify with their mothers – or perhaps just fail to identify with their fathers – and hence in later life come to recognize their sexuality in female sexuality.

Some researchers have listed hundreds of explanations that have been put forward – from genetic theories to masturbatory conditioning, and from being labelled by others and then taking on that label, to sibling rivalry. The truth is that nobody is really sure, and it is likely that there are many different explanations for different people.

Nevertheless, for whatever reason, many men and women do say they have been attracted to the

HOMOPHOBIA

Men seem more hostile to gay men than women, but many women are more hostile to lesbians than are men. Since the early 1970s, psychologists have studied this fear of homosexuality – or homophobia as it is termed in general. They found that people with negative rather than positive attitudes to homosexuals are:

■ *more likely to have friends with negative attitudes*

■ *more likely to be older and less well educated*

■ *more likely to be religious, more conservative, and also more authoritarian*

■ *more likely to have traditional stereotypical ideas about male and female behaviour*

SOME IMPORTANT DISTINCTIONS

A homosexual *Someone who is primarily erotically and emotionally interested in the same sex*

A heterosexual *Someone who is primarily erotically interested in the opposite sex*

A bisexual *Someone who is erotically interested in both sexes*

A transvestite *Someone who finds pleasure (often erotic) in wearing the clothes of the opposite sex. Transvesitites are usually heterosexual but can be gay*

An effeminate man *A man who adopts some of the characteristics of women. This is, however, no guide to sexual interest. Masculine-looking men can be gay and effeminate-looking men are sometimes heterosexual*

A transexual *Someone who feels they are in the wrong sex and who thus live a life as the opposite sex – often with the help of sex surgery to change their genitals*

A paedophile *Somone who is erotically interested in children. They are most commonly heterosexual men*

A code system has developed in the gay sub-culture which allows men to indicate their sexual proclivities. There are regional variations, but objects in the left pocket usually mean the man takes a passive role

same sex as far back as they can remember. In one United States study, 70 per cent of the sample group of homosexuals knew that they were gay before they were 15 years old.

GLAD TO BE GAY?

What is important for them is not what caused such an attraction in the first place, but how they are to handle this feeling through their life.

Some just deny it. They push their feelings away. They may seek a partner of the opposite sex to prove to themselves they are not really gay. And some may become 'homophobic' – hating gays, because they awaken their own attraction to the same sex.

Some may experiment with homosexuality, but not see themselves as gay. Many may go to other men for sexual release – often in parks and public conveniences – and go home to their wives as a 'happy heterosexual'. One United States survey looked quite closely into the backgrounds of the men who had sex in public places and found that about half of them were married, living a publicly heterosexual lifestyle and had no other contact with the gay world.

Some may seek to change. There are some therapists who think that they can change early homosexual attractions into heterosexual ones.

And some will decide to accept their sexuality. This is often called 'coming out'.

COMING OUT

The most important moment in a gay person's life is when they decide to 'come out' – to identify themselves as a gay person, meet other gay people, feel good about their gayness, and perhaps adopt a gay lifestyle.

This can happen at any age, but most commonly these days it happens in the late teens and early twenties. This may follow a painful and lonely adolescence, when the boy or girl becomes aware of their attraction to the same sex, but simply does not know what to do about it, and is too frightened to tell parents or friends for fear of rejection.

The teenage years can be a lonely and sad time when sexuality is kept secret. And it seems that to 'come out', people need some way of finding other gays or lesbians and being able to identify with them.

Research in the United States found many different routes towards coming out:
■ Through books, gay magazines and pen-pal 'contact' advertisements.
■ Through telephone help lines, gay counselling agencies, women's organizations.
■ Through gay bars, gay community groups and gay discos.

These lesbians from the Netherlands had their relationship 'confirmed' in church, although it was officially against Catholic law

It is more difficult for gay men and lesbian women to settle down with a long-term partner, partly because there is no social institution such as marriage for them

In the past it was relatively difficult to 'come out', but it is becoming easier – especially in the larger cities, where there is a fairly large and visible gay scene.

THE GAY COMMUNITY

Each big city has its own gay community, but some are more well organized than others. San Francisco, for example, is the 'gay capital' of the world – research suggests that well over 20 per cent of the population there is gay and leads a gay lifestyle. In such a community it is very easy to 'come out'. Indeed, many people move there because of its reputation.

After coming out, many gays spend a considerable time on the 'gay scene'. The 'scene', however, is fairly youthful – as gays grow older it is more common to have a network of close friends.

Many gays, of course, eventually settle down with a lover or partner, although women seem more likely than men to have a really long relationship with a single partner. For men, the relationship is often more flexible than a conventional marriage – they may choose not to live together, and they will often have other outside emotional and sexual relationships.

In some ways it is obviously harder for gays and lesbians to be in couples – there is no law to bind them together, little support from families and only occasionally is it possible to rear children.

THE GAY MOVEMENT

Homosexuality has come out of the closet in the past 20 years. It is more talked about, more visible and more accepted. Gay people have become a political force and struggled for social change.

The gay movement is particularly strong in the United States, where there is a gay lobby which scrutinizes election candidates.

And for many lesbians, being gay has actually come to be seen as a political choice – a public statement that one prefers the more gentle qualities of women to the aggressiveness of men.

Nevertheless, political and visible gays are only the tip of the iceberg. The majority of gay men and lesbians live out fairly quiet and ordinary lives – not easily identifiable and, perhaps, not wishing to be identified.

HOMOSEXUALITY AND THE LAW

Homosexual behaviour between males is no longer a criminal offence in England, Scotland or Northern Ireland – providing it occurs between two consenting adults aged over 21, in private.

It is still, however, a serious crime in many parts of the world. In Moslem countries it can lead to execution; in New Zealand it remains an offence, and even in the USA it is still theoretically criminal in about half the states.

In the UK, it has never been a crime to have lesbian relationships. This is almost certainly because the Victorian males who were responsible for homosexual legislation thought women to be less sexual and could not think of lesbian relationships as ever happening.

As the law stands in the UK, there are three main homosexual offences; buggery, indecent assault and indecency between males.

The most serious offence is buggery – or anal intercourse – which also involves the smallest numbers (588 cases in 1983).

The other two offences are more numerous, but less serious legally. Indecent assault on a male can include homosexual acts with a willing male less than 16 years of age – the age of consent. Only about 1 in 5 offenders go to prison.

Gross indecency is the offence most frequently occurring in public – toilets, or car parks. 1,362 cases were recorded in 1983.

In 1895 the playwright and personality Oscar Wilde (shown here with his friend Lord Alfred Douglas) was prosecuted under the British Law Amendment Act of 1885 which made private homosexual acts a criminal offence. This law remained in force until 1967.

LESBIANISM

More than ever before, lesbianism is out in the open. So why do many women who choose same-sex partners still find their lives restricted by social prejudice?

What do you think of when you think of a lesbian? Is it the stereotyped image of the 'butch' mannishly dressed dyke, or alternatively the unhappy woman who 'can't get a man'? Or do you see lesbians as aggressive, manhating feminists?

With few exceptions, the images of lesbians presented in the media, in literature and in theoretical explanations are very negative. In novels, for example, lesbians have often been portrayed as sick and unhappy individuals engaged in relationships which are doomed to failure. It is only recently that lesbian relationships have begun to be seen as a valid choice for women and as positive and fulfilling.

The idea that lesbians are all alike is something else that has been challenged recently. As more women have 'come out' as lesbian it has become more and more obvious that lesbians constitute a highly diverse group.

There is no such thing as a 'typical' lesbian in the same way that it would be nonsense to talk about 'typical' heterosexual women.

The jobs, interests and lifestyles of women who identify as lesbian vary as much as anyone else's. Rather than the stereotypes, real-life lesbians are more likely to be the young woman next door, the harassed mother in the supermarket or the woman who served you in the department store yesterday.

HOW MANY?

It is impossible to say how many lesbians there are in Britain, or elsewhere. Most researchers agree on a number somewhere between one in ten and one in twenty. The Kinsey report – based on interviews with thousands of women in the United States – showed that 13 per cent of women had had sex to the point of orgasm with another woman at some time during their adult lives. First published in 1953, Kinsey's findings demonstrated that lesbian experience is vastly more common than had previously been thought.

With the liberalization of social attitudes

Far from being doomed to failure, lesbian relationships can be as loving, 'ordinary' and long-lasting as their heterosexual equivalents

towards both lesbian and gay male relationships since the 1950s, today's figures are almost certain to be higher. As it becomes easier to be open about one's sexuality, more people are likely to experiment and also to admit to their experiences.

No fixed proportion of the population is lesbian. The numbers will vary according to the way lesbian relationships are seen by society and the opportunities for women to form them. Over the last 20 years, for example, the women's movement has helped to make a lesbian lifestyle more possible,

FACTS ABOUT LESBIANISM

■ *A large number of lesbians are or have been married. In* Homosexualities *(1978), the researchers Bell and Weinberg quote a number of studies which found that more than 20 per cent of lesbians have been married at least once. Their own study of approximately 300 lesbians from the United States reports that more than a third of them have been married*

■ *Of the married women interviewed by Bell and Weinberg, half had one or more children (this figure was higher for the black women). Of the group as a whole (married and unmarried), at least one in five were mothers*

■ *From the same sample, the average age of first steady relationship with a woman was 22 years old, although the age of first lesbian sexual experience was often younger (about 17 years old)*

■ *In another study, 50 per cent of women identified themselves as lesbian before having a sexual relationship with another woman, and 50 per cent only did so afterwards*

■ *An interesting aspect of recent studies is that – despite obvious social pressures – lesbians report satisfaction with their lifestyle. In a large-scale United States survey published in* The Gay Report *(Jay and Young, 1979), in answer to the question 'If you could take a pill to make you straight, would you do it', 95 per cent of the lesbians interviewed said 'No'.*

by recognizing lesbian relationships as 'normal' and encouraging financial independence from men.

BECOMING LESBIAN

There are many different theories which attempt to explain what makes a person lesbian or gay. These include genetic theories which suggest that one is 'born that way', hormonal explanations and theories which focus on early childhood experiences within the family.

None of these theories, however, adequately explains the diverse nature of women's experiences of becoming lesbian. Neither have researchers been able to demonstrate that lesbians are biologically different from other women or have been affected by a different upbringing. There seems to be no 'recipe' for lesbianism.

The married woman whose children are leaving home and at the age of 48 falls in love for the first time with someone of the same sex obviously has a very different experience of lesbianism from that of a 15-year-old girl who feels attracted to other girls, or that of a 27-year-old woman with a lesbian-feminist analysis of her sexuality.

MAKING THE CHOICE

For some women being a lesbian represents a

THE HISTORICAL VIEW

Research suggests that although homosexual behaviour has probably always existed, the idea that there exists a certain sort of person – the lesbian – is a fairly recent one. Until the latter part of the 19th century people did not think of themselves as either homosexual or

Radclyffe Hall (on the left) in 1920, eight years before publication of her lesbian novel

heterosexual.

It was not until the turn of the 20th century that sexologists such as Havelock Ellis began to write about homosexuality and lesbianism in terms of what a person was rather than what a person did. Love between women was no longer romanticized. On the contrary, lesbians were seen as both biologically abnormal and mentally sick. They were called 'inverts' – women who were like men in their interests and desires.

Stephen, the main character in Radclyffe Hall's classic lesbian novel The Well of Loneliness *published in 1928, saw herself as a man trapped in a woman's body. The novel was a passionate plea, the first of its kind for such women and their sexuality to be accepted by society.*

More recently the women's and gay movements have challenged the view that homosexuality is an illness. Lesbian feminists in particular see their lesbianism as a way of life or a political gesture rather than just a sexual preference.

personal and a political decision. They see themselves as chooing a lesbian identity and lifestyle.

Cherryl was in her early 30s, married with two children, when she first began to think of herself as lesbian. 'When I say I have chosen to be a lesbian,' she explains, 'I don't mean that I woke up one morning and thought "Today I'll be a lesbian". It was much more complicated than that. In fact, I never considered having a relationship with a woman until about three years ago.'

'I think what happened was that I gradually became more and more dissatisfied with the roles that women are expected to take on in heterosexual relationships. I also began to meet women who were lesbians. Their relationships seemed more equal to me. They were very happy and very positive about being lesbians. It was in that context that I was able to think about a lesbian lifestyle for myself.'

Lesbian feminists such as Cherryl are likely to have a very strong commitment to being a lesbian. This is not because it is any more 'in their nature' to be a lesbian than other women, but because lesbianism is fundamental to their political beliefs. Other women, whether they are feminists or not, may have a strong commitment to a lesbian identity too, but for different reasons. They may feel that they were born lesbian and that it is a fixed part of their personality that cannot be changed.

After five years of quite a happy marriage, Connie left her husband to live with another woman. 'I think in my case,' she says, 'I've always

More and more women are finding that they do not have to make the choice between lesbianism and motherhood – they can enjoy both

been a lesbian, though it's only dawned on me recently. Don't ask me why – perhaps it had something to do with my childhood. All I know is that I didn't choose it, it chose me.'

COMING OUT

Coming out is a continual process. It will involve first identifying oneself as gay or lesbian and then making that knowledge known to others. This is much easier for a woman if there is a gay community where she lives. In the past, gay pubs, clubs and social events tended to be dominated by gay men, but recently far more venues have opened in larger cities and towns which cater specifically for women.

But there may still be particular problems for young lesbians and older women. Young lesbians may have the problem of explaining to parents where they are going and with whom. Older women may feel out of place in the youth-orientated atmosphere of gay discos and clubs.

The majority of lesbians do not find it possible to come out beyond the gay world. They are therefore forced to lead a double life, and 'pass as straight' for most of the time.

There are many problems which can arise from choosing to remain 'in the closet'; having to invent lovers of the opposite sex as a cover for lesbian relationships – 'I have a boyfriend in London, but he can't get away very often' – is a particularly common sort of excuse.

There are also lesbians who have not even come out within the gay community. They are usually accepted by their families and friends as heterosexual, although they may see themselves as lesbian. Such women are at risk in terms of their emotional stability, simply because of their social isolation, and because they may feel they are 'living a lie'.

Understandably, one reason why very few lesbians come out to the world at large is that they fear rejection from parents, friends and work-mates. There may also be concern that parents will blame themselves for their daughter's lesbianism, or a very real fear of being sacked. In some jobs it is virtually impossible to come out. There have already been cases of women losing their jobs as care workers with children when it became known that they were lesbian.

LESBIAN MOTHERS

In the past, society has actively tried to deny lesbian mothers their right to exist. The media has frequently portrayed lesbian motherhood as something sensational. Many doctors and social workers are unwilling to offer information and services to lesbians wanting to become pregnant or wishing to adopt or foster a child, and the courts are very reluctant to grant custody or access to lesbian mothers.

Nancy Manahan and Rosemary Curb, former Roman Catholic nuns and editors of the US bestseller Lesbian Nuns: Breaking Silence – *a collection of essays by 42 ex-nuns whose new vocation is their lesbian activism*

Behind these actions lies the assumption that lesbians do not make good mothers. This is based on a concern that children of a lesbian mother will grow up to be gay. There is, however, no evidence that children raised by lesbians are more likely to become homosexual than children living in a heterosexual family.

ARTIFICIAL INSEMINATION

More and more lesbians are questioning the assumption that they must choose between lesbianism and motherhood. Artificial insemination has been used by lesbians who wish to conceive a child without heterosexual intercourse. Although this might sound strange to some, wanting to have sex with someone and wanting to have a child can be quite separate desires.

Another reason why some lesbians may prefer to have an AID (artificial insemination by donor) baby is to try to ensure undisputed guardianship and custody of their child. This is very understandable given the court's reluctance to grant custody and, very often, access to lesbian mothers.

BISEXUALITY

Bisexuality in adult life is rare, but sexual experiences with both men and women can be a normal part of growing up

Bisexuals are people who are equally attracted sexually to men and women. This completely balanced sexual preference actually applies to relatively few people. But there are many who, although they are predominantly attracted to one sex, do recognize a degree of attraction to the other.

According to the Kinsey Report, one-quarter of the population admit to having had at least one homosexual encounter (to orgasm) in their lives. Kinsey devised a sexual rating scale which has been used in research. Consisting of seven points, at one end – 0 – are the exclusively heterosexual, at the other end – 6 – are the exclusively homosexual. If equally homosexual and heterosexual (bisexual) you score 3. There are a further two intermediary grades on both the heterosexual side (1 and 2) and homosexual side (4 and 5). Using this scale it is possible to see that the exclusively heterosexual or homosexual is in a minority – more people have the potential to be bisexual, whether they actually express this sexually or not.

THE BEGINNINGS OF BISEXUALITY

At the time of sexual awakening, around puberty and during adolescence, strong bonds are often formed between young people of the same sex – crushes, emotional friendships, strongly romantic feelings. In some cases this includes physical expression – girlfriends who walk arms entwined, touching and cuddling each other, dancing together,

sometimes sharing a bed. It is not uncommon for this to include some form of sexual contact – for example, boys comparing the sizes of their penises and experimenting with mutual masturbation.

In single-sex environments, such as boarding schools, this is even more common. Philip went to public school, and he remembers that sexual liaisons were considered pretty normal. 'I did it too. It was a bit of fun I suppose. I thought it was a little like being a prisoner of war – there weren't any girls so you had to make do with what you could get. I don't feel ashamed of what happened – but now that I

'I thought it was a little like being a prisoner of war – there weren't any girls so you had to make do with what you could get. I don't feel ashamed of what happened – but I don't think I'd ever relate sexually to another man'

have the choice I don't think I'd ever relate sexually to another man. But one of my close friends at school is now a committed homosexual. Another man I've kept in touch with because we are in the same business is married – but his 'bits on the side' are always men. He's a bisexual I suppose.'

Before long, as in Philip's case, the adolescent usually accepts the view of society that these sexual or quasi-sexual contacts are wrong, physical affection between young friends of the same sex diminishes as they form more acceptable heterosexual relationships. For the majority, these new relationships are far more satisfactory, and they dismiss what went before as an unimportant part of growing up.

THE FEELINGS THAT REMAIN

But some people are unable to consign their homosexual feelings to the past. A minority of these never wish to succeed in making the transition to 'normal' heterosexuality and remain homosexual for life.

Dan knew that he was homosexual when young, but he could not accept the fact. When he was 19 he became engaged to a girl that he had been out with a few times – and had slept with once or twice. The engagement was broken after a very short time, and he is in no doubt now about his sexual orientation. 'I think that managing to have sex with the other

sex does not constitute a bisexual. I dare say I could still achieve and maintain an erection with a woman – but I haven't the slightest wish to. A bisexual fancies and also wants sex with both sexes. In the same way, I don't think that a single homosexual encounter makes a man bisexual – whatever the Kinsey report seems to suggest. People experiment, and then find they don't like it that much – continuing is what counts.'

A larger minority become to all intents and purposes heterosexual after adolescence, but they never forget or get over the powerful sexual feelings for members of their own sex. These feelings can remain, whether they are acted on or not.

Conducting sexual affairs with members of both sexes depends partly on sexual preference and partly on attitudes to your own sexuality. People who feel guilty, confused or uncomfortable with their own sexuality may never want to explore the homosexual side of their natures. But even if this lies dormant, the potential is there.

THE TRUE BISEXUAL

Most people's idea of a practising bisexual is of someone who sets up home with a homosexual and a heterosexual partner at the same time. This is called troilism, and in fact is is very rare.

A bisexual who is genuinely equally attracted to

'Sex is sex, isn't it? It feels good, it's a release – I don't see why it's just supposed to be men and women together. Another woman would be trouble, she'd want to muscle in on my marriage, that's for sure'

both sexes is still most likely to be in a single close relationship with a partner – either homosexual or heterosexual. He may, however, seek sexual gratification with a member of the other sex.

This is the situation for Winston, a West Indian who is married with six kids. 'Sex with my wife is normal. OK – like what you would expect for people married as long as we have been. But for the past 18 months I've been involved with a white man I met in a pub near where I work. It's straight sex, no emotions – he lives with another gay guy and they feel married. Sex is sex, isn't it? It feels good, it's a release – I don't see why it's just supposed to be men and women together. Another woman would be trouble, she'd want to muscle in on my marriage, that's for sure.'

Also common is the sequential bisexual. Faithful to one sex at a time, he or she may finish a long-term relationship with a woman, to be followed by a similar relationship with a man.

Alice has always conducted her relationships like this. 'I don't think of it as bisexuality. When I'm involved with another woman I think "yes, this is how it should be, I'm a lesbian." Yet a year or so later when I may be living with a man, I think that that is all in the past, and I am now completely "straight". I can't imagine living with a woman, say, and sneaking off for an affair with a man. I commit myself, totally and faithfully, to a partner and for the time that relationship continues, that is my sexual orientation.'

Alice, who has had two long affairs with women, and three, shorter affairs with men, believes that she relates to the person first, the sexual body second. 'I fall in love with that person, sex comes next and grows out of my feelings for him or her.'

DEGREES OF BISEXUALITY
It is harder to classify the intermediate stages of bisexuality – the predominantly heterosexual person who occasionally has homosexual flings or crushes. Or a mainly homosexual person occasionally attracted to members of the opposite sex. Sometimes these people have a genuine, but fairly weak, bisexual urge. With other people the urge or desire is stronger but other factors influence their expression of it.

Some gays, for instance, choose to keep up a 'heterosexual' front – they have fallen into a heterosexual way of life and their homosexual nature has to take second place. That is what Sharon says is so in her case. 'It took me time to realize it, but now I am sure that I am sexually gay. Previously I believed I was just frigid and didn't like sex. If I could start over again I would probably "come out" and live my life with another woman. But I'm married, I have children, I have a life I enjoy. It's a waste of time to think of what might have been. I do, however, have a very warm and sexual relationship with a lovely woman, but she understands why I could never live with her. Outsiders might classify me as bisexual, but I know that I am a lesbian who happens to be married'.

It is the same for Frank. 'In my line of work you can't expect to "come out" and get on. You need to be seen to live a normal life, you need to entertain the boss, and have intimate little dinners with other married colleagues. I'm fond of my wife, but our sex life is virtually nil and I see our relationship as essential to my career in the same way a good briefcase is. When it comes to sex I'm only turned on by men and I get my sex as and when I can. My lifestyle is bisexual, but my nature is homosexual.'

But other people are genuinely bisexual to a greater or lesser degree and feel that they need both types of relationships in their lives – limiting themselves to either men or women would not be enough for them. Bob is an example of someone who is mainly heterosexual but occasionally feels the urge to have sex with a man. 'On the whole I prefer women, but sometimes I get turned on by a man, particularly if it's obvious that he really goes for me – women never send out such blatant signals. What I like about it is that it feels so illicit – it's like the feelings you get about sex when you're a teenager – that somehow it's very wrong, which makes it doubly exciting.'

THE SEQUENTIAL BISEXUAL
Alice was quite an extreme example of someone who was a sequential bisexual – sometimes homosexual, sometimes heterosexual. Her pattern, through accident, was quite symmetrical – a relationship with a woman followed closely by a relationship with a man and so on. But some people can also be described as sequential bisexuals even if they only have one major homosexual relationship, the main distinction being that they do not run homosexual and heterosexual relationships at the same time.

Most of Karen's relationships have been with men, but she has had two close, loving, sexual partnerships with women, both during the time when she was most involved politically and socially with the women's liberation movement.

'At the same time that I was living, breathing, thinking feminism, a sexual relationship with a man seemed really out of the question. For three years my partners were women, and it seemed absolutely right then. Subsequently, since my involvement has dropped to a less intense level I have returned to a heterosexual way of life. My sex life with my female partners was good, but I suppose I actually fancy men more. The dynamics of a male/female relationship are right for me.'

'When the chemistry is there between me and a man it's great. And if he's skillful it's wonderful. But with some men you've had it after ten minutes, it's all over once they've had their fun. Or else you get the mechanical stud. . .'

THE NEED FOR RELATIONSHIPS WITH BOTH SEXES

Practising bisexuals often have a number of explanations for why they need partners of both sexes. But these reasons divide broadly into two main areas – sexual and emotional.

Len sees the split as essentially emotional. 'It's fair to say that I am attracted to men and women equally, but there is a different quality to the relationship. There is a kind of protective element in the male/female relationship, and sometimes I feel pressured to be always in control with a woman – though that can be nice. With men I feel it is less complicated, we're just mates together sharing things, it's more equal.'

Nick's explanation of his bisexuality is predominantly sexual. 'Making love to a woman is very different from sex with a man. With a woman I am able to be more tender, sex is sweeter. On the minus side some women just want you to play the experienced lover – they lie there and let you get on with it, then act hurt when you want to catch a bit of kip afterwards. With her you're not thinking about your own sexual pleasure but technique. With men I find sex almost "sporty", sometimes brutal. "Cottaging" [finding sexual partners in male lavatories] is raw sex, it's about me, what I feel, the intensity of my orgasm. Fundamental sex with no frills.'

CELIBACY

After the permissive sixties and the promiscuous seventies, will it be the abstaining eighties? With new and incurable sexual diseases rampant, celibacy is coming back into vogue

After many centuries out in the cold as far as society at large is concerned, celibacy – the conscious decision to live without sex – is coming back into fashion.

The twin spectres of AIDS and herpes appear to be terrifying the formerly promiscuous into a life free from sexual contact. Also the pervading climate of opinion is gradually shifting towards abstinence. Increasing numbers of the famous proclaim their lack of interest in sex without fear of public disapproval. One notable gender-bending star is widely quoted as saying he prefers a nice cup of tea.

But while the arguments rage as to whether this new-found obsession with self-denial is merely a recognition of the dangers of venereal disease or a more deeply seated backlash against the sexual revolution of the 1960s and early 1970s, celibacy remains shrouded in myth.

Many non-celibates find it impossible to believe that a man or woman can forgo sex indefinitely without risking emotional disturbance. Others mock the celibate as a closet homosexual or victim of insurmountable hang-ups, in dire need of psychiatric help. Even the religious celibate sometimes becomes the object of sly humour based on people's suspicions of dubious sexuality or thinly veiled hypocrisy.

Yet celibacy is by no means 'abnormal' and is practised by large numbers of people. As such, it deserves a sympathetic airing and better understanding.

WHAT IS CELIBACY?

Consciously deciding not to have sex should not be confused with being unable to partake of sex – either through lack of opportunity or available partners, or because of subconscious fears which may effectively inhibit sexual expression.

Celibates are people who exercise their freedom to choose. They are individuals who are aware of the sexual world, but who, for reasons of their own, opt to reject it. In this sense, celibacy can be seen

Cliff's life sex, by D

By ALEX HENDRY

POP STAR Cliff Richard "does not have any sex life," according to American evangelist Dr Billy Graham.

The astonishingly frank and personal remark about the private life of the 42-year-old singer was made during a Press conference in London yesterday.

The conference was held to ma the end of Dr Graham's three-mon "Mission England" crusade, with Cliff, a born-again Chris associated.

Last n said he w

Sex

as a way of life in the same way as choosing to live on a remote island or devoting one's life solely to a particular profession.

Neither is celibacy an irreversible decision to be entered into solemnly and for life. Just as celibates may choose to be so, they are also free to change their minds. This at least puts to rest the myth that all celibates are prisoners of their own repressed sexuality, locked in a dungeon of tortured self-denial, from which they cannot escape.

REASONS FOR CELIBACY

An increasingly common reason for periods of celibacy among single men and women is simply a desire to be more selective about whom they sleep with. Although this may spring from fears of veneral disease or emotional hurt, it is more likely

to be a reaction against the sexual freedom and consequent promiscuity which they enjoyed in younger life.

Unlike their parents and grandparents, these people may have had a wide variety of sexual experiences and the sex act itself has long ceased to be a mysterious delight to be savoured at every possible opportunity. They have come to the conclusion that sex alone – in casual flings or one-night-stands – is not enough, and that in future they will only consider it as part of a deeper, and more emotionally satisfying relationship.

Contrary to popular belief, the 'temporary' celibate is unlikely to be racked by feelings of frustration. Occasional sessions of masturbation can be used to relieve any sexual tension should it occur. But in general the desire to find what they are searching for overrides their basic sex drive. There is no reason why they should not be as happy as anyone else who is striving to lead a more fulfilling life and is prepared to make some sacrifices along the way.

REDUCED SEX DRIVE

Aside from religion or conscience, celibacy in the longer term is more likely to be the natural consequence of a lower-than-average sex drive.

Quite why individuals vary so much in their sexual needs largely remains a mystery. As yet there is no evidence that having sex serves any physiological requirement other than reproduction. The human sexual urge appears purely psychological, and research is now directed at establishing connections between sex drive and culture and upbringing and experiences during the formative years.

Nevertheless, sexual desire still appears to be – and feels – a part of our constitution. Just as the

Left *Soviet cosmonauts endured more than 211 days of enforced celibacy during their record-breaking stay on Salyut 7 space station in 1982*

Above *Even the newspapers have caught on to the new fashion for celibacy, spurred by the revelations of trend-setting pop stars*

DID YOU KNOW?

Many eastern societies have a concept of 'semen power' – strength gained by the non-spilling of seed – and practise celibacy to store up the body's strength.

The Ancient Chinese engaged in forms of coitus reservatus *and* coitus interruptus, *ways of having intercourse without ejaculating. They believed that through extreme self-discipline they could force the semen to return to the stem of the penis and from there back into the brain. Similarly today, some sects of Hindus, Jains and Buddhists extol intercourse as a union with God, but encourage the man not to ejaculate to avoid dissipating his strength. Other Asian ascetics practise celibacy in order to develop and perfect their physical and psychic powers.*

Most societies view chastity – living completely without sex – as abnormal and even dangerous. It is such a bizarre concept in some parts of the world that no word for virgin exists.

perpetual cold-sufferer marvels at those who never so much as sneeze, so it is hard for the highly sexed individual, whose body positively aches for gratification when deprived for a day or two, to comprehend the feelings and motives of the confirmed celibate.

Those with low sex drives are unlikely to advertise the fact, simply because they feel it will make them 'the odd one out'. They may be quite happy to laugh and joke about sex, or even to enter into quite serious discussion on sexual matters, but beneath the bravado is a quiet detachment stemming from the fact that ultimately, it does not concern them.

Like everyone else, the low-sex-drive celibate has a need for companionship and may well have close friends among both sexes. The absence of sexual stimulus, however, can restrict encounters with the opposite sex and many celibates prefer the company of their own sex, with whom they feel they have most in common.

However, this does not preclude celibates from forming longstanding and extremely close relationships with the opposite sex, perhaps even ending in marriage. Those with a low sex drive often attract or actively seek a partner with similar feelings, and although the question of having sex may arise during the courtship and the early months of marriage, it will quickly be set aside – often via excuses on both sides – to the point where the relationship settles into one of close understanding and non-sexual mutual comfort.

To the outside world the marriage will appear a happy one. And, indeed, so it will be as long as both parties' sex drives remain low. For such people, the pleasure and reassurance of sharing life with a loved one is infinitely more important than sex.

CELIBACY AND RELIGION

By far the most well-known group of celibates are those who abstain from sex as a condition of their religious order – monks, nuns and priests. For them, celibacy is a physical sacrifice to God made of their own free will. By forsaking the desires of the flesh, they seek to liberate their minds from the shackles of worldly pleasures and thereby heighten their own spiritual awareness.

Celibacy in religion has a chequered history, orginating among the Eastern religions around the 4th century AD. Its adoption by priests of the Catholic Church may well have had practical origins, for by publicly divorcing himself from the sexual obsessions of his congregation, the priest automatically gained mystery and spiritual authority. In

Religion can be a powerful reason for remaining celibate. Nuns are 'married to Christ' and dedicate their abstinence to God

practice, clerical celibacy was unenforceable and frequently flouted, giving rise to a thousand and one stories of the licentious priest whose pent-up frustrations caused him to run rampant among his flock.

Ironically, today, when celibacy among the Catholic priesthood is under attack from many quarters as being no longer relevant in a modern world, those who choose it probably adhere to it more strictly than ever before.

CELIBACY AND SPORT

Finally, and in a sense connected to religious celibacy, are the people who become celibate for a certain period in order to channel their sexual energies into a specific goal or achievement. It is not uncommon for athletes to abstain from sex while in training for an important event, or for artists to do likewise when embarking on some special project. A scientific explanation for such courses of action was put forward by Freud, who surmised that sexual desire was a form of psychic energy that could be channelled to express itself in non-sexual ways.

It now appears that while for some individuals self-denial can indeed be a spur to achievement because it gives positive manifestation to mental effort, there is no reason to believe that having sex dissipates our creative energies in any way – in fact for some people it may have quite the opposite effect.

CONSEQUENCES

So far, there is no evidence to suggest that abstaining from sex is physically harmful, nor that people who renounce celibacy – for example Catholic priests who renounce the cloth to marry – experience any particular problems of a physical nature.

World-champion boxer Muhammad Ali once claimed that he abstained from sex for six weeks before a title fight

MAHATMA GANDHI – PORTRAIT OF A CELIBATE

The great Indian religious and political leader Mahatma Gandhi became celibate at the age of 37, having married at 19 and fathered four children. He later wrote that the realization that he must adopt celibacy came to him one day while making love to his wife in the knowledge that his father lay dying. This aroused in him a deep shame which through sheer force of character he translated into a quest for higher spiritual awareness and he even went as far as to test himself by sleeping naked with young women.

While it is impossible to say for sure what brought about Gandhi's drastic decision, there seems little doubt that for him celibacy represented a tangible commitment on his own part to achieve a spiritual goal, and that this in turn helped give him the strength to perform the incredible feats which marked his later years.

Likewise, the true celibate – as opposed to the person forced into celibacy through sexual suppression – is unlikely to experience any deep psychological problems, other than those caused by pressure to conform to what is considered normal. This is hardly surprising if you consider that, to most celibates, sex is a relatively unimportant part of their lives – in the same way that some people never care to own their own house, car or travel abroad.

Research has shown that if anything, continued abstinence from sex actually lowers the sex drive, although this cannot be said to apply to people forced into temporary celibacy by their work.

INDEX

This material was previously published in the Marshall Cavendish partwork *Face to Face*.

ACKNOWLEDGEMENTS

Allsport: 188/9
BBC Hulton Picture Library: 180
Phil Babb: 168
Bob Carlos Clarke: 88
Jean Loup Charmet: 22, 23
Mary Evans Picture Library: 29, 177
Martin Evening: 61
Format: 180 Brenda Prince
John Frost: 186/7
John Garret: 123

Image Bank: 24/5, 27, 44, 50, 51, 53, 57, 66/7, 69, 71, 185(tr)
Dave King: 30, 74, 75, 77
Peter Knapp: 31
Kobal Collection: 18 Band Wagon, 19 Lets Make Love, 21(t) Tom Jones, 21(b) Samson & Delilah
Ranald McKechnie: 4, 34, 35, 92, 95, 107, 109, 113, 114/5, 126/7, 131/2, 134/5, 136/7, 167
Mansell Collection: 91
Eamonn J McCabe: 42

Robert McFarlane: 43, 45
Byron Newman: 89, 90
Novosti Press: 186
Helen Pask: 80/1, 84/5
PhotoLibrary International: 88
Colin Ramsay: 117
Alan Randall: 122, 125
Rex Features: 33, 174, 176, 178
Steve Smith: 38, 39, 40, 40/1
Frank Spooner: 175, 178/9, 181, 185(tl)
John Topham: 189

Dep. Leg. B-30074-87